Girls Who
Went Wrong

Girls Who Went Wrong: Prostitutes in American Fiction, 1885-1917

Laura Hapke

Bowling Green State University Popular Press
Bowling Green, Ohio 43403

Grateful acknowledgment is made to the Library of Congress for permission to reprint the *Police Gazette* drawing, to the Research Division, New York Public Library, Astor, Lenox and Tilden Foundations for permission to reprint the Buel and Campbell guidebook illustrations and poem from Myers's *Midnight in a Great City,* and to Hearst Magazines for permission to reprint the *New York Journal* page and *Hearst's* illustrations.

Acknowledgments

I am grateful to Pace University and to the National Endowment for the Humanities for summer grants which supported my research. I extend my thanks as well to the Scholarly Research Committee for released time, to the Word Processing Center, particularly Blanche Amelkin and Jackie Myers, for manuscript preparation, and to the staff of the Pace Library, especially Laura Manzari, for assisting me in tracking down information on this elusive topic.

I would also like to thank Richard Fabrizio, Brad Schultz, Jean McConochie, Nikki Manos, Barbara Horn, Joseph Salemi, and Brett Sherman for their helpful comments during various stages of this project.

Some of the material in Chapter 2 appeared in earlier form in "Maggie's Sisters: Nineteenth-Century Literary Images of the American Streetwalker," *Journal of American Culture*, Vol. 11, Summer 1982. Scattered paragraphs in Chapter 3 are adapted from "The Alternate Fallen Woman in *Maggie: A Girl of the Streets*," *The Markham Review*, Vol. 12, Spring 1983 and in Chapters 2 and 5 from "Girls Who Went Wrong: Fallen Women in Turn-of-the-Century Fiction," the Vol. 11, Summer 1982 issue of *The Markham Review*.

Contents

She Is More to Be Pitied Than Censured (1898)

At the Old Concert Hall on the Bowery
Round the table were seated one night
A crowd of young fellows carousing;
With them life seemed cheerful and bright.

At the very next table was seated
A girl who had fallen to shame.
All the young fellows jeered at her weakness
Till they heard an old woman exclaim:

She is more to be pitied than censured,
She is more to be helped than despised,
She is only a lassie who ventured
On life's stormy path ill-advised.
Do not scorn her with words fierce and bitter,
Do not laugh at her shame and downfall;
For a moment just stop and consider
That a man was the cause of it all.

                                    William B. Gray

Chapter One
Imagining the Prostitute

Americans expressed concern about prostitution in fervent reform movements from the mid-1880's until the nation's entry into World War I in 1917. During the three decades preceding the war, American alarm at the prostitute produced a wealth of literature. Reformers of every stripe—among them feminists, social workers, clergymen, physicians, police detectives, and journalists—endlessly debated the causes, effects, and regulation of the "great social evil."[1]

In fiction, however, it was an entirely different matter. Most serious late-nineteenth- and early-twentieth-century novelists refused to imagine the prostitute at all. In fact, she had been mentioned only in passing from the inception of the nation's literature. The eighteenth-century novelist Charles Brockden Brown, for example, includes a very tame brothel scene in one of his works; his contemporary William Hill Brown makes a quick reference to the prostitute.[2] In the next century, a Hawthorne story describes her briefly, and reformed prostitutes figure in works by Harriet Beecher Stowe and Louisa May Alcott.[3] Yet, by and large, the subliterary Gothic thriller, which, as Janis Stout observes, "skirted pornography," accounted for the fiction of prostitution until late in the nineteenth century.[4]

By the end of that century and the beginning of the twentieth, reputable writers who did describe the prostitute, wary of increased censorship and the unwritten laws of the genteel literary marketplace, followed their predecessors and relegated her to the status of a minor character. The exception was one group of novelists, some of enduring reputation, some all but forgotten. Joaquin Miller, Stephen Crane, Harold Frederic, Reginald Wright Kauffman, and David Graham Phillips placed the prostitute center stage as a poignant anti-heroine or even as a heroine. These men, their textual strategies, and their struggles—with the literary establishment, with the prudery of their culture, and, most importantly, with their own contradictory feelings about the prostitute—are the subject of this study.

This is necessarily a study of the masculine literary response to prostitution. In the decade following the Civil War, reform-minded novelists like Louisa May Alcott in *Work* (1873) and Harriet Beecher Stowe in *We and Our Neighbors* (1875) added secondary plots which

1

traced the lives of penitent young prostitutes in novels associating prostitution and other forms of feminine economic exploitation with the harshness and the lack of Christian charity in the new industrial city. Stowe and Alcott were unwilling to be hemmed in by the taboos surrounding such a controversial subject as the prostitute. They refused to kill off their fallen characters and provided compassionate portraits of these women's largely unsuccessful attempts to win social acceptance. Yet Stowe's Maggie and Alcott's Rachel are minor characters, and most other female novelists did not provide further lessons on urban indifference to the prostitute.[5]

Such reticence did not characterize the non-fiction published under the aegis of women's moral reform movements. Detailed accounts of prostitutes were published, for example, in the pre-Civil War journal of the Female Moral Reform Society, in post-war writings of women anti-prostitution crusaders, and in the work of Josephine Butler, a celebrated British befriender of prostitutes widely read in late-nineteenth-century America.[6] The next century saw studies like New York City probation officer Maude Miner's *The Slavery of Prostitution* (1916), in which she recorded the many interviews she had conducted with young prostitutes. A few women novelists of the Progressive era gave the prostitute attention, but their talent was minimal and their fiction thinly disguised polemic. Like their nineteenth-century predecessors, they feared the death to a literary career experienced by Kate Chopin, the author of *The Awakening* (1899), the story of an adulteress, a woman perceived as one remove from a prostitute.

The two generations of male writers to be studied here produced the first group of American novels on what one period commentator, voicing a common view, termed the "hideous subject" of prostitution.[7] This was the work of the classic writer Stephen Crane; two writers of enduring reputation, Harold Frederic and David Graham Phillips; and the "lost" novelists Joaquin Miller, Edgar Fawcett, and Reginald Wright Kauffman. Their concerns were neither sensational, as in the Gothic thrillers of the mid-nineteenth century, nor pornographic, as in the underground fiction of the same period. Instead they made the prostitute the subject of serious literary attention: a woman constantly threatened by entrapment, economic exploitation, and her own naiveté and vulnerability.[8]

In exploring so daring a literary subject, however, these novelists inevitably played out their own late-Victorian conflicts about woman's sexuality. If women were, as all of them believed, either chaste or fallen, how could the prostitute be defended? Was she not a volitional sinner as much as a scapegoated victim? As sinner, what did she suggest about the potential waywardness of all women? As victim, how could her depravity be ignored?

All of the writers to be scrutinized answer these questions by covering over their ambivalence about her real nature. They "solve" the problem of depicting her in all her complexity by removing her from the knowledge and often the consequences of carnal experience. She becomes in effect desexualized: in the work of Miller, Fawcett, and Crane, a traumatized seduction victim; in Frederic, a saintly sufferer; in Kauffman, an oratorical witness to social injustice; in Phillips, a triumphantly manly heroine. Such "solutions" are actually her creators' attempts to defend the ultimate fallen woman without acknowledging the hired sexuality of which her profession consisted.

The career of the flamboyant sagebrush romantic and self-styled frontier hero, Joaquin Miller, was marked by self-advertisement as much as literary talent. With an eye to bolstering his sagging reputation, he transferred his attention from verse narratives of the California mountains to an urban frontier. His *Destruction of Gotham* (1886) places the prostitute in a New York City wilderness more savage than that on which this "Byron of the Rockies" based his fleetingly celebrated poetry. One of the few period novels centered on the American prostitute, it views her as a casualty of city life who loses her wits in addition to her virtue. In adapting the popular mid-century "wicked city" thriller, Miller could not escape the Virtue Betrayed stereotype which characterized it.

Also with an eye to the literary marketplace, the well-to-do New Yorker and Columbia graduate Edgar Fawcett expanded Miller's focus by a more extended description of the prostitute's tenement milieu. *The Evil That Men Do* (1889), often mentioned as a precursor of Crane's more famous *Maggie: A Girl of the Streets* (1893; rev. ed. 1896), excoriates predators who ruin young girls and leave them to lives of street prostitution. Like Miller, Fawcett recycled the formulaic plot of the seduced innocent driven mad by city villainy. The strategy would prove as much an artistic compromise as an innovation.

Stephen Crane—the journalist, war correspondent, and author of *Maggie: A Girl of the Streets*—was the most talented of the American prostitute's nineteenth-century imaginers. He elevated the slum novel, and with it the streetwalker, to art. Indeed Crane developed a literary strategy which, in attempting to protect the deserted street girl, bore a marked resemblance to the chivalric rescues of red-light district women he actually conducted. Yet Crane too relied on the sentimental harlot's progress tale which had characterized prostitution fiction from the mid-century thriller to the work of Miller and Fawcett.

Another of the more celebrated nineteenth-century American writers, Harold Frederic also wrote a novel which centers on the prostitute. The title character of *The Lawton Girl* (1890) is a young woman who comes home to her small upstate New York town to "live it down." Still, the novel acknowledges her life as an active prostitute only in passing.

Though Frederic did place his repentant heroine in the believable social context of an upstate New York manufacturing town, his dominant need was to sanctify the woman whose brothel life so unsettled him. Ironically, Frederic was quite a sexual rebel in his own life, but his fiction made the prostitute pay for redemption with hers.

Like Crane and Frederic, Reginald Wright Kauffman was a small-town boy from the East who found success as a journalist and writer of fiction. As part of the response to Progressive era campaigns against the imagined evils of "white slavery," this investigative reporter took up the prostitute's defense and refused to kill her off, as had his literary predecessors. His best-seller *The House of Bondage* (1910) attempts to exculpate her by giving her a voice to defend herself. Kaufmann did succeed in legitimizing the white slave narrative, but he turned his heroine into a soapbox orator at great cost to verisimilitude. Still, *The House of Bondage* went through 16 printings in two years and paved the way for the controversial *Susan Lenox: Her Fall and Rise* (written 1911; published 1917), by David Graham Phillips.

A midwestern patrician's son credited with being the "man with the muckrake" irately described by Theodore Roosevelt, Phillips went beyond most muckrakers in his desire to expose urban corruption, most notably the sexual exploitation of poor women. Yet, unlike Kauffman's white slaves, his prostitute heroine Susan Lenox is a model of fortitude. Belying his novel's claim to document the horrors of forced prostitution, he insists that her life in the sex trade has not tainted but strengthened her: she emerges as innocent and hopeful as when she entered it. Paradoxically, rather than acknowledge in Susan what his novels with more conventional female characters argued was the "sex trickery" of women, Phillips defended his streetwalking protagonist against charges of sexual professionalism and immorality. He even mythified her as a mixture of purity and endurance: ideally female in virtue, ideally male in strength. From Miller to Kauffman, writers had presented the prostitute as a victim; Phillips carried her defense much further and made her a heroine. But in so doing, more than any other author to be studied here, he romanticized her as well.

These were not, of course, the only writers to create fiction about prostitution. The naturalist Frank Norris warned against the sharklike barroom harlot in his beast-in-man novel, *Vandover and the Brute* (written 1894; published 1914). The crusading photo-journalist Jacob Riis pictured the streetwalker as a snarling animal in a vignette from *Out of Mulberry Street* (1898). The half-novels, half-tracts of Socialists Walter Hurt (*The Scarlet Shadow*, 1907) and Estelle Baker (*The Rose Door*, 1911), employed hortatory white slaves to criticize capitalist excess. The politician Brand Whitlock included an equally exploited "Girl That's Down" in his collection *The Fall Guy* (1912) to urge reform of laws victimizing the prostitute. These and other writers will receive mention, though they either truncate their presentations or lack the vision of a Crane, a Phillips, or even a Kauffman.[9]

The very limited American pornography and erotica of the period will not be considered.[10] With titles like *Maidenhead Stories* and *The Story of a Slave*,[11] these works presented the prostitute as merely another female citizen of what Steven Marcus in his study of British erotica terms "pornotopia." It is a world in which the "essential imagination of nature" is an "immense, supine...female form."[12] Indeed, pornography, in Victorian times as in our own, is in no way an interpretation of life. It is a genre dedicated to arousing a specific and limited physiological response, despite the eloquence of many modern critics defending its supposed imaginative vision and artistic worth. American erotica, from books of sheer crudity to the eccentric works of utopian free love movements, might at times have intended more than titillation. Yet such books cannot help us understand what the prostitute meant to the above-ground literary imagination.

For this understanding we must turn to the prostitution novels of Crane, Frederic, Phillips, and their contemporaries. Most often, with the exception of *Maggie: A Girl of the Streets*, these works have been glossed over or ignored. What is more, there has been little attempt to locate *Maggie*, Crane's celebrated slum novel, in the context of his other writings on prostitution. The famous solicitation scene, excised from all but Crane's privately printed 1893 edition, was only republished fairly recently. Apparently, there has been critical reluctance to acknowledge Maggie's streetwalking.[13] Virtually no attempt has been made to study prostitution novels such as those by Miller or Kauffman primarily as literary works about women paid for sexual services.[14] Acknowledgments of these works, when they do occur, are usually buried in discussions of the rise of the urban social protest novel. The choice of topic—the prostitute—is usually dismissed as a minor example of literary rebellion, a daring choice but one lacking wider significance.[15]

Turning to the novels themselves, we see that Miller's *The Destruction of Gotham*, though less valuable as art than as an index to prevailing attitudes, is no weaker than his other work, which has been carefully scrutinized. Fawcett's *The Evil That Men Do* is actually better than much of his other fiction, but it too has received minimal attention in the only book-length study of his work.[16] Although Frederic's *The Lawton Girl* is equal if not superior to some of his other work and received a good deal of attention in its time, in our time critics prefer to comment on far more obscure novels by this writer. Most of these analysts have simply hidden the fact that Jessica Lawton is a prostitute. One commentator informs the reader that *The Lawton Girl* presents an "unsentimental and unconventional treatment of sex";

another prefers the ambiguity of calling Jessica a girl who returned home in "courageous shame."[17]

In their embarrassment over the topic of prostitution, critics have avoided discussing the texts of the Progressive generation as well. Kauffman's sympathy for his trapped prostitute heroine, lured to a brothel by a procurer, is either seen as evidence of his radical political beliefs or dismissed as an example of his era's peculiar "white slave" fixation.[18] Certainly no critic has analyzed *The House of Bondage* for literary technique or dominant imagery. Critics have brushed over the most controversial prostitution novel of the early twentieth century, *Susan Lenox: Her Fall and Rise,* in a similar way.[19] When they do mention Phillip's massive novel about an alcoholic streetwalker who climbs to success, they emphasize her economic exploitation, as if she were a worker like any other.[20]

Everett Carter's attitude toward Harold Frederic best summarizes the standard critical view of the fiction of prostitution. It is one which feminists, their attention focused on re-evaluating American classics or works by neglected women writers, have done little to alter. In a lengthy critical introduction to the writer's most famous work, *The Damnation of Theron Ware* (1896), Carter argues that Frederic brought "the power of sex from the background to the foreground of realistic fiction."[21] Yet Carter, instead of citing *The Lawton Girl,* turns to Frederic novels which offered much less discussion of the sexually unorthodox woman. His introduction makes no reference to either the prostitute Jessica Lawton or the novel in which she figures.

The censorious attitude of modern critics extends beyond glossing over the prostitute in the works which form the subject of this study. Granted, the small number of American novels dealing with prostitution might justify the omission of the subject from standard literary histories and bibliographies. But such an omission also reveals a critical prudishness which has obscured the importance of this group of works. By their very focus on the prostitute, these novels question an American literary tradition reluctant to discuss the sexually wayward woman. This tradition needs some brief explanation, and to it we now turn.

* * * * *

It is a critical commonplace that nineteenth-century American literature lacks fully realized women characters. In Joyce Warren's words, it "did not grant the individuality to women which [it was] willing to grant to men," which resulted in a "literature of female nonpersons."[22] This omission is particularly telling when these writers attempted to depict the sexually active woman. Their fear of female carnality, derived from a puritan heritage, was reinforced by a dedication to the myth of American innocence and their celebration of a frontier without women.[23] This literary inheritance not only made the prostitute an invisible figure but also limited the treatment of her spiritual cousin, the seductress. With sensual women all but absent, the "mystique of the virgin" dominated classic fiction.[24]

When she does appear, there is certainly a lack of credibility about the seductive woman. Whether Melville's "overpowering nightmare figures" or Hawthorne's tormented anti-heroines, their sensuality is "limited in its expression to atmospheric effects, insinuations, and rumors."[25] Other Dark Ladies, such as Hawthorne's unwilling Beatrice Rappaccini or Oliver Wendell Holmes's Elsie Venner, are equally unreal. An involuntary dweller in her scientist-father's poisoned garden, Beatrice is forced to lure the Adamic Giovanni to his death. Yet, as Judith Fryer has observed, she was "as much seduced as seducing."[26] When she falls in love with the young man, she poisons herself rather than have him die. Elsie Venner, whose mother was bitten by a snake while pregnant with her, also lures for reasons not of her choosing. Holmes prefaces his 1861 novel by insisting that she exists to pose a moral question:

The real aim of the story was to test the doctrine of "original sin" and human responsibility.... Was Elsie Venner, poisoned by the venom [of a snake]...before she was born, morally responsible for the "volitional" aberration, which translated into acts become what is known as sin....[?][27]

Holmes answers his question with a resounding no, establishing his character as a victim rather than a *femme fatale*. Her need to entrap men really signals, he contends, a genetic inheritance combined with a misplaced search for parental affection.

Within the context of such literary squeamishness about woman's sexuality, Hawthorne's passionate, dark-haired Hester Prynne seems an exception to the allegorical American seductress. Yet Hester is only introduced after her affair, and her story is one of transformation from adulteress to uplifting presence—she becomes a true mother to Pearl and Sister of Mercy to those in need. Only briefly, in a forest scene with Dimmesdale, does she stray from the penitent's role. She defends their sexual past and asks him to flee with her and their daughter. However, even in this she acts as a maternal figure urging the tortured man to renounce his bondage to Puritan thought, rather than as a former mistress seeking a renewed conquest.

If mid-century writers balked at portraying the power of seductive womanhood, some of them at least drew strong women whose lives were shaped by their forbidden love. The increased prudishness of the closing decades of the century deprived the fallen woman of whatever character or distinctiveness she had. American literature disdained the European interest in the desperate promiscuity of the Flaubertian adulteress or the unthinking sensuality of Zola's Nana. The literary context in which

Crane, Frederic, or lesser writers like Fawcett and Kauffman could imagine any sexually deviant woman was a circumscribed one. If they looked to popular fiction, they would only have found what Frank Norris, lamenting the debased romanticism of the period, deplored as the "onrush of works of ideality and romance."[28] Historical fiction like Charles Major's *When Knighthood Was in Flower* (1889) and George Barr McCutcheon's *Graustark* (1901) or Francis Marion Crawford's stream of romances claimed popular success and critical attention. When the *femme fatale* does appear, she embodies the sterile conventions offered by Mark Twain and Charles Dudley Warner in their portrait of Laura in *The Gilded Age* (1872) ("whenever she took a prisoner he remained her slave").[29] She is the coquettish but prudent Mrs. Farrell, the title character of a Howells novel, or the cardboard vamp of a number of forgettable works with titles like *A Modern Circe* (1887), *Mrs. Sparks of Paris* (1888), or *Delilah of Harlem* (1893). Or she is like DuMaurier's celebrated Trilby, the altruistic and virginal artist's model who only leads a Bohemian life because she does not know any better.[30]

Despite his adherence to the new creed of realism, William Dean Howells applauded such artistic self-censorship. To him, "erotic shivers and fervors" were tabooed subjects. Howells was certainly correct when, as the influential *Harper's* editor and arbiter of literary taste, he bragged that "an American novelist may not write a story on the lines of Anna Karenina or Madame Bovary. Sappho they put aside, and from Zola's work they avert their eyes."[31] He concurred with Henry James, who remarked acidly of the French writers Zola and Maupassant that they "picture a world where every man is a cad and every woman a harlot."[32]

Behind the American critical attack on European fiction was a genteel distaste for the subject of sex, particularly prostitution. At a time when estimates of American prostitutes averaged 40,000 in New York, and 10,000 to 20,000 in other large American cities, Howells disingenuously argued that "it is quite false or quite mistaken to suppose that our novels have left untouched the important realities of life." As if prostitution were non-existent, he continued, "they have relegated illicit sex in their pictures of life to the space and place they occupy in life itself, as we know it in America."[33]

Malcolm Cowley offers perhaps the best definition of the philosophy informing genteel literature and not without its effect on the prostitution novels of this study. There was, he contends, a pervasive

attempt to abolish the evils and vulgarities and the changes in American society by never talking about them....[Literature] focused instead on the American middle-class home and its presiding spirit, the pure young girl...[and] was characterized by an innocently hopeful atmosphere...absolutely divorced from daily life.[34]

This genteel influence was especially felt in literature which purported to describe the lower depths. H.H. Boyesen, the author of *Social Strugglers* (1893), published the same year as the unabridged *Maggie*, was in his day considered a social realist. Early in his novel, a slumming party of socialites and their jaded escorts enter a Lower East Side bar. Boyesen wishes to show compassion for the impoverished slum dwellers gawked at by these insensitive aristocrats. Yet, like the work of many period writers, his novel becomes a travel narrative of curious sights. Toughs and derelicts are the subjects of fairly thorough "local color" treatment. However, two women found in a seedy bar— the word prostitute is carefully avoided—are given a few lines at most. A "dreadful young woman" and her companion, "a pallid and stunted female creature with tousled hair and snaggled teeth," is all the description they receive.[35]

A similar obliqueness characterizes *The Golden House* (1894), a novel by Mark Twain's friend and sometime collaborator, Charles Dudley Warner.[36] Warner briefly pictures the prostitute as the guilty bearer of an unnamed sin, a sickly young girl wearing a tawdry hat and tight clothing. She is not otherwise identified, although her costume signals her profession to the reader. Warner comments that she has the eyes of a "troubled and hunted animal," but he does not discuss what those troubles are. He merely allows the reader a glimpse of the woman in her streetwalker's garb. He ends the scene by reforming such a potentially threatening figure. He has her seek out the neighborhood priest and inquire wistfully, "Do you think, father,...that I can be forgiven?" This abbreviated tale of a lost woman concludes with Father Damon looking down sadly at her: "Yes, my daughter, if you repent. It is all with our Father. He never refuses" (60).

If Warner only hinted at the harlot's life, James W. Sullivan, in the popular *Tenement Tales of New York* (1895), omits any mention of it at all.[37] The collection contains a far more acceptable period type, that of the girl who almost fell, but was saved by love of virtue. "Minnie Kelsey's Wedding" represents a prime example of the evasive literary attitude toward the sexuality of the working-class girl. There is an initial resemblance to Crane's *Maggie*: Minnie, a factory worker tired of her unrewarding life and wrongly suspected of waywardness, runs to the river to consider her plight. But the resemblance to Crane's heroine soon ends. When the city swell Tom King approaches her, she speaks with the voice of injured innocence: "I have been made the victim of my own vanity. I have suffered in my reputation through you." Rather than consign her to a more believable fate, Sullivan has Minnie say: "I shall never again be caught in such a trap" (60). In the sugary ending, Tom King, converted by such virtue, proclaims Minnie "a good girl" (61) and promptly marries her.

The young sweatshop model in another Sullivan tale, "Cohen's Figure," Ernestine Beaufoy, is not so fortunate, although she represents another tepid period alternative to the prostitute. In one passage, Sullivan titillates the reader with a vision of what Ernestine would have to endure should she sell herself to her "foreign" employer. The sweaty Cohen pretends to measure a dress on his new model:

He put the tape-line across her bosom in full—halfway above the swell—higher—lower. Next up-and-down measurements from the neck; in the middle; at one side; at the other; in close against the arms. At last he stopped....His expression...was at once lascivious, brutal, and gloating...The bloom was rubbed off Ernestine Beaufoy. (85)

Having ventured so far into dangerous literary territory, Sullivan prudently censors himself and kills off the now-tarnished girl. A moment after her degradation (though still a virgin), Ernestine leaps out of a window. Her decision relieves Sullivan's narrator: "She had chosen between death and degradation...[and] at the culmination of her tragic life, Ernestine Beaufoy was victor" (88). Presumably, it frees Sullivan as well.

As the works of Boyesen, Warner, and Sullivan suggest, the growing interest in the slum as a legitimate subject for local color fiction sent uptown socialites on slumming parties. It even allowed for occasional sensational passages, provided the old "wages of sin is death" formula was appropriately invoked. Yet these writers—less rebellious than Crane, for whom poverty, alcoholism, and crime were acceptable literary subjects—only hint at prostitution, in large part to avoid the censorship which had been steadily growing in power since the end of the Civil War. To better understand the kind of literary cautiousness from which even the prostitute's most daring imaginers would not be exempt, a brief analysis of the censors' power is in order.

* * * * *

Before the Civil War, there was little organized censorship. A small trade in erotica—chiefly foreign, since there was almost no tradition of indigenous erotic fiction—flourished.[38] But by the 1870's and 80's, censorship laws were stiffened in response to a new Social Purity fervor. The movement reflected unrest at the new moral relativism of urban communities, alarm at rising divorce rates, and an obsessive interest in promoting chastity and curbing sexual fulfillment, even in marriage. Included under the Social Purity umbrella were groups as diverse as the moderate Federation of Women's Clubs, the more radical National Purity Congress, and the fanatical Society for the Suppression of Vice. All campaigned against prostitution and for a single standard of sexual morality. Differences aside, they wished to impose the values of the village on big-city America, or as one modern analyst has phrased it, to "restate the Puritan view of society in social terms."[39]

Many in these movements saw literature as an index of moral purity or its lack. Any novel dealing with extra-marital sexuality aroused ire. One convert to the creed wrote in *Publishers' Weekly* in 1889: "The taste for unclean literature is confined to a very small part of the sixty millions of the inhabitants of this country. The vast majority are in sound moral health."[40] Sound moral health evidently required that *The Scarlet Letter* and *Leaves of Grass* be condemned (Walt Whitman was dismissed from his job for creating an "indecent" book), that a reference to semi-clothed Marquesan girls be omitted from a revised edition of Melville's *Typee*, and that Kate Chopin's *The Awakening* be removed from the library shelves of at least one major American city and probably other cities as well. European literature fared no better. Tolstoy's novel of a disastrous marriage, *The Kreutzer Sonata*, was banned. Arnold Bennett's *Old Wives' Tale*, guilty of no more than descriptions of a passionate elopement and lower-class French hotels, was rejected by *Scribner's* magazine for American publication. Hardy's *Jude the Obscure*, although *Harper's* offered to serialize it in abridged form, was castigated for its "abnormal eroticism."[41] As one representative censor proclaimed, "The flashy novels...that glow with the fires of impure passions, are to be relentlessly proscribed."[42] Classics with prostitute characters, such as *Moll Flanders, Roxana,* and *Tom Jones*, were now banned as well (though underground booksellers continued to be jailed for selling them).[43]

The censors' attacks on Alphonse Daudet and George Bernard Shaw best illustrate the cultural climate which gave warning to American writers wanting to deal with the prostitute. Daudet's novel *Sapho* (1884) is the story of a courtesan moving in a Parisian artistic milieu who falls in love. She talks her young artist into living with her, only to lose him to the forces of convention. The novel is a rather pedestrian imitation of Dumas' *Camille*. Still, it has one scene which many found particularly shocking: the young man carries Sapho upstairs to a bedroom. "We have seldom seen a book more objectionable," concluded the literary critic of *Publishers' Weekly*.[44] A Philadelphia court sentenced the news dealer who sold it in America to a year in prison. In 1900 the Clyde Fitch adaptation played in New York until censors, bolstered by reviewers who considered it lewd and obscene, succeeded in temporarily closing the play down. The lead actress and stage manager were arrested. A Michigan town was liberal enough to let a local company put on the play, but such was the furor that they could not finish the second act.[45] Five years later, Shaw's *Mrs. Warren's Profession*, its title character a capitalistic madam, opened in New Haven. The critics, missing the satire, railed against "dramatizing vice" and called the play a "wholly nasty justification of prostitution.''[46] The authorities again jailed members of the cast. Shaw himself wrote in 1907, "I do not go to America [because] I am afraid of being arrested...." "I cannot fight Comstock," he complained, "with the American nation at his back and the New York Police in his van."[47]

Shaw was referring to Anthony Comstock, the nation's chief censor and the leader of the watchdog Society for the Suppression of Vice. A special agent for the Post Office Department from the 1870's until his death in 1915 when his successors took up the cudgel, Comstock enforced the law named after him which prevented sending obscene matter through the mail.[48] He was credited with having caused the arrest of three thousand booksellers, authors, and publishers. He also reportedly destroyed 50 tons of books and almost 30,000 plates for printing objectionable literature—not to mention 4 million pictures.[49] Predictably, he labeled as a prostitute any woman who did not dress or talk the way a "pure, noble, modest woman" should.[50] Claiming to protect Christian youth against "traps for the young" (the title of one of his books), he made no distinction between pornography and the classics. Any literature about sexuality was dangerous:

The effect of this cursed...[literature] on our youth and society, no pen can describe. It breeds lust. Lust defiles the body, debauches the imagination, corrupts the mind, deadens the will, destroys the memory, sears the conscience, hardens the heart, and damns the soul.[51]

Works by Boccaccio, Maupassant, and Tolstoy were "little better than histories of brothels and prostitutes in...lust-cursed nations."[52]

In a nation which H.L. Mencken accused of being a land of moral censors, Comstock became a respected if controversial national figure. He was even perceived in many quarters as a social reformer. As late as 1930, the *Dictionary of American Biography* praised him because he "removed from circulation many items which have not been missed."[53] In his own time, publishers feared legal action if they did not send "questionable" manuscripts to him and his Society readers for criticism. Anticipating Comstock's response, the important publishing house of Appleton, for example, insisted on deleting potentially explosive passages before they would issue *Maggie: A Girl of the Streets* (which Crane had privately printed a few years before). A decade later, Comstock's successor John Sumner successfully blocked full serial publication of *Susan Lenox* and took Appleton to court to have the book version withdrawn from circulation. Eventually Appleton had to permit Sumner to delete all passages he felt were "unfit for publication and distribution" before the book could be reissued.[54]

When writers like Crane and Phillips risked this kind of censorship, they were upsetting prevailing attitudes about female sexuality. To get at the root of these attitudes, however, it is necessary to understand why, besides the feeling that to write about her was to produce pornographic or semi-pornographic material, the prostitute posed such a threat to the American imagination. To do so involves a brief history of reigning theories about woman's nature, particularly the Victorian emphasis on her passionlessness. Ironically, such an ideology would inform the fictive descriptions of the prostitute as well.

* * * * *

By her very nature the prostitute—and the fiction which dared to describe her—called into question two cherished period ideas: that woman had a higher moral sense than man and that she was innately chaste. *Woman, in Her Social and Domestic Character* was a popular discussion of woman's social role reprinted frequently in the nineteenth century. Its author, Mrs. John Sandford, observed that woman's "presence...[was] a pledge against impropriety and excess, a check on vice, and a protection to virtue."[55] Many moralists explained how women could be such paragons: they were simply "by nature and education less selfish."[56] Nature was, indeed, often invoked to describe feminine purity. To one representative mid-century essayist, chastity was "the natural inheritance of woman."[57]

There were those who challenged the vision of woman as too pure to be tarnished by the world's evil, too innocent to imagine evil of others. Yet the "Angel in the House"—"sweet, innocent, gentle, modest, selfless...pretty, dependent, and a staunch preserver of society"—was a fixture in discussions of feminine sexuality in fiction and prose literature well into the next century.[58] Certainly the pronouncements of influential writers such as William Dean Howells and muckraking journalist George Kibbe Turner suggested the enduring power of equating femininity with sexlessness. Skillful at giving ideology the force of fact, Howells in 1905 rejoiced in woman's "moral and spiritual superiority."[59] Five years later, despite the agitation of feminist and Social Purity groups for a single moral standard for men and women, Turner, whose white slave exposés were avidly read, proclaimed: "A woman's chastity...[is] the foundation of Anglo-Saxon society."[60]

Medical theory shored up the feminine purity philosophy. Dr. J. Richardson Parke, in his 1906 textbook *Human Sexuality*, claimed that woman had "[i]nnate modesty, and...normal feebleness of sexual desire."[61] Yet Richardson, who subtitled his book "Medico-Literary Treatise in the Laws, Anomalies, and Relations of Sex with special reference to Contrary Sexual Desire," was as perplexed as most analysts by prostitution. Invoking the good woman-bad woman Victorian dichotomy seemed appropriate. Still, it did not explain whether prostitutes actually felt sexual desire. Richardson focused on their interest in money, and thus, by evading the issue, left his innate chastity argument more or less intact. He was more cautious than noted medical historian of prostitution and resident physician at the Blackwell's Island women's detention center, Dr. William Sanger. After interviewing thousands of prostitutes, Sanger found that a number of them cited "inclination" as a cause for entry. Yet Sanger, rather than try to account for such sexuality, used these responses to reassure himself about normal women: "the full force of sexual desire [is] seldom known to a virtuous woman."[62]

Physicians like Parke and Sanger expressed the dominant view when they swept prostitution aside as abnormal. Only a few such as Dr. Elizabeth Blackwell, the first woman doctor in the United States, felt that sexual feeling existed in all women. She argued against "the very sandy foundation of the supposed stronger character of male sexual passion."[63] A minority of male physicians also acknowledged the sexual instinct in women who were not prostitutes or otherwise abnormal. Too, modern historians have questioned whether the traditional code matched the reality of feminine sexuality. Relying rather heavily on the Mosher Survey (a small study covering the years 1892 to 1920 relying on the responses of upper-middle-class women who described active sexual lives), Carl N. Degler contends that women's sexuality was far different from the official version in the best-known prescriptive literature.[64] Another modern historian of sexuality, Peter Gay, surveys the bourgeoisie through the prism of a well-documented adulterous affair between such models of married gentility as Mabel Loomis Todd and Emily Dickinson's brother Austin. Gay cites America as the "first (as impressionistic evidence strongly suggests) to encourage, or at least wink at, premarital erotic experimentation."[65] Yet he too bases his generalizations on limited evidence. We join a 1984 *New York Times* reviewer in wondering "why that [feminine purity] code was defended and justified with such passionate anxiety and such distinctive zeal."[66]

Granted, the revisionist view of Victorian sexuality had a measure of insight into the actual practices of some women. What is more significant is the insistence on the Chaste Heroine in everything from conduct guides and marriage manuals to gift-book poetry and magazine fiction. She must have concealed a wealth of anxieties. Certainly, when confronting the prostitution phenomenon, the concept of female passionlessness was reassuring. The language in which the pure woman was actually implicitly compared to the impure one by the celebrated British student of prostitution and venereal disease, Dr. William Acton, embodied the fears about the true relation of good and bad women. Acton's *Functions and Disorders of the Reproductive Organs,* which went through many American editions and was still in print twenty years after its 1875 publication, comforted male readers. They "need not fear," he wrote, "that [a] wife [would] require the excitement, or in any respect imitate the ways of a courtesan."[67] Although "need not fear" is a common enough construction, Acton recognizes that men would be frightened to think that a good woman was passionate, i.e. whorish. Behind chastity lurked the possibility that if women acted naturally, they would all act like prostitutes. Acton's American counterpart, Dr. William Sanger, cautioned that "were the passions in both sexes equal, prostitution would be far more rife in our midst than at present."[68]

Whether nineteenth-century chastity apologists realized it or not, their insistence was a radical departure from a dominant strain in Western thinking about woman. Although feminine virginity had been prized from earliest Christian times, there was a parallel belief in women as licentious creatures. Identifying woman's physical beauty with the dangers of the flesh supported the belief that man could control his urges but woman could not. Her lust was insatiable. Such reasoning informs works as diverse as Rabelais' bawdy fictions, the fifteenth-century witchcraft guidebook *Malleus Maleficarum*, and the writings of the Church Fathers.[69] Indeed a standard religious view was that woman originated sexual sin because of her lack of self-control. All women, "daughters of Eve," inherited her "demonic sensuality."[70] This demon-Eve solution to the problem of evil, building as it did on the myths of Lilith, Pandora, and the pagan goddesses of pre-Christian religions, universally linked women with evil sexuality. Thus, when a character in Elizabethan playwright Thomas Dekker's dark comedy spoke to his Magdalen daughter, he voiced a prejudice already age-old by the Renaissance:

Say thou are not a Whore, and that's more than fifteen women (among five hundred) dare swear without lying....[71]

Despite the corollary view that women embodied God's grace and were more spiritual than men, they were defined traditionally as particularly sexual.

Such a definition seemed far removed from the idea of the sexless Victorian lady, who, in poet Coventry Patmore's phrase, was "marr'd less than man by mortal fall." Numerous reasons have been advanced for this shift in thinking about woman, evident during the Enlightenment eighteenth century, which reached its flowering in the Victorian nineteenth.[72] Some modern analysts argue for a new bourgeois cult of domesticity, itself a reaction against aristocratic excess. Others contend that purity ideology was born with the Evangelical movement, which relied on the idea of the pious woman to shore up the religious revival. Whatever the cause, as soon as woman's nature was rewritten, there was a corresponding need to elevate her above man. Simple moral equality was not considered.

This leads us back to the fear of female promiscuity, a fear too frightening to acknowledge, but one which would inform the works of all the literary rebels to be discussed in this study. Clearly the division between chaste and unchaste women, though modified somewhat in early-twentieth-century discussions of prostitutes, was predicated on fears of the sexually active woman. As one modern student of this ideology remarked:

When woman is regarded as an asexual being, devoid of all erotic desire and capacity for fulfillment, again there is no need to be concerned about her sexual satisfaction....[H]er lack of desire endows her with a certain moral superiority over the carnal male, [but] [r]educed to moral, instead of sexual, superiority; reduced to a primarily spiritual, instead of a primarily sexual being, she of course is much less threatening....Yet even a chaste woman is dangerous, since a man may still sin by regarding her with lust. Therefore [the doubt that] any woman is truly pure. [Even women who] do not engage in sexual intercourse...are guilty of possessing a nature that incites the male to lustful thoughts.[73]

The prostitute called up the specter of a sexually destructive Eve, a Circe, a *femme fatale*. An ideology, moreover, which helped men deal with their own sexuality would be threatened if the prostitute were viewed in any other way than as depraved.

Thus when writers like Crane, Frederic, and Phillips decided to place the prostitute center stage, their work called up fears, evoking the horror of censor and genteel author alike. Even had there not been the official censorship of Comstock's Society for the Suppression of Vice, American writers worked within a context in which it was difficult to find a non-moralistic description, even if the focus was sociological, economic, or medical.[74] Critics consistently employed the language of sin: "depravity," "lewdness," "immorality," and, a term of equal opprobrium, especially for women, "sensuality." Mindful of the prostitute as a carrier of venereal disease and a criminal consort of thieves, even the more compassionate observers would have approved of the nineteenth-century historian William Hartpole Lecky's famous summation of her as "the supreme type of vice."[75] (Lecky himself felt that the prostitute, though a sinner, was a scapegoat for the sins and hypocrisies of man.) Her chief sin—variously termed "vicious sensual indulgence," "sexual perversity," and "licentiousness"—was rarely labeled the more straightforward term lust. Rather, these writers added a cluster of other deadly sins to explain her fall: greed, sloth, vanity.

In histories of prostitution, medical treatises on venereal disease, and newspaper exposés of bordellos, writers depicted the prostitute with revulsion and scorn. Most echoed the sentiments of the popular 1888 discussion of New York City red-light districts, *In Danger!,* that the prostitute was a moral menace because, "stripped of that alone which can retain and purify her influence," she acted her part "in the demoralization of society."[76] Reverend Matthew Hale Smith learned from his underworld tour that she was "lost to all moral feeling, and to all sense of shame."[77] The author of one description of urban poverty, *Vices of a Big City* (1890), bluntly warned against prostitutes because they were "degraded women." The author of *Lights and Shadows of New York Life* (1872), a popular guidebook, employed the "wages of sin" convention when describing beer garden waitresses who doubled as prostitutes:

The women known outside the city as pretty waiter girls are simply a collection of poor wretches who have gone down almost to the end of their fatal career. They may retain faint vestiges of their former beauty, but that is all. They are beastly, foul-mouthed, brutal wretches. Very many of them are half dead with consumption and disease. They are in every respect disgusting.[78]

The new spirit of sociological inquiry ushered in by the Progressive era attempted to replace such didacticism with social scientific observation. Vice commissions to study the conditions responsible for prostitution and tabulate statistics on commercialized vice proliferated.[79] Armies of investigators gathered and analyzed data on virtually every aspect of the sex trade, chief among them the prostitute's motives, wages, and working conditions. Now she was less the sinner to be blasted than the witness to be interviewed. Her recital of white slave entrapment appeared in every forum from the vice commission inquiry to the Progressive novel. But the language of moral condemnation lingered. The prostitute was defended as an economic victim but condemned as one who practiced "vile methods" and encouraged "vicious pleasures."[80]

Many observers who judged her harshly, indeed, still followed the influential Dr. Sanger, author of the first serious American history of prostitution. Sanger, faced with the specter of sexual volition, simply explained it away. When 513 of the 2,000 Blackwell's Island prostitutes he interviewed claimed voluntary entry into the trade, he responded that many were the victims of seduction before such inclination existed.[81] Seasoned red-light district journalists concurred. "Cases of voluntary prostitution are rare," one argued, for woman is "naturally chaste." Another commentator on the subject concluded: "at least six in *every two* are forced by sheer necessity to become confirmed prostitutes."[82] James Buel, a well-known late-nineteenth-century student of prostitution, altered the statistic but not the sentiment: "It is a well ascertained fact that more than three-fourths of all bawds in New York City are the victims of libertines, and almost entirely blameless for the first evil step taken."[83]

Late-Victorian thought could not resolve the contradictions in the phrase "almost entirely blameless." Was a prostitute a pure girl gone astray, a young woman tricked into the trade, "without...libidinous desire to prompt her to [such] self-immolation?"[84] Writers like the outraged conduct book writer Elizabeth Evans denied it: "courtesans follow their infamous trade because they enjoy it."[85] Yet the certitude and clarity of such naysaying were atypical. Far more representative was the opinion of B.O. Flower, editor of the reform journal *Arena*. Prostitutes were, in his view,

children of lust [because]...they had inherited the violent...passions of their fathers, which, in their case, when aroused, rendered them powerless to resist the cunning, determined advances of their polluters.[86]

British physician Bracebridge Hemyng agreed:

[T]here must be something inherently bad in her nature, to lead her to abandon her person to the other sex, who are at all times ready to take advantage of a woman's weakness and a woman's love.[87]

Both writers struggled with motive. To Flower, a woman acted licentiously but could not help it because she had inherited her father's lust. To Hemyng, her sacrificial devotion contended with her wickedness. The reasoning in both cases is cloudy.

The next century also vacillated between innate depravity and victimization. As social worker Annie Allen explained in 1910, a prostitute "has not chosen, she has merely fallen."[88] In addition, the language of involuntary sacrifice was still employed. Maude Miner, another noted Progressive analyst of prostitution, observed, "Before knowing the meaning of morality or immorality, young girls sacrificed their virtue."[89] The seducer was replaced by the white slaver, the madam, and the environment itself. Such influences joined the sweatshop to produce the fall. But, like the reformers of the previous century, Progressives could not reconcile the supposed passivity of the victim with the mercantile assertiveness of the soliciting prostitute.

Such were the cultural contradictions that inevitably influenced the writers to be studied here. What in our national ideology was a double vision of the prostitute became in our fiction conventions of denial. Her literary imaginers were sympathetic to and unsettled by prostitution. Resistant to genteel stricture, these men were nevertheless unable to create prostitutes that they could acknowledge as such. In their work these women appear as crazed or alcoholically remote seduction victims, saintly penitents, outraged orators, even, paradoxically, as manly heroines. They are either too traumatized, or too removed from their experience, to be engaged in a sexual life. In the rare event that they are not killed off, they emerge from "the life" as innocent of knowledge as when they entered it.

Joaquin Miller, an ostensible defender of the outlaw and pariah, was still faithful to the sentimental seduction fiction of the mid-century popular novel. His hapless rural ingenue endured urban sexual mistreatment she was too maddened to recall. Edgar Fawcett, though claiming to study the effect of environmental determinism on the New York working girl, traded his objectivity for a similar drama of betrayal and spiritual deadness. In short, both writers, despite their claims of social consciousness and verisimilitude, resurrected the clichés of the popular mid-century anti-urban narrative: the metropolis is a hell on earth, the prostitute a seduced innocent turned into an hysteric or alcoholic. Continuing the cliché, Miller and Fawcett defused their errant Dotties and Coras when they threatened to act as sexual beings.

Stephen Crane was personally fascinated by prostitutes. He interviewed them, toured and possibly patronized brothels, helped a known prostitute escape arrest, and entered into a common-law marriage with a madam, Cora Howorth Stewart. Nevertheless, in *Maggie* and his sketches on the Tenderloin prostitute, he used the same stereotypes as had Miller and Fawcett, though he employed these images with far more artistry. His women were either deserted innocents or, as in the *Maggie* subplot concerning Nell, bloodless predators. Unlike Miller and Fawcett, Crane wished to protect his prostitute heroines. He minimized their professional sexual activity, much as he had that of their real-life counterparts, by stressing their vulnerability and need for a male rescuer. Yet, he was troubled by the mercenary streetwalker, channeling these feelings of condemnation into the portrait of the villainous Nell. In art as in life, Crane never resolved his ambivalence about the impure woman, an ambivalence which his fiction embodied.

Crane's future friend Harold Frederic created an American Magdalen, Jessica Lawton, when, as European correspondent for the *New York Times,* he was condemning British evangelical crusades for social purity. In pseudonymous articles published in the *Pall Mall Gazette,* Frederic argued for tolerance of prostitutes. However, these articles revealed a double fear of feminine promiscuity and of economic self-reliance. We find Frederic's ambiguity surfacing in the lead character of *The Lawton Girl,* a prostitute-turned-settlement worker. The idea of a former prostitute teaching economic independence to oppressed factory girls was too unsettling. Frederic turned her into the outmoded Magdalen of mid-century fiction. In other words, he "resolved" his conflict between forgiving and condemning, a conflict also apparent in his novels featuring coquettish *femmes fatales,* by purifying and then killing off his prostitute heroine.

By the early twentieth century, increased interest in abolishing prostitution prompted extensive study of the prostitute herself. Fiction could now, ostensibly, analyze prostitution without didacticism. Newsman Reginald Wright Kauffman, the author of *The House of Bondage*, claimed to present sociological truth. He viewed himself as an investigator, like muckraking journalists and vice commissioners, reporting on forced prostitution. Kauffman saw the prostitute as a worker in an underworld sweatshop, a child-woman coerced into the trade by white slavers or economic need. His white slave novel, by insisting on the prostitute as a researcher or soapbox orator, sanitized the very woman he claimed to depict truthfully. He turned the prostitute into a witness to social injustice rather than a carnally knowing participant in commercialized vice. Kauffman, in short, validated the *idées fixes* of the Progressive era.

The social protest writer David Graham Phillips was the only Progressive novelist to challenge late-Victorian ideology. In contrast to his predecessors and contemporaries, he elevated the streetwalking prostitute to financial success and refused to moralize about her life. His *Susan Lenox: Her Fall and Rise* was the subject of fierce censorship battles which resulted in a bowdlerized final edition. Still, Phillips made a heroine of the prostitute by unrestrainedly praising her virtue and endurance. In so doing, he too evaded acknowledging her. Despite initial economic exploitation as a streetwalker who maintains a pimp, his Susan is variously an innocent small-town girl, a lady, and a manly heroine, a character untouched by experience and above time. Though Phillips stressed her femininity, she rather inconsistently had the courage and endurance of a man. Her survival was linked to such heroism rather than to the successful manipulation of sexuality.

The writers discussed in the following pages discovered the prostitute as a legitimate subject for American fiction. To a certain extent they succeeded in their war on the repressive literary and cultural traditions outlined in this chapter. Yet whether they were conscious of it or not, they revealed in their evasive attitude toward the prostitute both the genteel influence and their own ambivalence about the quintessential fallen woman. Despite their rebelliousness, they created prostitution novels that were neither artistic triumphs nor recognizable reflections of a complex reality. Nevertheless, these writers were more than mouthpieces for the repressive conventions of their time. In their struggle to defend the very woman of whom they disapproved, they illuminated powerful literary, ideological, and psychological forces. Ultimately, these forces compelled them, in creating the sanitized prostitute, to deny the very reality of woman's sexuality itself.

Chapter Two
Joaquin Miller, Edgar Fawcett, and the Wicked City

In an 1889 lecture series surveying notable American writers, the influential midwestern realist and exponent of literary innovation, Hamlin Garland, included the California author Joaquin Miller and the New York City novelist Edgar Fawcett. Garland lauded Miller for legitimizing the West as a literary subject and Fawcett for dramatizing the stark class differences of urban life.[1] Despite such praise, by the late 1880's the reputations of the two men had faded. Miller was rightly accused of imitating Byron's poetry and Bret Harte's stories. Fawcett, with equal justice, was criticized for contrived plots, flat characters, and a superficial knowledge of the New York poor.[2]

What they lacked in literary distinction, however, Miller and Fawcett made up for in daring. With the publication of their respective works, *The Destruction of Gotham* (1886) and *The Evil That Men Do* (1889), they became the only novelists of the 1880's to cast the tormented urban prostitute as a heroine.[3] Miller had already written comic tales of mining camp "soiled doves"; Fawcett would soon produce an essay on the causes of city prostitution. An interest in the subject aside, the two men were gambling that their novels would create controversy and revive their reputations.[4] Still, they hedged their literary bets by resurrecting the crazed or spiritually deadened seduction victims of the mid-century urban thriller. Before analyzing how Miller and Fawcett employed and expanded these stereotypes, it would be useful to provide brief biographies of two writers otherwise so divergent.

Well before *The Destruction of Gotham*, Joaquin Miller liked to advertise himself as a man who made his own rules. An ardent self-promoter, he was always at work on what one biographer called "his legend about himself...reflecting an American dream of epic adventure in the days of frontier life."[5] To suggest that he was a born pioneer, Miller switched the date and place of his birth from an 1837 Indiana farm to an 1841 covered wagon, going west. He claimed he fought Indians in California and accompanied a self-styled conqueror named Walker to Nicaragua, both of which strengthened his identification with the romantic personae of his poems. He further served this mythic self-image by replacing the sober name "Cinninatus Hiner," given him by his Quaker schoolteacher father, with Joaquin for its association with the colorful

Mexican bandit Joaquin Murietta, the subject of one of Miller's most famous poems. In the 1870's, at the height of his fame as "Byron of the Rockies," he even shocked literary London by appearing at dinner parties in frontier dress, playing on the western iconoclast of his poetry and tales.[6]

Predictably, Miller's art embraced the loner and the rebel. His *Songs of the Sierras* (1871) earned him great popularity abroad, particularly in England, where he was lauded for his individualism and wilderness authenticity.[7] Many of his "songs" depict American Childe Haroldes wandering the mountain vastnesses of Oregon and California haunted by the bloody battles they have fought and the impassioned Indian women they have loved and left. Long verse narratives of frontier clashes with or by the side of Indians preface remorseful epitaphs for these volatile jilted maidens. Reflections on the past are punctuated typically by such effusions as

> Sierras, and eternal tents
> Of snow that flash o'er battlements
> Of mountains! My land of the sun,
> Am I not true? (50)

Americans were less impressed by Miller's verse than by his rough-and-ready novel, *First Fam'lies of the Sierras* (1876).[8] In the comic-sentimental manner of Bret Harte, Miller celebrates the brawling gold-miners of a wilderness Eden. These are "hairy, half-savage, unread" (12) types whose bellicose women definitely belong to the oldest profession. The prostitutes are comic figures, especially in contrast to the doomed beauties of Miller's poetry. Yet, like the overly passionate Indian maids of the *Songs*, the "soiled doves" of his western fiction also fall short of the ideal Victorian woman discussed in Chapter One. In this they anticipate Miller's Dottie Lane, the brothel dweller of *The Destruction of Gotham*. In the 1880's, when he would write of the prostitute as a woman "lost in the wilds of civilization" (19), he would draw on his Byronic and Hartean anti-heroines, relying as well, as we shall see, on a literary tradition of urban female wickedness which predated them both.

If Miller was the rebel, the outsider, Edgar Fawcett was the patrician, the man on the inside. Born in New York in 1847 to a wealthy English father and an American mother, he graduated from Columbia in 1870, around the time that Miller was living in Oregon territory and engaging in real or imagined skirmishes with the native tribes there.[9] Although Fawcett never earned the reputation as an American original which, at least in the 1870's, made Miller the welcome guest of Rossetti and Browning, he was accepted by the aristocratic London and New York circles which echoed his disdain for the flamboyant western poet. Not surprisingly, he scorned Miller as a poseur who walked the "realms of art" in "cowhide boots."[10]

Fawcett was best known for work satirizing the vulgar *parvenus* of the Gilded Age for their "plutocratic self-adulation" and indifference to the poor.[11] Many of his novels rage at the social-climbing families who worship materialism and purchase husbands for their crass daughters from the old New York families. In his 1884 novel *Tinkling Cymbals,* one of his characters laments the pompous display of the New Money. When so many "are shut in hot garrets, not knowing where they shall get their next crust," Fawcett's spokesman storms, this Gilded Age vulgarity is "an injustice...an outrage!"[12]

Fawcett's own sense of class superiority, however, largely vitiated such social protest. A fortunate marriage in *An Ambitious Woman* (1884) and a stage career in *Miriam Balestier* (1888) magically extract the protagonists, who in any case are from impoverished gentility rather than the underclass, from the slum. Rather than analyze the lives of those born and forced to stay in poverty, Fawcett approves the few who, superior to the masses, escape from the "little yellowish-drab wooden houses...the stupid, haggling neighbors," and the "ugliness and stagnation and poverty."[13] Significant too is that, unlike the unfortunate heroine of *The Evil That Men Do,* who declines from a virtuous seamstress to an alcoholic streetwalker, the Fawcett heroines who climb out of squalor never sacrifice their virtue. While he acknowledged that drink and the tenements were often the shabby lot of those compelled to be poor, his belief in the rewards of womanly virtue precluded his admission that women might profit from their earnings as prostitutes. He preferred, as did Miller, to resurrect the outworn model of the harlot's fall, first to emotional, then literal death.

Despite obvious differences in temperament, background, and literary interest, Joaquin Miller and Edgar Fawcett used a similar method of depiction when they chose to imagine the New York City prostitute. Although they claimed to provide a graphic picture of the conditions propelling women to the trade, they were unable to translate sociological insight into fictional portraiture. Rather, they retreated before their own disapproval of feminine impurity and the pressure of the puritanic literary climate outlined in Chapter One. Caught between a need to defend and a refusal to acknowledge the prostitute's real activity, they employed desexualizing strategies which expanded the mid-century stereotype of the prostitute as Ruined Innocent. Ironically, for all their desire to be known as innovators, they largely adapted the anti-urban exposé of the mid-century in which the prostitute is a cancelled personality, bestialized by seduction and street or brothel life. A brief review of the form clarifies and highlights the compromises Miller and Fawcett made as well as the limited innovations their characteristic literary concerns prompted them to introduce.

* * * * *

To the nineteenth-century popular imagination, the city was as much a symbol of moral evil as economic good. Young rural women corrupted by urban life were particularly pitied for coming to the metropolis. "Happy had it been," remarked the author of one anti-urban tract, had they "never exchanged the starry skies for the lamps of the town, nor...left their quiet villages for the throng and roar of the city's streets."[14] Well before Miller used the term Gotham to signify immoral New York, one representative author warned, "if Gotham does not pass through some kind of change for the better, she may meet the fate of the once renowned and glorified city of Babylon!"[15] As Eugene Arden points out, by mid-century this characterization of New York as the center of American evil had "achieved the proportions of a national myth," though literary indictments of other large cities were also quite common.[16]

Distrust of urban deception and greed, based both on fear of the unfamiliar and resentment at urban economic dominance, thus created a hostile fascination with urban life which, as early as the 1840's, was heightened by the newly emerging slum and vice districts.[17] Soon a flood of cheap novels and semi-fictional exposés appeared, claiming to provide a lesson to the unwary that the city was the "home of the damned."[18] In a period when the anti-obscenity forces were not the powers they would become under Comstock's aegis, such thrillers—which stopped short of actual descriptions of the sexual encounter—enjoyed lively sales. These exposés were largely modeled on Eugene Sue's *The Mysteries of Paris* (1842) and G.W.M. Reynolds's *The Mysteries of London* (1845), in whose Gothic vision the city was a repository of shocking secrets. Sue and Reynolds unraveled the mysteries of "unbridled depravity among the rich and squalid wretchedness among the urban poor." They influenced American writers like E.Z. Judson ("Ned Buntline" of dime novel fame), Joseph Holt Ingraham, and Osgood Bradbury.[19] These three, among the most successful practitioners of the form, achieved commercial success by adapting the labyrinthine plotting and lower-depths subject matter of the Old World writers. Although authors like Judson employed the "city mystery" phrase in their titles, others like Ingraham and Bradbury prompted curiosity about urban excesses by their respective *Frank Rivers; or the Dangers of the Town* (1853) and *Female Depravity; or, the House of Death* (1857). Indeed the form might as aptly be termed the "wicked city" warning novel. Its ostensible aim was to "make the city be virtuous once more" by exposing the libertine and the pickpocket, the lustful power broker and the maddened streetwalker, the crooked financier and the inveterate drunkard.[20] It was more likely, however, that by chronicling the "shady sides of the great underworld," these books titillated more than muckraked, providing mighty inspiration for unsatisfied provincial longings.[21]

At the heart of this sensational form was the story of Ruined Virtue. As George Lippard explained in his best-selling Gothic exposé of Philadelphia, *The Quaker City* (1845), there was no event more symbolic of urban evil than the "seduction of a poor and innocent girl."[22] Particularly, he might have added, when she ends up on the pavements of the Tenderloin, as she does in typical period favorites like *New York by Gaslight* (1850), *Celio, or New York Above-Ground and Under-Ground* (1850), and *Frank Rivers; or, the Dangers of the Town* (1853).[23] In fact, the seduction-of-innocence theme had been a staple of popular fiction since the late eighteenth century, when American Clarissas like the doomed heroines of Mrs. Rowson's *Charlotte Temple* (1791) and *The Coquette* (1797), by Hannah Foster, made an avid feminine readership weep. In the hands of these domestic sentimentalists, girlish victims succumb to roués who promise marriage, then impregnate, and abandon them for a socially advantageous match. The villains even ignore such prototypical pleas as Charlotte Temple's "suffer me not to expire in the street."[24] The male-oriented warning novel of the next century, however, mixes such melodramatic sentiment with sensation, adding what Leslie Fiedler has termed the "darkness of the urban underworld" to the by-then-hackneyed seduction plot.[25] Now the betrayed girl does not perish as she did in Rowson or Foster. Instead she walks the gin-and-sin-soaked streets to which her despair at abandonment has led her.

In this guise, she is one of the chief moral dangers of the town, filching youth of "money...sense...and virtue."[26] *New York by Gaslight*, by George Foster, one of the most successful city thrillers, warns of her in this manner:

From the moment the prostitute ensnares a customer, his doom is sealed. Need we follow him to the filthy street, the squalid chamber where Prostitution performs her horrid rites? (7)

Often the answer is a prudent no. Instead the focus is on prostitutes as lunatic predators who hover "around the corners of the streets, cursing their fates in the bitterness of their hearts."[27] Vowed to wreak vengeance on all men for the sins of one, these women are maddened to the point of bestiality. The demented though still-beauteous title character of *The Life and Sufferings of Cecilia Mayo* (1843), not content with entrapping young men and procuring country girls for brothels, confesses that she killed and ate raw rabbits and sucked their blood.[28] Although few of her fictive peers become such beasts disguised by a female's form, many are depicted as seductive she-devils whose beauty cannot conceal their evil intent.

Those not powered by lunatic hatred are just as removed from rational conduct. Alcoholics seeking escape from the knowledge and the consequences of their sins, these wretched creatures, commented one journalistic observer employing the literary conventions of the thrillers, "maddened themselves with drink in order to become sufficiently immoral" to ply their trades.[29] Another satirically concluded that most prostitutes were "candidate[s] for admission into the Inebriate Asylum."[30] From the waterfront's "weazened...travesties on woman"[31] to the more successful Tenderloin saloon habituées, all are so narcotized by liquor that it is surprising they can solicit anyone.

Decades before Miller and Fawcett employed what Osgood Bradbury called the "old stereotyped story" of the prostitute's transit from rural innocence to urban dementia or spiritual deadness,[32] works like his *Female Depravity* capitalized on it. One prostitute's lust for vengeance is described thus:

Like most others of the unfortunate class to which she belonged, she had once loved a young man who seduced her under the most solemn promises of marriage, and then abandoned her to her fate. Such conduct goaded her to desperation...(34)

E.Z. Judson's monstrous streetwalker Big Lize, who has the strength of two men and walks the streets with a club, takes a rare non-violent moment to explain that she "wore the stamp of innocence" before encountering a "lawless, heartless, God-forsaken" libertine.[33] Joseph Holt Ingraham, another who wrote fiction on city perils, argued that even the most artful adventuress, obsessed with ruining the young manhood of the town, had once been tricked to a seducer's apartment. As the narrator of *New York by Gaslight* phrased it, courtesan and drunken waterfront harlot alike came to prostitution "invariably as the result of man's individual villainy" (36).

The mid-century anti-urban thriller was crowded with everything from serial seductions to labyrinthine tours of vice dens, from diatribes on the narcissistic rich to horror at the lives of the undeserving poor. Even had there been the wish to do so, there was little time to analyze the prostitute's transformation from seduction victim to urban menace or to present her thoughts or feelings beyond her formulaic castigation of a long-fled betrayer. She is not a character but a cautionary type, a lesson on the corruption of innocence, both her own and that of the youths she debauches. Her "depravity," more alluded to than dramatized, issues not from her flagrant sexuality but from a lunatic desire for revenge or a drunken quest for oblivion. Furthermore, for all their sensationalism, her mid-century explicators take care to invoke the "wages of sin" formula and defuse the threat she poses by killing her off.

By the end of the nineteenth century, the characterization of the prostitute as a traumatized victim of city wickedness had a renewed value for Joaquin Miller and Edgar Fawcett as they sought to account for the legions of women who walked the red-light streets of New York. Unwilling to confront the waywardness of the prostitute or to gather the facts of her life in the vice trade, they chose to adapt mid-century stereotypes by building to an extent on their own earlier work. Miller breathed some life into the outworn image of the lunatic seductress. Fawcett did the same with the stereotype of the dead-alive alcoholic. Such recycling of popular literature provided a way of controlling the quintessential fallen woman by placing her unorthodox sexuality within a reassuringly formulaic mold. Yet as their fiction amply demonstrates, it inevitably restricted any exploration of the prostitute who had propelled these writers into such conventions of denial.

* * * * *

As its title suggests, Miller's *The Destruction of Gotham* is in the tradition of Osgood Bradbury and Joseph Holt Ingraham. "This is a most graphic story of the times," read an advertisement which capitalized on the novel's association with the sensational urban exposé, "showing the conflict between the upper and lower stratas of society in New York, ending in a great disaster to the city itself."[34] Actually, as the prostitute Dottie Lane is the chief representative of the lower stratas, and her seducer of the upper ones, the publisher's statement was a disingenuous one. Like Miller's "Prologue" to the novel, it seemed designed to pull in readers while disarming the forces of Comstockery. The "news articles" of female drunkards, broken families, and rich debauchees which preface the narrative itself strengthen Miller's claim that the story of Dottie is one of documentary truth. But his hyperbolic style and introductory references to "poor 'Dot' in flight up Broadway[,] pursued by the agents of city evil" (8), are pure mid-century.

In the narrative which follows, Miller describes the city which engulfs female virtue in a manner which belies his claim of truth. As in the work of his predecessors, New York is so immersed in "drunken and devilish pursuits of power, pleasure, and gold" (8) that only apocalypse can save it. In fact, Miller enacts a Last Judgment at the novel's end, when a mob of the oppressed storms the homes of the rich and burns down much of the city. Dottie Lane has already met the standard literary fate of ruined innocence, but her little daughter is rescued from the flames. Her savior is a fictive version of Miller himself, an anti-urban writer disgusted with the "thousands of filthy things which man...has allowed to accumulate" (213). He takes the child in his arms and leaves the burning island, having vowed to protect this daughter of the city from the fate of her mother.

Long before Miller purges urban vice by setting New York afire, Dottie Lane becomes a sacrifice to the devilish city. When the countrified young woman, with her "Madonna face" (46) and trusting nature, sets foot in Gotham, its monsters lose no time in pouncing on her. A madam who is a composite of the sadistic Cecilia Mayo, the grotesque Big Lize, and the drunken waterfront prostitutes of other antebellum fare soon spies the defenseless girl. Under orders from the shadowy plutocrat John Matherson, heir apparent of the rakes of Ingraham and Bradbury, this gin-and-garlic-scented procuress lures Dottie to a Tenderloin brothel. The place is depicted in the familiar language of warning literature:

From every door, window, cellar, or garret peered painted faces of all shades of complexion....Was Dottie to be watched and kept for days, weeks, years, with these strange and unearthly inhabitants, who are only visible at night? (45)

Matherson soon provides the answer. A Jekyll-and-Hyde type, he is, by melodramatic coincidence, engaged to Dottie's rich cousin Hattie, whom the orphaned girl has come to the city to seek. Matherson exemplifies the unprincipled man of the town, for he courts the affluent woman while he debauches the impoverished one—a strategy Edgar Fawcett's Casper Drummond also employs. No match for Matherson, his brothel prisoner Dottie quickly succumbs, both to him and the unscrupulous clients to whom he soon hands her over.

Rather than describe a young woman's life in a house of prostitution, or her subsequent trials in the underclass, as Progressive novelists do early in the next century, Miller cautiously brushes over the details of Dottie's two years in the trade. He picks up her story after she has fled— or been expelled from—the brothel. With her is a child she insists is Matherson's. Dottie herself has become a kind of lunatic Hester Prynne. She wanders aimlessly about with little Dolly, uttering disconnected sentences, her shabby attire in distinct contrast to the costly elegance of her daughter. What was once sweet passivity is now vindictiveness. "[R]ambling in her talk" (65), Dottie gestures violently and vows to ruin Matherson. Vengeance rather than motherhood seems to preoccupy her, for she carries a gun and threatens to waylay her seducer-procurer and his fiancée Hattie. Dottie thus calls up the maddened streetwalkers who people earlier works like *Female Depravity* and *Mysteries and Miseries of New York*. Her transformation from a hesitant innocent to a "half-wild creature" (80) is proof that her seduction and bordello life have unhinged her. Expressions of rage at poverty and rejection are viewed as insane rather than legitimate, the "fire" in her eyes that of derangement rather than self-expression. Her wandering the streets with her illegitimate child, forced from poor lodging to wretched employment, hunted all the while by Matherson's agents, are props for her mad scenes rather than, as in Progressive fiction, factors contributing to her loss of sanity.

What has caused her dementia, as it did her mid-century predecessors, is the fall from virtue.

When Miller enters the mind of this woman who, in his veiled reference to the brothel, had not "opened her eyes on honest surroundings" (75) for years, he has reached the limits of the mid-century popular influence. Writers like Bradbury and Judson were not interested in providing psychological portraits so much as including the prostitute in an urban rogue's gallery. As her character develops, Dottie instead reminds the reader of the crazed Dickensian prostitute Martha in *David Copperfield* (1850). Both desperate wanderers are found by charitable men, Martha by the kind-hearted Uncle Peggotty and Dottie by Walton, a reporter sympathetic to the oppressed. Like the incoherent Martha, Dottie responds to male compassion by revealing a mind reduced:

You see these people on this big island send people over yonder to that little island when they want to get them away, because there are more of them than on the little island, and they can do as they please. That is why I was sent there. Oh, it was dreadful—it was dreadful! (51)

Properly decoded, Dottie's childlike speech describes her time in a prison hospital for prostitutes, although the experiences which led her there clearly limited her ability to describe them.

Both Dickens and Miller skirt the issue of the prostitute as a woman with a sexual history by presenting her as crazed by a past she has difficulty comprehending, much less recounting. The differences, however, are significant. In a suicidal frenzy at the side of the Thames, Martha commands her would-be redeemer, "Throw me away, as all the world does. Kill me for being what I am..." (680). Still, she recovers her reasoning powers sufficiently to listen to the Christlike Peggotty and to undergo a conversion and a return to sanity. Later she marries and begins a new life in Australia. Miller, in contrast, sees neither redemption for the urban prostitute nor a way out of her mental limbo. Dottie has been lost, he insists, since the first night at the brothel which had "burned away the supports of her bewildered brain" (101).

Miller and Dickens thus translate the troubling sexuality of the prostitute into irrationality and violence. But whereas the Dickensian prostitute directs her violent anger inward, planning her own death (or expressing a suicidal fidelity to a murderous lover), Miller's prostitute poses more of a threat to others than to herself. Dottie roams the metropolis gun in hand. She even turns on her own child when they seek shelter in a tenement, threatening to kill Dollie if the little girl makes noise. Not only has she vowed to ruin Matherson by exposing his double life, but she makes an unsuccessful attempt on the life of her rival, Hattie Lane.

That encounter, playing on nineteenth-century visual associations of female vice and virtue, is particularly significant. Eyes aflame, Dottie enters the Lane mansion during a glittering social evening to confront the blonde Hattie, whose ordered passivity Miller approvingly associates with the calm perfection of classical sculpture. Dottie is the unwomanly woman of anarchic sexuality, her black mane disordered, her beauty savage and terrible. Hattie, her carefully arranged golden hair surrounded by a halo of light, is her chaste antithesis. Enraged by the purity no longer hers, Dottie springs forward, the avatar of vice, to destroy the incarnation of virtue.

If Dottie in this scene is an object lesson on the effects of sin on the female psyche, she is something else as well. First of all, she almost succeeds in her murder attempt. She certainly strikes fear into the crowd of fashionable people attending the soirée, who stand by powerless to control her. The ubiquitous Walton tries to defuse Dottie's manic force. But "she was so wild, so desperate and determined, that the girl was soon the master, in her madness" (91). Deadly weapon in hand, she is a kind of metropolitan Medea, jealous, inexorable, and beyond control. Only Walton's appeal that she not kill Hattie improbably stays her hand, sending one who "had come to be as a wild beast" (193) back to the darkness and anonymity of the New York streets.

In her work on British culture, Nina Auerbach argues that, from Rossetti's painting *Found* to Eliot's *Adam Bede*, the Victorians' repeated visual and literary images of the debased and grovelling fallen woman are reactions to the perceived danger of the type. "[P]erceptions of her power," she remarks, "cannot be untangled from the impulse to suppress it."[35] That is, the insistence on the powerlessness of the sexual pariah conceals the fear that she is all too powerful. Of course Miller's portrayal of Dottie lacks the verisimilitude, not to mention the symbolic richness, of a Dickens or Hardy character. Unlike a Nancy, a Tess, or a Hetty Sorrel, Dottie does not move from debasement to transcendence. Yet one can apply Auerbach's perception to this American anti-heroine nonetheless. No matter how disoriented by the traumas of her entrapment and seduction, she is enraged at Matherson's farming her out to his colleagues. Her recent brothel life, in fact, has made her more potent than when she entered Gotham in virginal innocence. No longer the gullible virgin, she is not yet the unsightly Water Street harlot either. She possesses a dangerous combination of beauty and manic energy. The repeated insistence on her bestiality indeed masks the real threat she poses, one that issues as much from her sexuality as from her madness. The prostitute who tries to murder women and little girls, her rivals, after all, for male attention, may very well lure men to death too.

As will Fawcett and other turn-of-the-century portrayers of the prostitute, Miller dispels the anxiety she provokes in him by suppressing her. His fictive ego Walton offers aid to Dottie, now in flight from reprisals by Matherson for her attack on Hattie Lane. In the name of helping her, Walton approves her decision to become a pieceworker in the cigar trade by finding her a cheap tenement room in which to work and live with her child. By the 1880's the cigar industry was notorious for the exploitative nature of its work. One cigar roller noted that the pressure of the job "could make a nervous wreck out of you."[36] Dottie herself complains that she is paid only for the work accepted by the managers rather than by the hour. She becomes increasingly debilitated by the job and depressed by the rat-infested garret in which she lives. Still, her trials deflect her attention from further attempts at vengeance or resumption of her old trade. When Walton visits Dottie, it is clear that her anger has turned to terror:

"You see, I put tobacco-stems here, around Dollie's side of the bed. That will keep them from eating her first....But...I know they will bite our feet and our faces when—— when——"
"Dottie, it's the old foolish fear. Now be calm. Rats don't bite people, not live people, I reckon."
"But,—but they do bite dead people, Mr. Walton."
"Well, you are not dead, Dottie." (192)

Walton's surprisingly callous remarks and cold comfort suggest Miller's own punitive attitude toward the erring Dottie. Like Miller himself, this author's surrogate dooms her to a garret atonement. Her "madness"—if, as Walton seems to believe, madness it is to fear rat bites— is now safely contained; her dangerous beauty and fiery rages are now spectral paleness and paralyzing depression. Accepting Walton's advice that she remain in a virtuous, if harsh, life, Dottie quickly perishes— possibly of starvation, possibly by her own hand. Walton then rescues her child without a backward glance and (as would Miller soon after completing *The Destruction of Gotham*) flees the city that corrupted the mother.

Dottie Lane was not the first of Miller's wild, dark heroines to be brought to a sad but supposedly just end. Women driven to frenzy for love of a mysterious Byronic figure appear in two of his most famous *Songs of the Sierras*. An Indian woman who loves the title character of "The Arizonian" is spurned for a fair blonde of his own race. Like Dottie when cast off for her wealthy cousin, the Indian maiden, in her rage at the man who jilted her, is "livid," her eyes "afire" (20). But fury soon turns to self-sacrifice. As storms break out and she is trapped by a flood, she saves her betrayer's life, then drowns herself. The Indian maid "with the coal-black eye" (20) in "The Tale of the Tall Alcalde," while not rejected for a pure woman, also reacts suicidally to her own loss of innocence. She has set free the handsome warrior captured in her tribe's battles with their foe, and, presumably, has had an affair with him. Calling herself "impure" for betraying her virtue as well as her people, she builds her own funeral pyre. In a passion of remorse, to be doubly certain of her own death,

> She caught a dagger from her side
> And plunged it to its silver hilt
> Into her hot and bursting heart
> And fell into my arms and died
> Died as my soul to hers was press'd.
> Died as I held her to my breast,
> Died without one word or moan,
> And left me with my dead—alone. (27)

Whether jilted or not, these Dark Ladies of the Sierras, like Dottie Lane herself, are propelled to self-annihilation by their uncontrolled natures. Yet whereas the urban prostitute only provokes horror in a Walton, Miller's manly wanderers experience grief for the woman who has sacrificed her life to passion. Unlike the roving madwoman of the horrific city, these women can be idealized. Their torrential passion only threatens *their* well-being, not that of the outsider whose life they have saved. A lesson to the female revenge-seekers of Gotham, they punish themselves instead of men. If it is a tragic ending, their creator suggests, it is also an appropriate one.

In Miller's western poems, then, the passionate woman destroyed by masculine rejection anticipates Dottie Lane up to a point. Still, perhaps because she is the unrequited lover rather than the embittered sexual professional, she lacks the urban prostitute's manic desire for vengeance. That quality surfaces instead in the mining camp prostitutes of Miller's early novel, *First Fam'lies of Sierras.* The work is set in the Harte-like landscape of the Howling Wilderness (shades of Roaring Camp) where semi-savage miners brawl, drink, and visit "soiled doves." Two of these tainted women are Bunker Hill and Captain Tommy, whose very names rather jokingly tell how little of the conventional feminine is left in them. While no seduction tragedy connects them to the roughened types who frequent them, the women have the same psychic scars as does Dottie Lane. Angry, hating men, Bunker Hill wallows in unhappiness; the equally misanthropic Captain Tommy has violent fits of temper and lashes out at the men in her intimidating way. Like their revenge-driven New York City counterparts, their inner chaos pushes them to keep the miners vying for their favors. Thus they incite battles and take grim satisfaction from the "constant state of uproar" (13) their presence in camp creates.

If the maddened desire for vengeance proves tragic in urban prostitutes like Dottie Lane, it is comic in wilderness ones. For one thing, Miller employs the folksy exaggeration of narratives like "The Luck of Roaring Camp" and Twain's *Roughing It* (1871). He satirizes both the "glorious climate of Californy" (14) and the dubious Circes of the western mining camp. Both have helped produce the "regular Sunday funeral" (14) which characterizes life in a place so aptly called the Howling Wilderness. Furthermore, Bunker Hill and Captain Tommy may share Dottie Lane's emotional turmoil, but they entirely lack her youth and beauty. Miller prefaces a series of jokes at their expense with the wry observation that these women are "in some respects worse than no women at all" (13). He finds humor in everything from Bunker Hill's humped back to Captain Tommy's six-foot frame. Not surprisingly in a national literature which associates darkness and sexuality, Tommy's hair, like Dottie Lane's, is black—but there the resemblance ends. Not only does she wear it in a "heap which seemed constantly in motion," but she has gathered some of it into a braid down her back. When this humorously grotesque figure wishes to speak, she pulls on her bell-rope of hair as if to wind herself up, talking nonstop until she decides to unravel the hairy coil and turn off the strange human wind-up toy she has made of herself.

In the universe of this Sierran "wild Eden" (38), the unwomanly woman need not meet the doom of an urban Big Lize or a Dottie Lane. Like Bret Harte's golden-hearted Miggles, who leaves prostitution to nurse a former customer, Captain Tommy undergoes a reform denied her city sisters. A long-suffering Good Woman comes to the camp, gives birth to a child, and inspires both Tommy and Bunker Hill to resurrect their maternal impulses. Bunker Hill abandons the oldest profession to rock the cradle "and coo and crow to little Half-a-pint" (185). Captain Tommy curbs her savage temper and is "dignified, sanctified...a better woman" (171) because of her concern for the new-born child. She shares her moral rebirth with the miner Limber Tim, and completes her conversion to respectability by marrying him.

Because they are figures of comic sentimentality, the promiscuous women of *First Fam'lies of the Sierras* are spared the fate of Miller's overly passionate heroines. Permitted to atone in a way his Indian maidens and streetwalkers are not, they are returned to grace through their own good deeds and the traditional western tolerance for those Miller calls the "fallen angels" (13) of the uncivilized frontier.[37]

As in Miller's western works, both the impulse to exonerate and to punish the illicitly sexual woman inform *The Destruction of Gotham*. Yet lacking the tragic sense he brings to the poetry or the comic tolerance he expresses for mining camp harlots, Miller mourns Dottie as a jilted maiden only to excoriate her as a maddened prostitute. One of his biographers aptly observed that when Miller tried his hand at urban fiction, he lost much of what he knew.[38] Thus while he drew on the women of his Sierran works, he needed something more to make sense of female moral ruin in the city life he found so horrifying. Like the mid-century sensationalists, he found it in the image of the prostitute as a rural *naif* whom the streets and brothels have transformed. His Dottie emerges, therefore, as a creature far more menacing than any of Miller's wilderness heroines.

Lacking the artistry and irony with which Stephen Crane would infuse the traditional seduction tale, Miller did little more than build on an earlier popular image of the deranged prostitute. He boasted that his reformist story of an impoverished girl driven to sin predated the Progressive exposé of white slavery,[39] yet he actually provided no analysis of adverse economic conditions forcing her to the brothel, much less the operations of white slavers. Nor did he attempt to place the prostitute in the subculture of the bordello or of the streets she paces as a woman with a child to support.

By Miller's time, lustful power brokers, sadistic procurers, and dehumanized prostitutes were familiar literary emblems of urban moral debasement. The betrayal which causes Dottie Lane's dementia occurs against the painted backdrop of mid-century warning fiction. Only when the anger of the rejected woman spills over into the sexual energy of the raging prostitute does Dottie begin to emerge as a distinct character. But her creator quickly contains so troubling a woman, finding in anti-urban popular tradition a reassuring way of controlling her sexuality by subordinating it to psychic disaster.

Only a few years after *The Destruction of Gotham*, Edgar Fawcett attempted to provide a more believable social context for the girl who went wrong. Cited as a precursor of *Maggie: A Girl of the Streets,* Fawcett's *The Evil That Men Do* lengthily charts a woman's fall from seamstress to kept woman to prostitute. Unlike Miller, Fawcett focuses on the conditions of the period sweatshop and the impoverished milieu which propels a working girl into the vice trade. His attention to economic factors anticipates Progressives like Reginald Wright Kauffman and David Graham Phillips, the subjects of later chapters. Yet like Miller and his predecessors, Fawcett still casts the prostitute as the disoriented seduction victim of a rake-infested city. *The Evil That Men Do*, as well as Fawcett's other writings on woman's imperilled virtue, reveals an uneasiness with the economic explanation which gives women a measure of volition in choosing prostitution. To meet the challenge to the late-Victorian insistence on woman's innate chastity implied by voluntary entry into the sex trade, Fawcett employs a strategy of personality cancellation. He punishes the unchaste woman while denying her conscious involvement in the sexual life; he acknowledges her paid professionalism only to undercut this admission by purifying her. Thus, like her other American imaginers, Fawcett works out his ambivalence toward the prostitute in ways both distinct and representative.

* * * * *

In "The Woes of the New York Working-Girl," an essay on prostitution written shortly after *The Evil That Men Do* for the reform journal *Arena*, Fawcett marvels: "The more one observes the lives of working-girls the more he wonders that so many of them [still have]...good names."[40] The essay was occasioned by his visit to a settlement house for poor working girls much like the one to which he would send his own Cora Strang. The women he observed there inspire compassion for those whom his novel had recently praised as "girlish bread-winners" (228). Among the women he describes are the young cigar workers, their clothes and hair reeking of the odors of the trade, who pass their days in poorly paid home piecework or factory sweatshops. (Miller's Dottie took on such work to her peril.) To Fawcett, such hard-pressed women symbolize the toiling daughters of the poor. What wonder, he laments, that they are tempted to fall?

In concluding his essay, Fawcett proclaims allegiance to naturalism, a scientific approach to the study of society urged by the Zolaesque disciples of Herbert Spencer. Fawcett was impressed by Spencer's belief that the laws of biology could be applied to society as well as to nature, an idea with which the opening chapters of tenement description in *The Evil That Men Do* experiments. Still, Fawcett's naturalism was always half-hearted. In this most naturalistic of his works, he sensationalizes the evils of poverty and stereotypes his characters. Even in his *Arena* essay, when he tries to analyze slum families, he conjures up a father who "reels into some saloon" after "wringing from a toiling daughter's lenient hand the coin he wastes there" (27)—a line more reminiscent of T.S. Arthur in the lachrymose *Ten Nights in a Bar-room* than Herbert Spencer or Emile Zola. Furthermore, despite his *Arena* essay's emphasis on the unwholesome conditions fostering prostitution, when Fawcett has to account for the "Carrie" or the "Fanny" who leaves domestic service to be a streetwalker, he returns to the language of antebellum fiction: "rake," "seducer," "enticement," "road to ruin." To better understand what led him to prefer the sentimental to the scientific explanation, it would be well to examine the novel which best exemplifies his conflict about the woman of the streets.

The Evil That Men Do opens with a graphic depiction of the life assailing Cora Strang. Like Miller's Dottie, Cora is an orphaned country girl recently come to New York. Fawcett, however, details the poverty Miller had largely chosen to pass over. He dwells on everything from Cora's sewing job at sixty cents a day to her $14 a week room in Mrs.

Slattery's apartment, from the advances of the landlady's alcoholic son Owen to the prostitutes who taunt Cora for her youth and innocence. In fact, Fawcett's dark and teeming Lower East Side is the one that Jacob Riis would more eloquently capture in the photographs and prose of *How the Other Half Lives* (1890). Like Riis in the photo-narrative which would become a landmark of urban social reform, Fawcett enters the cramped tenement rooms of the women pieceworkers, the filthy courtyards and back alleys, the dives of criminals and their prostitute consorts.

In his horror at poverty, though, Fawcett dilutes the verbal and visual power of a Riis by employing the inflated rhetoric of Joaquin Miller. Cora's tenement building provokes this hyperbolic response: "Sin rioted in the reeking house, whose very stairs had rotten creaks when you trod them, as though fatigued by sots and trulls." Fawcett's slum is thus as much a "cauldron-hell broth" (87) as an impoverished neighborhood. But the determinism is no less emphatic. In this morally chaotic world, Fawcett suggests, Cora Strang could hardly avoid the fate of the shrill prostitutes, "maddened" by alcohol, who live all around her.

In one proleptic scene, two of them drunkenly observe her with jeering amusement. Early in the narrative she enters a saloon to find refuge from the cold and attracts their envious notice. While the women have not yet entered the stage of insensibility which they seek, they become increasingly strident at the sight of her innocence. Soon they switch from glaring at this living reminder of their former virtue to fighting with one another like the animals Fawcett suggests they have become. The screams and profanity which they hurl at each other transform them into creatures "aflame with wrath, muttering and glowering" (17). Like Miller, Fawcett describes menacing, bestial prostitutes. Yet he departs from the stereotype enough to observe that their violence issues as much from anger at their plight as from animality. As they become enraged and taunt each other with stories of the worthless men who have jilted them, they seek oblivion, as will the fallen Cora herself one day, in an alcoholic flight from self.

Having emphasized that Cora could be corrupted by the scenes daily enacted before her, however, Fawcett undercuts his own determinism. He insists Cora is a "delicate blush-rose in the midst of mirk and soilure" (9), a phrase that Stephen Crane, familiar with the work, would play on in his own satiric slum novel *Maggie*. There is nothing satiric about Fawcett's insistence that Cora is a saint of the slum. Unlike Maggie, who recoils at the sight of dance hall prostitutes and fears she will soon join their ranks, Cora, secure in her chastity, pities the "poor creatures" she sees in the Bowery dives. While she acknowledges that they "wouldn't be what they are" but for the pinched life she herself has been forced to live, she reflects that "God somehow keeps me straight" (18). She proceeds to prove it as she eludes a string of seducers. They include her leering sweatshop boss, who calls her a "little trump of virtue" (9), a saloon bartender used to hearing prostitutes lament their lost virtue, and Casper Drummond, a worthless society type out slumming who will figure again in the narrative and who unsuccessfully offers her money. "I've seen other girls begin that way," she resolutely informs Drummond. "I don't want to follow in their tracks" (79).

If these encounters bespeak Cora's virtue, her relationships in the community attest to her goodness. Indeed, despite her pinched circumstances, Fawcett's heroine is a slum version of the ideal Victorian woman: pure, pious, and morally inspiring. She spreads the consolations of religion in visits to a tubercular neighbor and transforms a neighborhood beggar into the Deserving Poor by a warm smile and a cheerful donation. She inspires the slovenly women of her building to work through the night rather than carouse in beer halls, and supports her mean-spirited landlady Mrs. Slattery when she takes ill. More like a redeemer of the slum than one of its victims, she even has a magical effect on Mrs. Slattery's drunken son Owen, whose advances she has rejected. Awed by her, he reflects on his sensual nature and attempts to reform.

The savage conditions of slum life prevent her from exemplifying the sheltered Angel of the House celebrated in the British poet Coventry Patmore's oft-quoted line, "wrong dare not in her presence speak." Yet Cora does exemplify what many Victorian ideologues, both in England and America, believed was woman's mission. By lifting up the unfortunate, they argued, woman could extend her moral influence on the home to society itself. Cora's own poverty apart, she anticipates another Fawcett heroine, Doris Josselyn, the Lady Bountiful of his later novel *New York* (1898).[41] More fortunate than Cora but no less caring, Doris disdains society life to visit ragged children and found charitable institutions. Cora sympathizes with women who fall. Doris uses her money to reform them by supporting Magdalen homes. Cora converts the shiftless Owen Slattery; Doris inspires an ex-convict to a "passionate reverence" (54) for her and a new moral life.

Fawcett's argument that a poor woman can be as inspiring as a rich one makes Cora's fall more poignant. Unlike Doris Josselyn, who is insulated by affluence, Cora cannot remain Virtue Untested. Unable to pay her room rent on a seamstress's wage, she moves to a working girls' home. There a sinister "Mrs. Carr" visits her and tries to recruit her for a brothel. Other snares are laid as well. When she rejects this offer and takes work as a lady's maid, her virtue arouses the philandering master of the house and causes the jealous servants to slander her good name.

Cora is then "rescued" by a friend of the household, Casper Drummond. By melodramatic coincidence, he is the plotting sensualist whom she had already met in a Bowery dance hall. At this point, Fawcett's tenement novel disappears entirely in the familiar tale of a hapless innocent propelled to prostitution in despair at abandonment by her seducer. Whereas the betrayer depicted by Stephen Crane or the procurer of Progressive novelists like Reginald Wright Kauffman and David Graham Phillips was as stereotyped as any uptown lothario, at least he was a recognizable product of the slum. Fawcett's Drummond, in contrast, issues as much from the pages of earlier writers as from the right side of the tracks. Complete with cologne, curled moustache, and visiting card, he plies Cora with falsehoods while assuring her, "I'm not lying to you, my little darling! God knows I'm not!" (72). Like the "mellow-voiced" libertine of Joseph Holt Ingraham's *Frank Rivers* (26), Drummond's speech was seductive, his "eye quick and his ear sharp" (65). Cut from the same cloth as Ingraham's villain, who lures his prey to his rooms by tempting her with false promises and "winning smiles" (26), Drummond pursues Cora Strang. At first, much like her virtuous mid-century predecessors, she resists him. (The more pure the "virgin whiteness," Ingraham had reminded his readers, the more poignant the fall.) Indeed despite the "fascination of being with him" (234), Cora outdoes her predecessors in evading Drummond. Only when he plies her with the stock drugged glass of wine—shades of Ingraham's "he bore her half-unconscious to his chambers" (*Frank Rivers*, 31)—is her ruin accomplished.

In "The Woes of the New York Working-Girl," when Fawcett argued that young women flee poverty "for rakes whose very lust seems a heaven of refuge," he granted these "wretched starvelings" (34) a measure of volition. Yet in his art, Fawcett treats Cora's fall to prostitution as the predictable result of Drummond's departure. He does mention that she becomes increasingly alienated when she is robbed, has a miscarriage, and is only aided by a shopgirl friend turned prostitute. And he spares a few sermonic pages for her new life as a prostitute, her uncaring clients and vapid associates. But the change that has come over her, most notably a drunken face of "blotchy pinkness" and a wayward manner with men, issues from her cast-off status.

The emphasis on Cora as Virtue Undone continues well after she has drifted from mistress to streetwalker. Like her vengeful counterparts in Miller and popular fiction, Cora ascribes her fall, to the extent that she can reflect on it at all, to her deceiver. Concurring with another prostitute's summation of Drummond—"He sent you there...[H]e's ten times more to blame than you've been!" (312)—she seeks him out on his marriage day. Almost as furious at her rival as Miller's Dottie Lane, Cora rushes up to the newly-wedded couple and tears the veil from the bride's head. When the police remove her, she is unrepentant: "It let him know I was alive and the poor, mean thing he's made me" (324).

Such actions suggest Cora's resentment at rejection rather than, as Fawcett's own opening pages and *Arena* essay argue, the immorality fostered by a slum environment. Fawcett liked to proclaim the value of naturalism, but Cora is in distinct contrast to a true naturalist creation such as the title character of Edmond de Goncourt's 1877 novel of French prostitution, *Elisa*. In that work, Elisa's decision to become a prostitute is an imitation of those whom she has always observed. For years she has seen and heard the neighborhood women ply their trade and has come to regard the marketing of her body as a more lucrative form of work than the slums of Paris could otherwise provide. Thus she becomes a prostitute "quite simply and naturally, with hardly any feelings of conscience."[42] While no American writer would have felt comfortable with such a matter-of-fact explanation, in his initial focus on Cora as a member of the New York underclass, Fawcett was moving toward the idea that her prostitution was her adaptation to an impoverished environment. Yet faced with the paid sexual activity such a life involved, he first emphasizes her seduction, and then employs devices which distance Cora from the sexual activity in which, as a prostitute, she is immersed.

As in better days she was the personification of virtue, now she is the symbol of vice. Yet as such she is abstraction, not person who acts:

The *ruin* was complete. Every moral *beam* and *rafter* tumbled, every *clamp* and *stanchion* gave away... For a time she dwelt in *luxury*....A certain kind of *adoration* grovelled before her....*Pleasure* thrummed its viol in her ears, and *vice* dragged her by the waist with its rompish dance. The town blushed voluptuously before her sight; it had no more hints of want or *toil* in the hectic *joys* its days and nights proffered. *Experience* had flung aside its old austerities like the worn garments of a beggar suddenly dowered with millions. *Time* smothered his scythe in flowers, though the blade gleamed through their heavy tangles....There were hoarse notes in its cadence now and then, as harsh as when a grain of sand grits on the teeth in food cooked by the skills of deftest kitchens. Horrible moments of *fatigue* and *self-disgust* would be banished with draughts of a stimulant that made existence abnormally jocund. (306-307) (emphasis added)

Comparisons of Cora's behavior to a building whose "beam," "rafter," "clamp" and "stanchions" are in "ruin" furnish images of lifeless landscapes where crumbling buildings replace inhabited ones and where in effect there are neither human beings nor activity. As the passage continues, the very transformation of Cora to symbolic actor "dragged by the waist" by "vice" undercuts the idea that she is a person who practices it. The allegorical use of the nouns "luxury," "vice," and "time" distances her from prostitution, as does the substitution of the nouns "fatigue" and "self-disgust" for any verbs which might denote sexual activity. The idea of Cora's prostitution as the opposite of work and thus of action itself is underscored by the phrase "no more hints of want or toil." Finally, while the mixed metaphor of time passing as "a grain of sand grits" justifies his detractors' criticism of Fawcett's style, it also functions to further distance Cora from the action such convoluted constructions try to hide. As seduction victim reacting to Drummond's betrayal, Cora can act. As a working prostitute, she is a non-person, and cannot.

The strategy which suggests her sinful activity only to undercut it extends to her speaking of it as well. Cora's increasing verbal vindictiveness toward customers is relegated in passing to her "grudge against men and things" which would "prick through her attempts at jollity" (309). When Fawcett focuses on her reaction to betrayal, he legitimizes her rage and briefly allows her a voice. When he studies Cora as a working prostitute, he refuses to allow her to describe, much less justify, her life. Only when she re-encounters a man from her virtuous past does Fawcett permit her to speak. When she does, it is far more her creator's didactic summation of her life than that of the seasoned prostitute talking to an old admirer. "I've gone right down," she tells Owen, "I'm as bad as the worst now" (330).

Fawcett's refusal to let the prostitute defend her life is telling in light of the fact that but two years earlier, his novel *The Confessions of Claud* had no such reservations about a man who confesses to murder.[43] Indeed that work even employs a first-person narration to create sympathy for the homicidal Otho Claud. Fawcett prefers to humanize the masculine rule-breaker rather than the feminine one. He also permits the murderous Claud, who has killed a rival in a fit of jealous rage, to find a rationalization for the crime in an ungovernable temper inherited from his father. Claud, it seems, has the "curse of heredity" (331).

It is noteworthy that Fawcett can explain away the murder of an effete aristocrat, a type which he had often satirically attacked in his fiction, as evidence that a murderer can lack free will. But he shies away from exculpating the slum prostitute as the victim of environmental determinism. His early descriptions of Cora Strang's impoverished milieu even foreshadow an exoneration of her. Yet a male murderer is less unsettling to Fawcett than a female prostitute. He can experiment with exonerating a confessed murderer, first stressing the curse of heredity and then suggesting that Claud can reform with the help of the trusting young woman who believes in his innocence. But in Fawcett's view Cora is not eligible for such reformation. Whether as mid-rung prostitute or the gutter streetwalker she eventually becomes, she is an obliterated personality, hardly human enough to articulate a sentence, much less escape the consequences of her sinful actions to begin life anew.

The defender of Otho Claud not only associates her with a death-in-life which is symbolic of her separation from society but punishes her with a literal death as well. She is murdered, her throat cut by Owen Slattery, who had pursued her in her purer days and who now appoints himself both judge and executioner. Much like Dottie Lane's mad scenes, the death scene of Cora has Dickensian overtones. But once again the contrast between it and the Dickens model reveals that for all his seeming sympathy, the American novelist condemns the prostitute even more harshly than does the British one. In the death of Nancy in *Oliver Twist* (1838), Dickens's prostitute, like Fawcett's, is killed by a drunken brute she had trusted not to harm her.[44] Unlike Cora, however, Dickens's Nancy has already been converted by the purity of Rose Maylie, whose white handkerchief she raises as she dies and which is the symbol of the redemption she will find in death. Given her new penitence, the violence she experiences from Sikes is a martyrdom:

[He] freed one arm, and grasped his pistol...and he beat it with all the force that he could summon, upon the upturned face that almost touched his own.

She staggered and fell, nearly blinded with the blood that rained down from a deep gash in her forehead; but raising herself with difficulty on her knees, drew from her bosom a white handkerchief—Rose Maylie's own—and holding it up, in her folded hands, breathed one prayer for mercy to her Maker. (422-423)

Although nothing in *The Evil That Men Do* rivals the power of Dickens in such scenes, Fawcett rises to uncharacteristic eloquence when describing the demise of his own prostitute heroine. Cora's death, like Nancy's, will be an expiation. Dickens, however, condemns the murderous Sikes more than the fallen woman Nancy, who is redeemed by death. For Fawcett it is the assassin who is spiritually ennobled, a deliverer washing clean the sins the tainted Cora Strang.

In the final scene of the novel, Owen has met Cora, a fellow alcoholic, in a Skid Row bar where she is looking for customers. He takes her to the house where she once lodged, now a ruin symbolizing the wreckage of their lives. In a foreshadowing of the oblivion which awaits her at his hands, she falls drunkenly asleep. Owen experiences a kind of lunatic epiphany:

For Owen the darkness had become luminous. And as though spirit had won the power to leap aloof from flesh and quite transcend it, all his foulness of the past few months fell away from him like a noisome garment. He felt crowned with hope and vigor; he was a man again, and more than this, an *impetuous, passionate lover*. The *woman whose arms clasped him was the unstained Cora of old, not a trace of sin had ever touched her*; she was and had always been a vestal that guarded the white flame of honor. Suddenly it seemed that her face, just as he had last seen it where their former home lay crumbled about them, bloomed for him from the darkness in a perfect similitude of what it once had been. The gold-brown eyes--the auburn hair, mutinous and fluctuant about her delicate head--the little mobile mouth, dearest of all, that pink of the eglantine on her milky cheek--these lived again with delicious restoration! This *lovely ghost* had come to take her place! The next instant she felt something cold against her throat. *Perhaps no pain followed,* for as she sank to earth, half supported by him who had given her the quietus that she craved, not a single shudder shook her frame... (338) (emphasis added).

On one level Cora's somnolence invites Owen to a more exciting conquest than would her paid and waking compliance. Yet the admission of her sexuality is undercut by the insistence that she is the "vestal" virgin of her youth, the unseduced Cora of Owen's memory. Ultimately, however, even a prostitute remembered in purer days is too unsettling. Owen's feverish brain turns to thoughts of executing her and conjures her safely disembodied "lovely ghost."

This bizarre scene reveals that, for all his emphasis on the prostitute's mental cancellation after seduction, Fawcett allowed his own anger at her impurity to be the province of her murderer-deliverer. It is not enough that her personality has been reduced by the sexual life; she must crave the "quietus" of death. Already too spiritually deadened, and hardly human enough ("[p]erhaps no pain followed") to feel the pain of Owen's knife, she is the blamed victim here, if the victim at all. Whereas in *Oliver Twist* the sadistic Bill Sikes is associated with the devil, Fawcett's Owen is an angel of mercy. Killing Cora is a loving act, an attempt to restore her to the "unstained Cora of old"; he gently helps her to the ground after he has slit her throat. When he joins her by killing himself, he falls with his arm across her neck, both concealing her wound and denying the violence of her death. Owen's subsequent suicide—he kills himself after he murders Cora—is his despondent admission of remorse. Yet Fawcett, who had defended another "justified" murderer, Otho Claud, belies this one's guilt as well. Cora's killer has, after all, the novel's last line explains, "given back much of her native beauty in tender resuscitation" (339). Death restores what prostitution, the fate worse than death, had stolen.

Fawcett's decision to transform Cora's death into a beautification is particularly revealing in terms of his ambivalence about the luring power of the prostitute. In his *Arena* essay on working girls who fall to prostitution, Fawcett expressed a horror of the prostitute's repellent physicality:

Their rouge and cosmetics are of so baleful a quality that you might fancy some bedraggled Quasimodo of the slums would alone feel a thrill of response at their pathetic lures. In the vanities of noxious rags, you might dream, they should deck themselves for ghastly coquetries, with but pools of gutter-slime as their mirrors, and as jewelry but the hideous ulcers here and there on their brutally envenomed flesh...(27).

How can one account for the hatred that fuels this passage? The ghastly coquettes depicted above may be as revolting as Fawcett insists, but they are still able to inspire a "thrill of response" in some customer. Fawcett's insistence on the prostitute's ugliness and diseased condition cannot conceal his fear that a cosmetic transformation can render Quasimodo's consorts active still. If, despite their unattractiveness, such is the force of those at the end of the harlot's progress, Cora in mid-career is far more alarming. Her threat, like that of Miller's Dottie Lane, must be defused by death. Only then can her attractiveness be acknowledged.

* * * * *

However much modern readers may feel that Miller and Fawcett censored the prostitute in an attempt to render her harmless, in the age of the Vice Society they had made a daring literary gamble by treating her at all. Fawcett in a sense spoke for both of them when, anticipating a negative response to his book, he satirically inserted a conversation in which a wealthy client complains to his demi-mondaine companion about the immorality of *The Evil That Men Do*. She replies, "the very people that know how true such a book is are always the first to stamp on it and shout it down" (305). "Authors are [so] afraid to speak out" about sexual subjects, Fawcett complained a few years later, that "no American writer today, though he should write another 'Scarlet Letter,' could gain the least vogue for it. . ."[45]

Such predictions proved true. Courting acclaim, Miller and Fawcett were condemned for sensationalism. The staid and influential *Nation* could not bring itself to mention the true subject of *The Destruction of Gotham,* but it did make a veiled allusion to it in deploring Miller's "vicious literary style."[46] *The Evil That Men Do* was similarly condemned as a work which was "unmitigatedly bad all through," inferior as art and lacking in moral instruction. It "pains without helping, and disgusts without teaching," the reviewer concluded.[47]

Neither author took up the subject of prostitution again. Miller returned to other frontiers. He became, among other things, the Klondike correspondent for Hearst's *New York Journal* before returning to California.[48] There he died in 1913, having resumed the mantle of the western artist and become a kind of sage to a new school of California writers.[49] Fawcett too left New York and slum fiction. Until his death in 1904, he produced a number of novels of the privileged classes, a subject from which he had only strayed to tell the story of Cora Strang.

Although their bid to be the *enfants terribles* of the New York literary scene failed, in imagining the prostitute, Edgar Fawcett and Joaquin Miller did succeed in demonstrating the durability of the anti-urban warning novel. They even expanded the form by focusing on the prostitute as a ruined ingenue whom metropolitan life had crazed or spiritually deadened. Their city is much the same moral wasteland it had been in the works of E.Z. Judson and Joseph Holt Ingraham, but they make some attempt to individuate the previously one-dimensional creatures who wander it.

Unlike their subliterary predecessors, Miller and Fawcett dramatized the rage of the prostitute as the Woman Scorned. Yet when Dottie Lane and Cora Strang threaten to move from menacing to sexually active characters, these erring women arouse their creators' hostility and are controlled, first by psychic, then by literal death. Still, such portrayals reveal authorial conflicts between repression and acknowledgment of the American prostitute's activity, between anger at the woman and defense of the victim. Such conflicts would be inherited by a far better writer in search of the literary truth of the city, Stephen Crane.

Chapter Three
Stephen Crane and the Deserted Street Girl

Maggie: A Girl of the Streets (1893) was the most notable nineteenth-century American novel of the streetwalker. Stephen Crane, the young newsman who produced it, also had the distinction of knowing the brothels, bars, and dance halls of New York's Tenderloin and Bowery better than any other well-known writer of his day.[1] There is no record, for instance, that Joaquin Miller's reportorial interest in depravity extended to more than a glance at the red-light district, and Edgar Fawcett's knowledge seemed limited to an occasional slum tour. Crane, in contrast, had been fascinated by the lives of prostitutes since his university days, when he interviewed Syracuse women who had been arrested for soliciting and sent to Putnam County Court. During his brief college career, in the recollections of a college friend, this work kept Crane "a good deal in the company of [such] girls."[2]

In 1892, a draft of *Maggie* in hand, the twenty-one-year-old Crane went to New York to seek publication and more lower-depths experience than that afforded by his Syracuse acquaintances or his brief explorations of the slums of lower Manhattan the year before. While he never limited his studies of human isolation to the female pariahs of red-light New York, he wrote a number of sketches between 1892 and 1896 based on his study of these women. Crane hardly restricted his information-gathering to tours of the Tenderloin, however. In 1896, the year Appleton and Company published a bowdlerized version of *Maggie*, Crane lived in a rooming house of streetwalkers, forming a friendship of sorts with one Amy Huntington. He was evidently undaunted by an encounter the year before with the prostitute Doris Watts, who apparently tried to blackmail him into marriage.[3] Crane later described Watts's attempt to extract money from him with a curiously sympathetic mixture of detachment and forbearance:

I leaned on the door and told her to drop [the blackmail] nonsense. There was...a shield stuck full of knives [in her room]. She lost her temper and grabbed a knife from the shield. It flew over my shoulder and stuck into the wood beside my ear and quivered so that I can still hear the noise.[4]

45

Doris Watts received her money, although from Crane's summation it is not clear whether the author of *Maggie* really understood the world of violence and instability that prostitutes like Watts inhabited.

In a reminiscence, Frank Noxon reported that Crane always treated Tenderloin women with "deference and respect."[5] Though in none of his extant writings did Crane condone prostitution, in his unfinished "Notes About Prostitutes" (1896), he stated matter-of-factly, "Prostitutes walk the streets," and went on to satirize their foes. Not content with crying, "Imprison them," noted Crane sardonically, such people cry "Hang [prostitutes]; brain them: Burn them!"[6] Whatever impelled him to seek out and study these women of the street, he obviously objected to the visceral hatreds they inspired.

One of the most memorable examples of Crane's rather quixotic dedication to justice for prostitutes was provided by the Dora Clark affair. Shortly after Appleton and Company issued his novel, the author of *Maggie* was touring the Tenderloin to gather material for future sketches. With him was the streetwalker Dora Clark alias Dora Wilkinson alias Rubi Young. Moments after she left Crane and her "chorus girl" friends, she was, for a change, wrongly arrested for soliciting. Crane came to her defense, chivalrously claiming that she was his wife and appearing in her defense the next day in court. Crane's testimony won Dora her freedom (though it was not long before her volatile personality caused her to be arrested for fighting with another prostitute).[7] In testifying on her behalf, Crane lost the friendship of two prominent admirers of *Maggie*, Hamlin Garland and Police Commissioner Theodore Roosevelt. He also earned the enmity of the local police themselves.[8] Prosecution witnesses, former red-light "friends" of Crane, attempted to discredit him, and for a time the papers were filled with their charges of his supposed drug addiction and patronage of brothels. "I well knew I was risking a reputation that I have worked hard to build," he told reporters, but "she was a woman and unjustly accused...."[9] Throughout her trial, he insisted Dora had been wrongly detained for soliciting, disingenuously claiming that he knew nothing to discredit her character. His *New York Journal* account of the incident was more frank: "This common prostitute is being done a wrong....[A] wrong done to a prostitute must be as purely wrong as [one] to a queen."[10]

Crane came to the aid of another prostitute he imagined as beleaguered in the late 90's. On one of his New York City ramblings with a fellow minister's son and news reporter, Robert Davis, he reportedly offered to "rescue" a streetwalker.[11] Not surprisingly, she refused his offer. One might even doubt the authenticity of the account were it not that soon after the Dora Clark episode—itself a rescue attempt of sorts—Crane left New York for Jacksonville, Florida to repeat the scenario with far greater success. There he visited a number of madams along the "line," as the red-light district was called, and made the acquaintance of Cora Howorth Stewart. Twice-married, her professional name Cora Taylor, she was the madam of a fairly luxurious brothel called the Hotel de Dream. Crane's friend Ernest McCready characterized her as the "Dame aux Camelias," and there is little doubt that the woman five or six years Crane's senior had worldly experience aplenty.[12] Crane seemed to view her as a victim of circumstances. In all of his recorded handling of the relationship—including his carefully ambiguous reference to a friend about Cora's unhappy past—he shielded her from condemnation. In 1897 he traveled with her to England, taking care that they voyage with chaperons as an engaged couple who planned to marry aboard. They disregarded those like Richard Harding Davis who sneered at that "bi-roxide blonde...whom I did not care to meet."[13] Although Cora could not obtain a divorce from her second husband, from 1897 until Crane's death three years later, she moved in English literary and social circles as Mrs. Stephen Crane. Crane's letters home, as one relative remembered, spoke of Cora as his wife and were careful not to mention her checkered past.[14] Her resurrection to respectability was to prove short-lived, however. Pressed for funds at Crane's death in 1900, she returned to Florida to run another house of prostitution, and became embroiled in a murder scandal a few years before her own death in 1910.[15]

Despite the idealizing tendencies exemplified in his dealings with a Dora Clark or a Cora Stewart, the man who defended the prostitute could also view her in far less positive ways. One of his last works, the hastily written potboiler *Active Service* (1897; published 1900), presents an aggressively unsympathetic *femme fatale*, Nora Black. Possibly modeled in part on Cora Crane, Nora tries everything from chicanery to seductive garments to win over a news reporter who is, significantly, alternately interested and repelled. Well before this portrait of the unscrupulous—and ultimately unsuccessful—Nora, Crane revealed he could be judgmental about both prostitution and promiscuity, a stance fostered by a religious upbringing he could never entirely escape. Crane was, after all, the son of a strict Methodist minister who was considered dogmatic even by those who praised him. Jonathan Townley Crane was the author of a number of temperance tracts and the book *Popular Amusements* (1869), which warned against unholy excitements, among them the dangers of reading novels. Crane's mother, as he himself noted, "lived in and for religion." She was a fierce supporter of Frances Willard's WCTU crusades, though, interestingly enough, she once defied her neighbors by taking in an unwed mother.[16] While her son would provide his own version of protecting the seduction victim, Crane demonstrated his parents' influence as well. He could be conservative about feminine behavior, for he disapproved of women smoking, drinking, or wearing revealing attire, activities inevitably associated with red-light women.[17]

Furthermore, in a letter to a friend describing streetwalkers as "just naturally unchaste," Crane provided a description of their aspirations which belied his own efforts at their rescue or protection. They would simply be courtesans or mistresses, he commented, "if they had the money."[18] He offered a similar assessment when he praised Zola for depicting the unsavory but affluent Nana. She was a "real streetwalker," not a defenseless creature seduced "by some evil man."[19] Cora Stewart's biographer speculates that Crane meant to praise the prostitute for her "mind and will of her own," and, by implication, to defend Cora Crane herself.[20] To this reader it seems far more plausible that Crane was offering an antitype of the seduction story prostitutes themselves so often told.

How, then, is *Maggie: A Girl of the Streets* a translation of Crane's contradictory attitudes towards prostitution? What does the text—and his other writings on the Tenderloin—reveal of his conflicts between defense and judgment, idealization and documentation? Malcolm Cowley has observed that Crane had an "obsessive notion about the blamelessness of prostitutes."[21] It is true that in his art he minimized the prostitute's professional activity much as he did in life. In chronicling Maggie's fall, he stressed her vulnerability, lack of success in the trade, and, above all, her need for a male rescuer. Yet despite an artistry in the portrayal of the psychological violence done to slum women which surpassed any other tenement novel of the 1890's, *Maggie* is a traditional tale. Like Miller and Fawcett, Crane sympathizes with but kills off the girl who goes wrong. Furthermore, as a subplot involving a cold-blooded dance hall woman suggests, the man who could envision Good Prostitutes like Maggie could blast others as mercenaries. Crane's disapproval of the "real" streetwalker prompted him to desexualize his own heroine, to employ a strategy of protection which refused to acknowledge her activity. Still, her creator felt compelled to punish the hired sexuality he tried to explain away. In this he displays an ambivalence about the prostitute which, his real-life rescues not withstanding, his art could only resolve by the same conventions of denial of her other turn-of-the-century imaginers.

* * * * *

If no censor pounced on *Maggie: A Girl of the Streets* when a medical-religious publishing house printed eleven hundred copies under a pseudonym (to save family scandal) at Crane's expense in 1893, it was because the book was doomed in advance to obscurity. His friend Wallis McHarg's warning that no publisher would print a novel about a prostitute proved correct. No newsstand or bookshop—with the exception of Brentano's, which gave back ten of the twelve copies it took—would have the book, and Crane eventually gave away all but one copy. He had anticipated "the sensation it would make," he wrote, and was disappointed that "[n]obody seemed to notice it or care for it."[22]

By 1896, however, both interest in slum fiction and Crane's reputation had surged. On the strength of the best-selling *The Red Badge of Courage*, which had appeared the year before, Appleton agreed to re-publish *Maggie*. This was, however, provided Crane delete the "hells" and "damns" that were considered profanities. More importantly, the publisher insisted that a paragraph describing Maggie's only successful solicitation of a customer be excised. It appears that an Appleton editor, Ripley Hitchcock, did this bowdlerizing, although Crane, anxious to have the book published, acquiesced.[23]

With or without its heroine successfully engaged in her trade, as slum fiction the short novel was quite different from the work of genteel depictors of the romance of the tenement like Edward W. Townsend and Charles Dudley Warner. As David M. Fine in his study of 90's tenement fiction has shown, writers gave middle-class readers "the kind of poor they wanted to believe in and expected in their fiction."[24] Even after Jacob Riis's ground—breaking *How the Other Half Lives* (1890), the novel of urban squalor was far less common than the local color tale of picturesque poverty. In the works of writers like Edward W. Townsend, author of the well-received *Chimmie Fadden* (1895), violent, depressing slum types like Fawcett's alcoholic Owen Slattery are entirely absent. Instead Chimmie's optimism, generosity, and amused tolerance of do-gooder "swells" place the slum "tough" in comic perspective. Here Townsend's dialect hero introduces himself to the reader:

"Say, you know me, when I useter sell poiper, wasn't I a scrapper? Dat's right, ain't it?....Well, say, dis morning I seed a loidy I know crossin' de Bow'ry. See? Say, she is a torrobread, an' dat goes....I've seed her feeding' dem kids wot gets free turk on Christmas by dose east side missionaries."[25]

In Townsend's earlier work, the popular *A Daughter of the Tenements* (1890), classed by Crane as an optimistic vision of slum life, the heroine's transit from rags to riches is accomplished with the aid of her protective family and a Horatio Alger work ethic. Surrounded by a family as caring as Maggie's is destructive, the virginal Carmelita makes her way through a beneficent slum and a world filled with lovable comic figures. The creator of a world awash in sentiment, it is no wonder that Townsend relegates the thieves, prostitutes, and other underclass types to a few asides. Nor, given the vogue for uplifting slum tales, is it surprising that a *Bookman* critic preferred Townsend's work to Crane's gloomy depiction. Commenting on both authors in the mid-90's, the reviewer found *Maggie* "among the saddest books in our language," and noted approvingly that Townsend's slum was a far more attractive place.[27]

Charles Dudley Warner and H.H. Boyesen joined Townsend in providing a cheery vision of the poor. The sun fell "lovingly" on the "pretty scene" of Warner's Lower East Side, reminding the narrator of *The Golden House* (1894) that those who toiled were free to appreciate the simpler pleasures of air and sunshine.[28] Their poverty, indeed, was a blessing in disguise, for it freed them from the "ennui" afflicting the more affluent. H.H. Boyesen claimed to recognize the poor of New York as "social strugglers," the title of his 1893 novel, but, like Warner, he viewed them as essentially untroubled. It was "extremely novel," he explained, "to see people in this...Puritanical land of ours so joyous...living expressive conversational lives, full of...happy irresponsibility."[29] No wonder *Century* editor Richard Watson Gilder refused to publish Crane's story of a girl from a squalid environment which forces her to streetwalking and suicide.

As the lurid tenement pictures painted by Joaquin Miller and Edgar Fawcett demonstrate, Crane was not the first novelist of prostitution to reject the fashionable slum novel. He rebelled against the convention of the picturesque poor, though with far more artistry. Maggie excepted, Crane's characters inhabit a back-street environment animated—and made more sordid—by their truculence and alcoholic self-assertion. They engage in endless physical and psychological warfare; at one point an old woman asks the long-suffering Maggie, "What is it dis time? Is yer fader beatin' yer mudder, or yer mudder beatin' yer fader?" (10). A composite din is produced by the wailing of abused children and the brawls of home, street, and saloon. The noise expresses the rage of those boxed in by their tenement world. Everyone screams, from the "howling urchins from Devil's Row" to their mothers, "formidable women, with uncombed hair and disordered dress," who engage in "frantic quarrels" (10), to the wagon drivers in perpetual anger. There is never any tenement quiet:

Above the muffled roar of conversation, the dismal wailing of babies at night, the thumping of feet in unseen corridors and rooms, and the sound of varied hoarse shoutings in the street and the rattling of wheels over cobbles...[t]he screams of the child and the roars of [a] mother died away to the feeble moaning and a subdued bass muttering. (10)

Such inspired impressionism is quite different from the picture presented by Townsend's *Daughter of the Tenements*. There the clean thoroughfare, though "thundrous," is like an "island beach." The urban roar is a kind of accompaniment to the neighborhood's "piping of museum and concert-hall orchestras" (92). All is made further melodious by the "scurrying games of thousands of children" (92). More tellingly, the author is reluctant to introduce the subject of prostitution into a story of the "beautiful little daughter of the tenement" (36). Townsend presents the novel's only reference as if in a hurry to get past it. Unwilling to delve into social distinctions or life histories, he gives a quick pair of phrases to the prosperous streetwalker and the woman she may soon become: "There were scarlet women in silks, with brilliant faces; scarlet women in rags, with pinched, unpainted faces..." (92). This cheerless allusion is immediately undercut by a description of energetic missionaries from the Salvation Army. Such optimistic redeemers set the tone for the rest of the passage, which soon shifts to Townsend's characteristic description of the innocent gaiety and local color charm of the slum street.

In his focus on the bellicose slum, in contrast, Crane trades sentimental didacticism for irony. When they are not haunting saloons, Maggie's mother, who is a frequent Police Court visitor, and her equally disreputable father and brother engage in lurid arguments. In some early scenes describing a day in Jimmie's childhood, he battles with other warlike children only to be beaten first by his father for being "disorderly" and then by his mother for his disheveled appearance. The violence is not yet finished, however, for he then must witness the blows his drunken parents deal each other. In the hands of Edgar Fawcett, such behavior would be condemned as animalistic. Crane, though, withholds authorial judgment, letting his characters damn themselves. Fawcett's seamstress Cora and her friends come home to oaths which the author claims "drained the lowest depths of humanity" (*The Evil That Men Do*, 39). Maggie confronts a similar scene unmediated by Crane's moralizing: "When Maggie came home...her mother lay asleep amidst the wrecks of chairs and a table....Maggie's mother, stretched on the floor, blasphemed and gave her daughter a bad name" (21).

Maggie was more than period slum fiction. Robert W. Stallman rightly concluded that it was "the first American novel to render urban slum life artistically."[30] Although Crane's characters and episodes are reminiscent of melodrama, Crane locates them in a nightmare world, an hysterical landscape. Through dazzling originality of image, described by Larzer Ziff as a "reality projected by...[his] will rather than one observed and ordered,"[31] Crane shapes a vision of the self-delusion and selfishness produced in part by poverty, in part by the human condition itself.

Yet as prostitution fiction *Maggie* was not the realistic novel for which many contemporary reviewers—as unfamiliar with the subject as with the slum itself—mistook it. Assuming Crane's distinct approach was truth, not artistry, the *New York Press* was convinced that Crane was "nothing if...not realistic...in every chapter."[32] A midwestern journal approvingly found Crane's characters and setting "true,"[33] and one Boston paper even praised the story as "so very real that its effect is almost harrowing," adding that the "pictures [were] vivid" and glow[ed] with "life."[34] Although *The Evil That Men Do* was not invoked by name,

Crane was deemed superior to Fawcett. That author had romanticized and "gilded" vice, whereas Crane "rendered the seamy side of modern existence, the real life of the slums...."[35] Even journalists like those from the *New York Home Journal,* who were revolted by the vulgarity of "lower depths fiction," found verisimilitude in Crane. They did not doubt the realism of *Maggie's* portrayals, although they wished for some "suggestion for uplifting so vile and debased a class" as Crane described.[36] One San Francisco paper alluded to his realism by noting that Crane had analyzed "an important social problem."[37]

While too squeamish or editorially forbidden to mention the word prostitution, reviewers perceived *Maggie* as realistic city fiction in part because it dealt with so daring a subject. What they viewed as realism, however, was basically a conventional tale of Virtue Overwhelmed and "ruined by the overwhelming forces of heredity and environment."[38] Maggie, lured by the slick Pete, is wrongly accused and cast out by her drunken family. She is then seduced and left to fend for herself, only to fall to a prostitute's brief life and watery death. The swiftness of her descent was that predicted by didactic period commentators like the Reverend Matthew Hale Smith: "Their bold and gay life is very short...some [women] breaking down in six months to descend to streetwalking, a few months of misery, and death."[39] In the despondency which caused her fall to prostitution, Maggie also calls up the melodramatic pronouncements of seasoned reporters such as James Buel, whose exploratory tour of the New York red-light district predated Crane's. In his *Mysteries and Miseries of America's Great Cities* (1883) Buel included many "factual" stories of women like Maggie. He concluded from such tales that a "very large majority" of prostitutes were "victims of a confiding trust in some loved one."[40]

Another important analyst who misread and sentimentalized the prostitute's motives was Dr. William Sanger, resident physician of Blackwell's Island. Sanger interviewed 2,000 New York City prostitutes and tried to provide a scientific analysis by charting their years in the trade, age, previous occupation and the like. When the majority of the women claimed they entered the trade voluntarily, however, Sanger reinterpreted the causes of their fall. His summaries of interviews read like notes for *Maggie:*

A sorrowing, heart-broken girl has been denied the opportunity of repentance, and driven from...home....A mother's ill-treatment has driven [another]...to ruin...False accusations and unkind treatment were resorted to, and, from their natural effects, drove a girl from home and virtue....Drunkenness and debauchery made home a hell upon earth....Prostitution was willingly embraced as an escape from parental tyranny.[41]

While there may have been a measure of truth in these responses, prostitutes could not usually be relied on for accurate personal histories, and the uniformity of their replies seems suspicious.

Like the many period observers who evaded the issue of volition by explaining it away, Crane cast Maggie Johnson in the mold of the heroine-as-victim. In the words of one sympathetic period reviewer, she was "sinned against...[and] cast adrift...friendless and helpless."[42] Reminiscent of Fawcett's Cora Strang, Maggie is vulnerable to a smooth-talking trifler who offers rescue from a sweatshop life. In contrast to the stunted types who surround her, Maggie is a "rare and wonderful production of a tenement district" (24). Like Cora she possesses beauty, goodness, and purity. Crane's rhetoric echoes Fawcett's; just as in *The Evil That Men Do* Cora was a "blushrose in the midst of...mirk and soilure" (9), Maggie, in the oft-quoted phrase, "blossomed in a mud puddle" (16).

Nevertheless, unlike Fawcett and his predecessors, Crane continues the defense of Maggie after she becomes a prostitute, employing a strategy which caused some of the more astute critics of the time to complain that she was more type than character. The 1896 *Literary Digest* pointed out that Maggie was "less important to the canvas than her brother Jimmie, or her sottish mother, or the...bartender who is...her destroyer."[43] Modern analysts have concurred, finding her mute and absent.[44] While it is certainly true that rather than becoming a personality reduced through seduction, Maggie is withdrawn and silent well before her fall, her presence is nonetheless felt in the battered way she responds to the "earth of...hardships and insults" (13) on which Crane places her.

The minimized Maggie becomes the very basis of Crane's protective strategy regarding the prostitute. Not only can he defend her effectively by contrasting her in scene after scene with repellent accusers and adversaries who reveal their immorality rather than her own. He can also make clear that Maggie is too reduced and passive to be a sexual aggressor, i.e. a "real prostitute."

Well before her fall to prostitution, Maggie is a woman in need of protection. The novel opens not with her, but with her tougher brother Jimmie, one of those "swearing in barbaric trebles" (3). Unlike Maggie, he will know how to survive in the Hogarthian Rum Alley of the Lower East Side. Crane makes it clear that even as a small girl, Maggie cannot fight the blows of her brother, who, as the world will, "advanced dealing her cuffs." When in the opening chapters both Jimmie and Maggie's drunken mother Mary strike her, Maggie's response is fearful. In a characteristically futile bid for love, she attempts to placate. She is mute, bewildered, and frightened of reprisal, in her very passivity one of the few Bowery denizens not engaged in vilification as self-defense. She never musters the animal ferocity to defend herself against the hostility of a world in which people feel "obliged to quarrel on all possible occasions" (14).

As a child Maggie is taught to fear physical and verbal beatings. As a young woman who is infatuated by the slick bartender Pete, she again trembles at the mother who wrongly accuses her of blackening the family name. By placing the familiar exhortation to chastity in the mother's mouth, Crane can both parody melodrama (the virtuous guiding mother often appears in fictions of imperilled innocence) and defend the daughter preached at by so flawed a parent. The mother, depicted as a monster, continues to rant, glowering at her daughter, eyes burning, and the issue of whether Maggie has "gone teh d' devil" (32) recedes before the savagery of the one who judges. Maggie's only "crime," in fact, is that she listens to what William Sanger, providing the period's standard explanation, termed "the specious arguments and false promises of dishonorable men."[45] Her bad angel Pete whispers he will protect her, and the eternally trembling girl exits to her mother's curses. The harpy neighbors take up the litany of condemnation and gleefully describe Maggie's predictable mistreatment: "she asked him did he love her, did he. An' she was a-crying' as if her heart would break...." They form a malevolent chorus, and the injustice of their accusations increases sympathy for Maggie: "She allus was a bold thing...Dat Johnson girl ain't straight..." (33).

By a series of pairings with other women involved in sexual relationships, Crane further develops the idea of Maggie's fall to prostitution as a response to desertion. In a proleptic dance hall scene which takes place after Maggie has fled her family, she draws back frightened, in horror of contamination from prostitutes seated with customers. As Maggie becomes more dependent on Pete for support, her innocence is contrasted with the experience of Nell, a confidence woman in both senses of the word, who will snatch Pete from Maggie. Crane establishes Nell, whom he half-ironically and half-grudgingly names a "woman of brilliance and audacity" (43), as the Bad Prostitute. Unlike Maggie, Nell has not been betrayed by a seducer. She has no guilty ties to the community or raging family to placate. A survivor, she can fleece a customer and exit laughing. She survives, distrusting men and earning a good living from them. Her saloon conversation with Maggie's lover Pete, whom she is sizing up, indicates her businesslike attitude:

"When did yeh get back? How did dat Buff'lo business turn out?" The woman shrugged her shoulders. "Well, he didn't have as many stamps as he made out, so I shook him, that's all." (43)

Nell is Crane's version of the "real streetwalker" that he praised in Zola's portrait of Nana. She resembles Nana in her unrepentant attitude, fashionable attire, and ability to play one customer off against another. Just as Zola's money-hungry Frenchwoman turns her aristocratic clients into fools competing for her favors, Nell, waving her arms with a "studied indifference," makes Pete and her drunken young escort Freddie jealous. For the moment, she chooses Maggie's lover, whom she will later rob and leave in contempt.

Still, nothing in Nell suggests the sensuality of Nana, with her blonde hair, "marble flesh," and "power to destroy...and remain unaffected."[46] Essentially Crane's hardened prostitute is a variant on the cardboard predator of mid-century warning literature, a type Joaquin Miller and Edgar Fawcett had also adapted. In her own way Nell is as grotesque as the clubswinging Big Lize of E.Z. Judson's *Mysteries and Miseries of New York* (1848) or the bloodthirsty title character of the fictional autobiography of Cecilia Mayo. She is certainly the "adroit adventuress who lays her snares" described by journalist Edward Crapsey, author of *The Nether Side of New York* (1872).[47] Crapsey castigated such a type for assignations in dance halls and cheap back bedrooms which culminated in her robbing the addled dupes she had ensnared. Much like the Tenderloin predator of guidebooks and Gothic thrillers, Nell, Crane noted satirically, took care to know the "amount of [a man's] salary" (58).

The alternate fallen woman in *Maggie*, then, is a hardened professional who reveals the true motives of the streetwalker. As a secondary character, she strengthens Crane's defense of Maggie, the deserted victim unable to withstand the unsavory conditions of prostitution or the ravages of remorse. In distinct contrast to Nell, the luckless Maggie is the amateur prostitute, cast off by her family and her lover and unable to survive very long. But by her very appearance in the narrative, Nell also reveals Crane's ambivalence about the defenselessness of prostitutes. Self-sufficient, cruel, and ruthless, she is a figure absent from serious American literature before David Graham Phillips's *Susan Lenox*: the thoroughly unrepentant prostitute. Yet, unlike Phillips, who finds a way of romanticizing the type, Crane does not develop the portrait. Perhaps in her bloodless adaptability Nell is far more unsettling to her creator than Maggie, whom with contemptuous accuracy Nell characterizes as a "pale little thing with no spirit" (49).

Moved in Nell to provide a richer dimension to the traditional story of ruined innocence, a counterpoint to the seduced Maggie, Crane tries to still the doubts she raises about the nature—and thus the imagined plight—of the streetwalker. Thus he highlights Maggie's inexperience rather than the expertise she might acquire or her resemblance to a Nell. Not only does he defend Maggie by contrasting her lack of experience with Nell's expertise, but he also blurs the distinction between the deserted woman and the prostitute. Between the dance hall scene in which Pete scorns Maggie for Nell and another one in which Maggie goes to beseech him a final time, Crane briefly introduces Jimmie's cast-off girlfriend, Hattie. She functions as Maggie's double, a "forlorn" woman with the fixed smile of the prostitute, "as if someone had sketched with cruel forefinger indelible lines about her mouth" (46). She mirrors Maggie's imminent rejection and subsequent streetwalking by walking endlessly, scanning the faces of men she passes. Yet Hattie is not—or not yet—a prostitute, merely a desperate girl searching for her lover. Hattie begs Jimmie for attention and support. The jilted Maggie does the same with Pete in the next scene, only to receive the identical irritated reply: "Oh, go teh hell" (47). Much earlier in the narrative, Maggie's brother, incensed that the young men of the neighborhood are beginning to chase Maggie, warned what would happen to her in similar terms: "go teh hell or go teh work!" (16). It is not clear why in the bowdlerized edition Appleton substituted "go on d'toif" (Va.,I,63), a more explicit reference to streetwalking, for Jimmie's injunction to his sister but left his later profanity to Mattie uncensored. What *is* clear is Crane's message: the woman bereft of male protection will end up in the hell of prostitution.

Furthermore, the pair of scenes with the supplicating women and their heedless ex-lovers foreshadows Crane's exculpating strategy once Maggie does take to the street. To defend her prostitution as a response to desertion, Crane minimizes Maggie's hired sexuality. Cousin to Miller's Dottie Lane and Fawcett's Cora Strang, Maggie in her robotic soliciting acts out a trancelike response to the trauma of abandonment.[48] Although Crane thus attempts to protect Maggie by stressing her blamelessness, he does so largely by expanding the idea at the heart of *The Destruction of Gotham* and *The Evil That Men Do:* the once-innocent prostitute as reduced personality. Yet, as in the lesser writers, such a desexualizing defense cannot prevent condemnation of her sexual guilt.

Before further analysis of *Maggie* as evidence of Crane's protective strategy as well as its limits, it is helpful to turn to his Tenderloin sketches. They were written during the early 90's when he was creating and revising *Maggie* and published in 1896, the year of the Appleton edition. In their repeated presentation of the slum woman at the mercy of actual or potential deserters, these vignettes reveal Crane's chivalric attitude toward the prostitute or otherwise promiscuous Tenderloin woman. As we shall observe, it was an attitude that *Maggie* would put to its most severe test.

* * * * *

Crane's sketch, "A Desertion," drafted around 1892 but not published until after his death in 1900, depicts the slum woman about to be an orphan in the Tenderloin storm.[49] Interestingly enough, she is named Nell, although she is the butt of the kind of malicious gossip which assails Maggie well before she succumbs to Pete. Unlike the Nell of *Maggie,* her namesake is certainly no seasoned Bowery prostitute. Perhaps Crane is suggesting that the hardened street woman was once a slandered innocent. Whether this is so or not, the young girl is clearly the prey of her sniping neighbors. They are bursting to tell her moralistic father that her only "crime" is coming home late from her factory job, much as a still-virtuous Maggie committed the sin of staying out with Jimmie's friend Pete. When Maggie's beleaguered counterpart comes home, she too fears her parent's reproaches. The neighborhood waits in malicious anticipation as, frightened of reprisals, she enters her tenement building. As if unconsciously anticipating the streetwalker's life to which she will be driven by parental rejection, she exhibits the same "peculiar fixture of gaze" as will Maggie when she plies the streets. Rather like Maggie in her desperate last days, the young woman is one who "saw a succession of passing dangers, with menaces aligned on every corner" (189). She tries to flee this vision of herself as a helpless prostitute by placating her father with apologies. His back is turned as if in angry rejection. Increasingly desperate, she reaches out to touch him—much as the seduced Maggie in her final return home will unsuccessfully reach out to Jimmie— only to find that the father has given her the ultimate rejection. He is dead and his eyes, "fixed upon hers," are "filled with an unspeakable hatred" (191).

As in *Maggie,* Crane shifts the focus from the young woman's ambiguous crime to her rejection by those she asks for help. Like Maggie, the young Nell has a factory job, but the stereotyped implication is that, now that her family's support is withdrawn, she will leave the sweatshop and take up prostitution. Certainly the final line of the sketch contains this grim prediction. A neighbor, unaware that Nell's father has died and thus of the irony of her remark, comments: "Ah th' damned ol' fool....He's drivin' 'er in teh th' street" (192).

Despite the fact that her namesake in *Maggie,* which Crane was completing around this time, does well enough fleecing clients like the drunken Pete in the saloons of the Bowery, the young woman in the news sketch seems headed for the fate of the undefended protagonist of another sketch of the early 90's, also entitled "A Desertion."[50] In it a young woman, her face painted, and thus presumably a prostitute, is attempting to interest a young man who may be her lover, pimp, or client. The sketch is a version of the dance hall scene in which Maggie, having begun to bore her lover, is about to be cast off for the manipulative Nell. In the short piece, the young woman combines Nell's chattering manner with Maggie's lack of allure. The young man "seem[s] about to make up his mind to something" (261), and looks over uneasily at the woman he will soon abandon. Not only does this unfinished treatment parallel Crane's slum novel in its emphasis on the cast-off fallen woman. The unsuccessful prostitute depicted in the sketch also anticipates Maggie at her next stage, when, despite her prettiness, she can lure none but the most repellent client.

Crane's association of the Tenderloin girl, whether virtuous or fallen, mistress of a criminal or a sexual professional, with feminine helplessness continued well after he published *Maggie* and revised it for Appleton and Company. A trio of sketches about her appeared in 1896. Two of them were published in the *New York Journal*, the same paper in which he defended his rescue of Dora Clark. The three sketches, which all depict the flawed male protector, provide further commentary on Crane's fascination with the rescue of tainted virtue.

The first of the three sketches, published in *Town Topics* in October 1896, "In the Tenderloin: A Duel Between an Alarm Clock and a Suicidal Purpose," is the only one in which, to use the phrase Crane employed to characterize his own championing of Dora Clark, a man has "done his duty" to an unchaste woman who cannot take care of herself.[51] Swift Doyer, though, is no minister's son compassionately observing the *demi-monde;* he is a jealous lover who tosses alarm clocks at his unstable girlfriend. Presumably more in the right than the self-righteous accusers Crane usually depicts, Swift resembles them in his violent willingness to hurl accusations at a frightened woman: "Lied to me, didn't you....Told me a lie and thought I wouldn't get unto (sic) you. Lied to me!" (161). Unlike the friendless *Maggie* and the waifs of the two "Desertion" sketches, Swift's woman—described as one of "these girls" of the Tenderloin and thus either a prostitute or one otherwise acquainted with the unchaste life—is given life by her male protector. In despair at her prospects or Swift's rage, she has attempted a return to purity by donning a white robe and taking morphine. Swift rouses her by blows and doses of coffee, calling her "soul back from the verge" (160).

For all his concern to save his mistress's life, Swift has much the same attitude toward the promiscuous woman as Maggie's scoundrel lover or the respectable men Maggie encounters in her wanderings. Swift initially scoffs at her lamentations about a broken heart by reflecting that "these girls have no hearts to be broken" (160). When he fears that she is indeed dying, he conjures up a damnation image—she will be doubly judged as both a fallen woman and a suicide. And he even resents that she does not offer a dying speech of repentance beginning with "Ah, once I was an innocent girl" (161). In a sense he is "dully conventional" type of which one modern commentator accused him.[52]

Nevertheless, Crane implies that Swift will be "black as a storm-god" (160) the next time his woman annoys him by her evasions.

Swift is Lochinvar himself, however, compared to his friend Bill, the failed guardian who is the title character of "Yen-Nock Bill and His Sweetheart," published a month after the first vignette in the *New York Journal*.[53] Bill is an opium-addicted confidence man and shoplifter. Reduced to snarling vulnerability by pneumonia, he taunts Julie, his devoted girlfriend, as she tries to save his life. Even in the throes of illness, with his eyes "turned in a way that was at once childish and insane," he rebuffs her when she pleads that he show some feeling for her. It is Julie who finds Bill a better lodging and arranges for his care. As he recovers, in response to her plea "be good to me; won't you, Billie dear?" he speaks in the tones of Maggie's Pete: "No, why should I?" (173). The sketch may well be a comment on the slum woman's passivity, but it is also a variant on the desertion scenario employed in other sketches. As if she were Maggie had Pete not cast her out, Julie is the woman consigned to the emotional Apache dance of the woman dependent on a sadistic lover.

Occasionally, as in "The Tenderloin As It Really Is" (1896), Crane departed from the vision of rejected womanhood.[54] Flossie's sobbing at the reproaches of her Johnnie demonstrates once again that here is a "girl whose sole anxiety is the man" (165). Yet it is she who listens briefly to the siren call of Bill Maconnigle, "this celebrated cavalier" of the Haymarket dance hall. Although the café is the haunt of prostitutes, Flossie's status is ambiguous. She seems simply to be flirting with another man, and when her Johnnie threatens Bill with "Youse gitaway f'm here an' leggo" (164), she is happy at the attention. A fight ensues, and Flossie scratches and kicks to help defend her brawling lover. As the story concludes, one of Crane's few contented dance hall girls helps her wounded lover to shelter down a Tenderloin side street.

In his news sketches, Crane expressed pity for the hard-pressed, often suicidal women driven to desperation as the consort of underworld men. While city-bred, these women were as much prey to the shocked despondency following rejection as their mid-century predecessors in "wicked city" fare. As much as Crane treated a woman's devotion to a rake with a good deal more irony than a Miller or a Fawcett, he was genuinely critical of the failed protection which was her lot. Even "A Detail," written during the early 90's and published the same year as the other sketches, inspires sympathy for two prostitutes.[55] Crane alludes to them as women whose faces demonstrated "personal grief" (278) as at the loss of a loved one. For a change there is no mention of an absent father or lover. The tiny sketch concerns an old woman who mistakenly assumes the women are respectable girls and whose naiveté produces their sad reaction. Still, Crane rings characteristic changes on the theme of the waif-life creature posing as the street professional. To determine how his lengthiest treatment of the failed protector and the deserted prostitute will—and—will not—sustain those ideas, we now return to it.

* * * * *

As Crane's most daring study of femininity at the mercy of failed rescuers, *Maggie* conflates its heroine's search for help with her prostitution. We recall that in one of the "Desertion" sketches the young woman with the judgmental father had walked anxiously home to him. Crane remarks that she looked as if she were protecting herself from the menaces of the slum, not the least of which is her parent's wrath. When Maggie, who has lost parental support because of her affair with Pete, is jilted by him, she adopts the same kind of self-protective look. Like the woman frightened of fatherly rage, Maggie reacts to Pete's rebuffs by adopting "a demeanor of intentness as if going somewhere" (50). Soon she becomes a prostitute, but her face still reflects her attempts at self-protection. She looks as if "intent upon reaching a distant home," rather an unwelcoming facial expression for one in search of customers. It is, however, the only defense left her, and one which she will continue to employ when she is not adopting the bolder, more seductive expressions expected of those in the trade.

Early on in her life on the street, Maggie again tries to avoid the label of prostitute by beseeching a clergyman for help, ironically only to be mistaken for a woman in search of clients. As an anecdote about Crane's Bowery ramblings suggests, he liked to imagine the streetwalker as in quest of redemption even when it was far from the case. The year after Appleton issued *Maggie,* Crane wandered the Bowery with Robert H. Davis, another minister's son and journalist. The men were soon approached by a streetwalker in search of customers. On seeing her, Crane placed his left hand on his heart, bowed, doffed his hat, and asked her if she were a stranger to the city. In response she offered the formulaic "Well, suppose I am a stranger. Can you show me anything?" Crane is said to have responded, "Yes, I can show you the way out, but if you prefer to remain..." After the girl quickly rejected his help and walked off, Crane remarked, "This is a long canyon. I wonder if there *is* a way out."[56] The story illuminates Crane's most characteristic response to the prostitute: he assumes the woman whom his companion Davis dubs "Maggie" is entrapped by the city. Despite the fact that she is the complete, unruffled professional, he speaks to her in the language of rescue. In *Maggie,* as in the anecdote, the perception is of the prostitute lost in an urban wilderness. Yet unlike his imagined Maggie, this one reportedly responded to Crane by reversing the roles. As she departed, she told him that he "shouldn't hang out in the Tenderloin" because he "can't stand it."[57] Having delivered such sage advice, she strolled down Broadway as if assured that her next meeting with a man would be more profitable.

The rather humorous story suggests that, as in his much-publicized rescue of the street prostitute Dora Clark (who was again arrested for soliciting the day after Crane's defense of her), Crane imposed a model of Maggie on an unlikely candidate. The Bowery prostitute far more resembled Maggie's antithesis Nell, and may well have been willing to turn the cautionary encounter with Crane into a more lucrative one. At the very least, with her the protector and Crane the potential victim, she is in stark contrast to the shrinking Maggie, who is indeed a pale little thing with no spirit.

For the Maggie who walks the mean streets of New York is a most reluctant prostitute. Although an early description has a few words about her in fashionable dress worthy of Nell, Crane seems to begin his harlot's progress tale in so hackneyed fashion to demonstrate that Maggie lacks Nell's skills. Indeed Crane protects her from the charge of being a sexual mercenary by turning her into an obvious failure at the trade. She attracts neither gentlemen in evening attire, nor businessmen, nor laborers, not even a penniless drunkard, a man with "blotched features," or a "ragged being with shifting, blood-shot eyes and eyes and grimy hands" (53). Until her last, highly symbolic encounter, Maggie's transit is not so much a harlot's progress as a series of rejections by the less and less affluent.

One modern student of Crane questions why a girl of Maggie's physical attributes is such a failure at the trade.[58] Hershel Parker and Brian Higgins try to account for her ineffectiveness in the vice world by calling her too eager. Such an explanation seems an odd one, for Maggie manufactures luring behavior according to the kind of man she encounters. For the unsophisticated she has open smiles, for the society type, fashionable indifference.

While Donald Pizer's statement that Maggie is an "expressionistic symbol of purity"[59] is a rather strong one, her lack of success as a streetwalker reveals Crane's need to insist that she labors in vain at impurity. Crane in effect tries to protect a prostitute from the actual experience of prostitution. Maggie thus fails at soliciting; at least until the encounter which prefigures her death, her creator cannot permit her to be other than the traumatized desertion victim, the child-woman of the streets.

So much is Maggie the amateur prostitute that her only solicitation is far more symbolic of her impending death than of her hired sexuality. In the original edition, this scene appears:

When almost to the river the girl saw a great figure. On going forward she perceived it to be a huge fat man in torn and greasy garments. His grey hair straggled down over his forehead. His small, bleared eyes, sparkling from amidst great rolls of red fat, swept eagerly over the girl's upturned face. He laughed, his brown, disordered teeth gleaming under a grey, grizzled moustache from which beerdrops dripped. His whole body gently quivered and shook like that of a dead jelly fish. Chuckling and leering, he followed the girl of the crimson legions. At their feet the river appeared a deathly black hue. (53)

Despite its foreshadowing of Maggie's river doom, the offending paragraph seemed to Crane's publishers an overly frank reference to the trade which led her there. Insisting that Crane sanitize Maggie even more than he had in his emphasis on her lack of actual activity as a prostitute, Appleton excised this "successful" solicitation.

Crane's publishers were only the first to evade the sole evidence of Maggie's acceptance by clients. Editors employed the expurgated rather than the original text for decades. It was not until 1979, with the publication of a Norton Critical edition, that the restored *Maggie* appeared. Significantly, the Norton book was offered as a kind of college text rather than as a definitive edition. It was as if the scholarly community would not accept a usurpation of the standard University of Virginia edition of Crane's works, published in the late 1960's with annotations, variants, and a defense of the expurgated text.[60]

It is worth commenting further on the modern debate about the solicitation scene, for to this reader those who defend the bowdlerized version seem guilty of a lingering Victorianism. Most who approve the omission have confused Appleton's censorious policy with Crane's intentions. Some, though, defend the expurgation on aesthetic grounds. To them, Maggie's act of prostitution, when she moves despondently toward the river, detracts from the unity of the presentation. Fredson Bowers, one of the most eminent of Crane's modern commentators, has contended that the chapter from which the scene was excised pictured a suicidal Maggie, "moving swiftly forward on a predetermined journey." Solicitation was "not the purpose of her movement" because there had been "no suggestion" that she was "seriously seeking customers" (Va., lxxxii). Bowers further claims that Crane, not Appleton, was responsible for the decision to excise: "By 1896 Crane had come to see the distracting effect...of the fat man" (Va., lxxxix). That is, since Maggie's was a movement toward death, the details of her solicitation were "absurd" (Va., lxxxiii).

Certainly the excised scene prefigures Maggie's death, and her solicitation itself, as Bowers himself points out, makes her a rather "sacrificial figure" (Va., lxxxiv). He has no difficulty acknowledging her as a prostitute during her earlier days. Indeed he emphasizes her affluence far more than Crane's fleeting reference to her fashionable attire warranted. Yet Bowers cannot concede that Maggie is still plying her trade while at the same time contemplating suicide. In his view, a prostitute cannot be both suicidal and sexual. It is more palatable to excise the scene in the name of her atonement than to retain it for what it demonstrated of her impulse to survive.

Bowers thus eliminates the solicitation scene for reasons less aesthetic than half understood. He expresses the anger that fueled this textual decision when he approvingly cites a colleague's damning reference to Maggie's "wretched little life" whose "only dignity" (Va., lxxxiv) would have been reduced had the solicitation scene been included in the authoritative text. Most importantly, Bowers reveals the way the offending scene crystallizes his own disapproval of Maggie when he considers the function of the fat man. With no textual evidence for support, he speculates that the man may have murdered Maggie after raping her. Bowers continues the judgmental fantasy about Maggie's offstage activity: "the possibility of murder is as present as that of suicide, given the degeneracy of the man in Crane's description" (Va., lxxxviii). While it is true that a prostitute's customer can turn violent, Bowers creates a version of Maggie's last night which is pure speculation. His drive to create his own version becomes clearer if one notes that he favorably compares Maggie's so-called murderer to the clergyman who refuses to redeem her: "the fat man is no more culpable than the clergyman in his treatment of her, but is no hypocrite" (Va., lxxxvi). Here Bowers seems to be providing unconscious approval of the assassin who ends Maggie's wretched little life. If this is the case, his insistence on removing the solicitation scene is a way of blocking out *any* action which does not conform to his view of a suicidal figure.

Those, among them Hershel Parker and Brian Higgins, who support the restored 1893 text, employ an argument which errs in the other direction. They argue that Maggie's solicitation must be included because it is proof that she is a skilled professional. Before the excised scene, her distant gaze "as if intent upon reaching a distant home" is termed a "stratagem" (242) to attract men, the lure of an increasingly desperate prostitute. Yet these critics seem at a loss to account for a woman who does not look and often does not act like a streetwalker, and who commits suicide after soliciting a repellent man rather than continue in the trade. Indeed their insistence on Maggie as a knowing participant in her own moral degeneration seems misplaced, based as it is on her consistently unsuccessful solicitations and the death which immediately follows the one sexual contact Crane permitted himself to allude to in the text.

What opponents and proponents of the restored solicitation scene fail to recognize is that is does not alter Crane's insistence on Maggie as spiritually dead rather than actively soliciting. Bowers does recognize that Maggie is a sacrificial, even a Christlike figure, but he concocts a rape-murder scene which belies Maggie's trancelike offering of herself to her repulsive client. He is caught up in arguing that the scene detracts from Crane's presentation of a suicidal Maggie on a "voluntary and preconceived journey to a distant home" (Va., lxxxviii). Parker and Higgins stress that in her last moments Maggie is still "obviously a whore" (242), yet they are as reluctant as Bowers to grant that Crane depicts her as she really is—a kind of moral sleepwalker robotically following a final betrayer.

The image of Maggie's beckoning her prospective customer reveals Crane's conflation of her mental deadness and willess sexuality. "His small, bleared eyes, sparkling from amidst great rolls of red fat, swept eagerly over the girl's upturned face," writes Crane. Maggie here is part prostitute, part innocent-come-to-the-slaughter. There is an added dimension as well. Whether the parallel was conscious or not, Crane later used the image in a story whose very title was "The Upturned Face" (1900). There he describes a battlefield corpse which shocks those who try to give it burial. It seems no coincidence that Maggie, a casualty of an inner-city battlefield, should also be depicted as dead-alive.

The association of the prostitute with spiritual death had long been a staple of anti-vice writers, among them Joaquin Miller and Edgar Fawcett and evangelical clergymen like Thomas DeWitt Talmage. Miller, Fawcett, and their predecessors have been scrutinized in an earlier chapter; suffice it to say that Crane was familiar with their imagery of ruined innocence. He would also have known of Talmage, who trumpeted his anti-prostitution message in the pages of the New York newspapers and in widely read diatribes like *The Masque Torn Off* (1879). Rather like the Reverend Jonathan Townley Crane, who wrote tracts on the dangers of alcohol, dancing, and novel reading and cautioned against a "morbid love of excitement," Talmage proclaimed his "divine commission" to condemn sin.[61] *The Masque Torn Off* explores the chief form of city iniquity: prostitution. Talmage lambastes the spiritually dead of a New York brothel. There, prostitutes and customers alike are "moral corpses":

There were corpses on the stairway...corpses in the gardens. Leper met leper, but no bandaged mouth kept back the breath.... (236)

While Crane as the renegade son of a preacher might well have scorned Talmage's heavy moralizing, the solicitation passage in *Maggie* has its own religious insistence of the wages of sin. Maggie, who is about to enter hell, meets a satanic figure. As a modern analyst of the scene remarks, he is a "a slovenly, night-wandering image of the devil himself."[62]

On one level then, Maggie is a lost soul, caught in the grip of the devil. She can only find deliverance in a river death. As Carol Hurd Green has observed, Crane "condemned Maggie to death with the same regretful stringency as the genteel reformers...."[63] As, for that matter, did the fiction of melodramatic sentimentalists like Wirt Sikes, the author of *One Poor Girl. The Story of Thousands* (1869), a well-known "trials of the seamstress" work. Sikes's heroine, though not a prostitute, is a precursor of Maggie. She falls through seduction from work in a sweatshop to suicide. Her creator intones:

It is a grave question whether any woman who seeks to kill herself because she has lost her virgin innocence is worth trying to save. I think not....The crime of the fallen woman is emphatically the crime of weakness too. That is why it and suicide go so much together.[64]

"Seek not," concludes the inexorable Sikes, "to breathe life into the Corpse of Virtue" (56).

It has been argued that by refusing to rescue Maggie from her corrosive environment, Crane reversed melodramas of hard-pressed young girls in which the heroine, whether in the dime novel or the tenement fiction of Edward W. Townsend, remained pure and escaped poverty.[65] Crane's treatment of the virtue-corrupting slum was an advance over the debased romanticism which refused to acknowledge the influence of environment in shaping circumstances. Furthermore, by locating the seducer within the milieu and criticizing Maggie's illusions about him, Crane provided a more believable model than did Edgar Fawcett of a slum woman's foolhardy receptiveness to bad influences. Still, by offering the death-as-judgment scenario, Crane undercut the very defense of the Good Prostitute on which the story of Maggie is based. Much like Miller and Fawcett, Crane provided the harlot progress ending which with few exceptions had characterized American fiction about the prostitute from its inception.

Clearly there was ambivalence in Crane's defense of Maggie as the deserted victim. But at the core he wished to protect the street prostitute from the loathsomeness of her life rather than, as his colleagues and predecessors did, protect the world from the moral threat she posed. Without even the dubious guardianship offered the Tenderloin women of Crane's news sketches or the chilling selfishness which insured Nell's survival, Maggie's only protection becomes death itself.

Perhaps Crane was dissatisfied with his inability to save his prostitute heroine, for he returned briefly to the issue of her redemption in *George's Mother*. He completed the novel in 1894; it appeared the same year as the expurgated *Maggie*.[66] George Kelcey, an alcoholic young man at odds with a mother dedicated to his moral uplift, idealizes Maggie much the way she does Pete. Maggie is utterly indifferent to the unprepossessing young man. He clearly cannot compete with the flashy type who will prove her undoing. Kelcey imagines scenes in which he "rescues the girl from her hideous environment" (138), her slum apartment, her monstrous mother. His resolve, however, is short-lived, for an encounter with Pete, who has come to see Maggie in the early stages of the pursuit, reduces him to despair. At the sight of the gaudy bartender, George slinks away "in the depths of woe" (139).

George's Mother is not another tale of Maggie's trials but of George's troubled attachment to a reformist mother who berates him for drunkenness but will never give him up to another woman. There is only one reference to Maggie's preference for Pete, and none to her subsequent sufferings. Still, the inclusion of Maggie is noteworthy. Having in one work consigned her to the "black river," Crane seems to be imagining an alternate fate for the vulnerable slum girl. To Kelcey, she is not the easy mark to be seduced and left to fend for herself on the streets, but a "goddess" (138) of the tenements. Still, like the failed protectors of Crane's newspaper sketches, Kelcey is too ineffectual to be of help.

Seen in the context of those sketches and of *Maggie* itself, *George's Mother* further explores the prostitute as victim. Crane briefly returns to Maggie's early life to demonstrate that even then her choices—a Pete or a George Kelcey—were tragically constricted. Woman or girl, there is no rescue for her.

* * * * *

As one sympathetic to the *demi-monde*, Stephen Crane, among other protective acts, refused to condemn a blackmailing prostitute, Doris Watts, testified in court for a roving streetwalker, Dora Clark, and proposed marriage to a veteran madam, Cora Howorth Stewart. Translating into art what one contemporary euphemistically termed his overriding "desire to save the helpless" was not as easy.[67] In his fiction and sketches he tried to defend the prostitute by dramatizing her victimization and minimizing her participation in the sex trade, but he could not still his disquiet about her impurity. Like Joaquin Miller, Edgar Fawcett, and countless "wicked city" sensationalizers, anti-urban guidebook writers, and evangelical moralists of the mid- and late-nineteenth century, Crane perceived the prostitute as a ruined woman. True, his Maggies are not the lurid grotesques of mid-century anti-vice writings, characters who resurface as Miller's maddened Dottie Lane and Fawcett's alcoholically remote Cora Strang. To an extent Crane humanized the prostitute. He gave his deserted street waifs a dimension lacking in the fallen creatures of his colleagues. Still, Maggie's psychic deadness and the suicidal resolve she shares with the hysterical heroines of his sketches hark back to the mid-century stereotypes. Even more clichéd is the adventuress, Nell. In depicting her, Crane channelled what he knew of the mercenary streetwalker onto a cardboard villainess whose nature he did not risk exploring.

Crane never resolved his ambivalence about the unchaste woman, a tension between idealization and condemnation which his work on prostitution embodies. These warring impulses are at their most evident in the character of Maggie herself. Killed off because she is the sexual sinner, Maggie also dies because she is not sexual at all, but unguided, unprotected, and cast adrift.

Chapter Four
Harold Frederic and the Cost of Redemption

When Stephen Crane arrived in England in 1897, Harold Frederic had reason to welcome him. Frederic, whose novel about a small-town seductress and a minister's crisis of faith, *The Damnation of Theron Ware* (1896), was for a time even more popular than Crane's acclaimed *The Red Badge of Courage,* had just smoothed the way for the British reception of Crane's Civil War novel.[1] He praised the work for its vivid characterization and effect of "photographic revelation," praise which Crane in turn gave Frederic's ironic fiction on the moral strictures of upstate New York.[2] Though less of a literary impressionist than Crane, Frederic shared the younger man's interest in depicting the effects of extreme or depressing environments on characters as diverse as the small-town *naif,* the Civil War soldier, and, last but not least, the city-dwelling prostitute.[3]

There was perhaps an added reason for Frederic's enthusiastic welcome. Like Crane, Frederic was living rather openly with a woman not his wife, causing rumbles even in the relatively permissive upper-crust circles he frequented and to which he would introduce his new acquaintance.[4] Crane had left America with the ex-madam Cora Howorth Stewart to escape the double notoriety of his common-law liaison and his recent rescue of wrongly-arrested streetwalker Dora Clark. He must have struck Frederic as admirably willing to risk scandal to defend women vulnerable to social ostracism. As the friendship between the men and the two unconventional couples developed, there was speculation that Crane inspired the affectionately satiric portrait in Frederic's 1898 novel *Gloria Mundi* of idealist Christian Tower, who wished to save his "sisters," the prostitutes of London's Haymarket district.[5]

Well over a decade before he met the defender of Maggie Johnson and Dora Clark, Frederic had covered Haymarket vice for the prestigious *Pall Mall Gazette.* Though lacking Christian Tower's naively evangelical belief in the redemption of the prostitute, Frederic's journalism revealed sympathy for her and the hope that she might leave the trade one day. In his now-forgotten third novel, *The Lawton Girl* (1890), he placed her American counterpart in the carefully delineated small-town setting for which he was becoming noted.[6] A personality study of the reformed prostitute, the novel dramatized the effects of Jessica Lawton's resolve on her flinty upstate New York hometown and the discontented factory girls she proposed to save from immorality. By 1896, the year the revised *Maggie* was published, Frederic was still sufficiently interested in the prostitute's redemption to publish *March Hares,* a light romance set in London which dealt with a young woman on the brink of streetwalking who chose a more savory eleventh-hour alternative.

We have already observed the pull in Crane's work between protecting and rejecting the prostitute. Frederic's treatment of Jessica Lawton and her coquettish sisters reveals a similar ambivalence. He also introduces a new dimension: many of his incipient or penitent prostitutes and egotistical coquettes fleetingly emerge as emancipated New Women of the 1880's and 90's and challenge woman's traditionally dependent role. Now the danger of woman's sexuality is magnified by her allied desire for economic freedom. To meet the dual threat, Frederic turns to images which punish as they purify. The near-fallen woman becomes the spinster or the chastened wife; the prostitute who seeks social amnesty is martyred and made a saint. To account for such deflating responses, particularly to his morally reclaimable prostitute heroine Jessica Lawton, it is necessary to comprehend Frederic's expatriate reaction to the London sex trade and the symbolic importance of the female promiscuity he observed there.

The title character of *The Lawton Girl* returns to the fictive American town of Thessaly as if she were the only prostitute, penitent or not, likely to reside there. In stark contrast to Thessaly, a town itself like the Utica of Frederic's boyhood,[7] London when he arrived in the mid-80's was quite open to the prostitute. From the fashionable West to the seedy East End, thousands of streetwalkers (estimates ranged from six to eighty thousand) competed with hundreds of brothels.[8] Women of varying degrees of affluence blocked the West End streets around what is now called Piccadilly Circus, alarming the respectable on their way to clubs and theaters with obscene gestures and profane language. Many observers deplored these "brazen-faced women, blazoned in tawdry finery," with their "painted cheeks and brandy-sparkling eyes."[9] "The fouled hindquarters of English life," the Frenchman Taine remarked in disgust; the "western counterpart of an eastern slave market," echoed *The Saturday Review.*[10] As Frederic walked to his own club, the Savage, he could well have been solicited by a succession of showily made-up women. They certainly did not escape his notice; his late novel *Gloria Mundi* includes a scene at the Empire, a West End vaudeville theater near Haymarket whose bar was popular with prostitutes in search of clientele.

This, then, was London as reformers stepped up campaigns to pass the Criminal Law Amendment bill to prevent juvenile prostitution and crack down on street and brothel vice. Women became increasingly interested in "saving the fallen."[11] Ellice Hopkins, whom Frederic would include in an article on the anti-vice movement, visited brothels with evangelical zeal; Mrs. Ormiston Chant addressed 400 Social Purity rallies in one year; the Salvation Army sent female crusaders out on "Piccadilly patrols" to warn or inspire the unredeemed.[12] While dukes paid to meet underage girls in "introducing houses," spend the night in Mrs. Jeffries' luxurious bordello (across the street from a police station), or indulge in the panoply of other sexual excesses chronicled in the eleven volumes of *My Secret Life, Pall Mall Gazette* editor W.T. Stead decided to rouse the conscience of Europe and America. He disguised himself as a rake, toured the underworld, and published his experiences to an avid reading public.[13]

Frederic took it all in: the great city was proving an excellent place for the budding American novelist to gain perspective on his own experience. The dual spectacle of jaded sophisticates and strident reformers inevitably evoked contrasts with the secretive sinners and back-fence gossips of his small-town adolescence. From this metropolitan and European vantage point, he could reflect on the reception an American town untouched by the social evil would accord a Prodigal Daughter returned from a city brothel. Soon he would begin notes for the story of Jessica Lawton, and his reflections would find a fictional embodiment.

Before Frederic the novelist imagined his chastened American prostitute, Frederic the reporter investigated the real-life inhabitants of London's red-light districts. His first year in England had been a productive one. He had earned international fame for his *New York Times* dispatches on cholera-stricken southern France and the Irish Home Rule question and praise for his *Pall Mall Gazette* portrait of the new American president, Grover Cleveland.[14] A man of inexhaustible energy, Frederic used his rapidly-gained entry into the leading social and intellectual circles to send back a stream of weekly dispatches on the political, literary, and cultural talk of London.[15] From society dinners to brothel tours, he seemed as acquainted with the *haute* as with the *demi-monde*.[16] Though only in England a year, he thus seemed eminently qualified when asked by W.T. Stead to write a pair of *Pall Mall Gazette* articles on the problem of London prostitution.[17]

Under Stead, that influential London paper was in the midst of a battle against juvenile prostitution. Stead himself was on a crusade to pass the Criminal Law Amendment Bill to raise the age of sexual consent for young girls from thirteen to sixteen and to increase police power over brothels and procurers. With the measured support of respected figures in the Anglican Church, the Salvation Army, and the anti-vice movement, the publicity-seeking editor undertook a muckraking tour of the underworld. He interviewed brothel keepers, pimps, and prostitutes—all of those who could testify to the procurement of underage girls. Stead's most sensational measure, however, was to "purchase" thirteen-year-old Eliza Armstrong for five pounds to prove that such a transaction could occur. His hyperbolic four-part "Maiden Tribute of Modern Babylon" series narrating the purchase and describing London's underworld appeared in the early days of July 1885. To Stead's satisfaction, the "Maiden Tribute" caused a furor which soon gave him and the *Gazette* international attention, forcing a Parliamentary debate and the August passage of the age-of-consent bill.[18]

Frederic's articles appeared in July and August of 1885, at the height of the Stead-created furor. As if in deliberate contrast to Stead's rabble-rousing rhetoric, they were sober responses to the phenomenon of London vice. Like many of his British colleagues, Frederic considered Stead's journalism sensational and his revelations offensive. In a September dispatch to his home paper, Frederic wrote of the "astounding, revolting, ridiculously overdrawn story of a Modern Babylon."[19] Years later he was still referring to the "stench of the 'maiden tribute' affair."[20] It is a testimony to Stead's interest in opposition views—as well as in fanning controversy—that he published Frederic's articles at all. As if speaking for Stead himself, his biographer termed Frederic's the "Devil's point of view"[21] for its calm acceptance of the prostitute's trade.

Frederic refused to romanticize. In the first of his pseudonymous articles, "A Saunterer in the Labyrinth," he seemed rather unconcerned with the age-of-consent legislation known as the Criminal Law Amendment Bill, to which he made fleeting reference. He preferred to refute Stead's contention that the time was ripe for a mass return to social purity, whether through the rescue of teenage brothel victims or the conversion of their middle-aged patrons. Stead felt compelled to preface a reprint of Frederic's second article, "Musings on the Question of the Hour," in the *Gazette's* weekly digest, the *Pall Mall Budget*, with this disclaimer:

The more painfully many of the remarks of 'A Saunterer' may grate upon the susceptibilities of many of our readers the more obvious is the necessity for reminding them of the opinions with which they have to deal.[22]

Frederic's *Gazette* essays, taken with his subsequent *New York Times* description of an enormous Stead rally, represent an attack on the anti-prostitution movement more daring than any of Stephen Crane's newspaper pieces. Frederic's liberalism, however, was not without ambivalence. As his defense of the prostitute anticipated the tensions of his later fiction, these articles repay closer scrutiny.

Frederic chose as his persona in the *Gazette* articles one of those journalists, lawyers, city men, and artists whom he met so often in that "world of Piccadilly and clubland which thought...[Stead] had done mischief" ("Saunterer," 22). Such a man was a British version of Frederic himself, appalled at what his *New York Times* piece termed "the vast vigilance committee to compel morality in England" ("Saunterer," 22). Disgusted that child prostitution, "unknown at the West end of London when I began life" ("Saunterer," 22), should prosper, Frederic's persona also casts a cold eye on the zealots who thought they could control the sexual instinct through religious conversion. Cynical too about an age-of-consent bill in the face of coverups by aristocrats who hamper police inquiries, he has a practical suggestion. Though phrased bluntly, Frederic's advice would have won approval from many in the Social Purity movement. Give sex education to young women, he advised, for it "seems hardly fair that a girl should be allowed to marry, any more than be seduced without knowing what a momentous business she is letting herself in for" ("Saunterer," 22). From this suggestion the Saunterer moves to a defense of the middle-rung prostitute. Whether she fell to prostitution from ignorance or economic necessity, such a woman was now the victim of official morality:

I quite agree with all that has been said in defense of the public women of London. I have never frequented the kind of houses which the Commission [Stead's self-appointed journalists' group] visited, but in the quieter regions of the calling which I know, I never found the women other than kindly and gentle, *by no means addicted either to heavy drinking or obscene conversation.* Hitherto the one official idea of promoting morality has been to hunt the poor creatures from pillar to post. This will surely be recognized as hard, once it is perceived that nearly all come into the business unwillingly and are *unable to escape* from it....The women thus persecuted often lose their furniture, which makes all the difference in the world between *possible escape* and certain ruin, and they lose their established friends....[It] will probably be conceded by all that a woman who gets a few friends around her and ceases to knock about and drink is a preferable manifestation of womanhood to a poor creature ever seeking strangers of whom she has no knowledge and for whom she cannot have the smallest trace of attachment. (22) (emphasis added)

For all its criticism of those who hound the prostitute, the passage dwells on her depravity as well. Frederic insists that the fairly affluent prostitute who, after all, entered the trade involuntarily, is neither foul-mouthed nor drunken. Yet despite his confidence in the steadiness of her nature, he warns that she could become an alcoholic should she suffer financial reverses. Frederic vacillates between the Good and Bad Prostitute here. The would-be escapee reminds him of the one bestially wed to the trade. The woman longing for a virtuous life calls up her drunken alter ego, the indiscriminate woman of the streets. The dominant image is of the "gentle, kindly" prostitute who desires and merits a better fate, a woman who "escapes" with her self-reliance and some savings as well.[23] Yet when, in his fiction, she becomes the penitential Jessica Lawton, she crystallizes Frederic's doubts about the prostitute's redemption.

Frederic's second *Gazette* piece, "Musings on the Question of the Hour," places her in the context of the age itself:

The tendencies of the age do not make for continence, either in men or women. The majority is growing up outside the influence of the Churches. The old fear of hell fire, as the reward of sinners, is dying, dying, dying.... (11)

Without condoning the "growing sensuality of the age," Frederic sees it as an outgrowth of the same sexual instinct which, a century hence, he boldly remarks, will replace hired female promiscuity with, among other things, men and women living out of wedlock. Even in Frederic's own time, he argues, the independent working woman who is not dependent on marriage is likely to be less chaste than the married one. Frederic all but links this unmarried woman, in that "thirst for finery and excitement" (11) which was considered one reason for a woman's entry into prostitution, to the prostitute herself. Certainly both women are willing enough to forget their "natural and indoctrinated tendency to chastity" (11).

For all its apparent tolerance of the prostitute, Frederic's first *Gazette* essay presents inconsistent images of her. His second one expands that inconsistency to include all wayward women. His Saunterer seems unaware of the contradictions in a phrase like woman's "natural and indoctrinated tendency to chastity." While assuming that "even among women we must look for less rather than more self-denial in the future," he finds polyandry, presumably whether in a prostitute or shop girl, "a low ideal of human existence" (11) and far more troubling than male licentiousness. Furthermore, although he hovers around it, he evades the issue of whether, if the prostitute *could* earn enough money to be independent of men, she would still engage in sex after she abandoned the trade. Given the vision of the excitement-craving factory girl, could an ex-prostitute reasonably be expected to practice chastity? Presented and then skirted, such ideas inform the portrait of Jessica Lawton, the prostitute-turned-shopkeeper of *The Lawton Girl*.

Whatever the moral reservations about female promiscuity discernible beneath the surface reasonableness of his *Gazette* essays, Frederic had a strong dislike of the professional reformer. He wrote sarcastically of one of Stead's influential allies in the movement: "Miss Ellice Hopkins has made so many converts, why should she not convert the nation?" ("Musings," 11). Frederic could better tolerate the prostitutes who consorted with men whom they disliked than he could those who felt that by the "flushing of social sewers" the sexual morality of the day would be altered. The phrase appears in his final essay on the British anti-prostitution movement, a September *New York Times* article entitled "Mr. Stead and His Work." It covered a triumphant August 21 Hyde Park rally of 70,000 people gathered "to denounce criminal vice" and to celebrate the recent passage of the age-of-consent bill.[24] To assess this flag-waving spectacle for his home audience, Frederic relinquishes his clubman persona. He becomes instead the indignant American democrat. These zealots could learn from Americans, Frederic storms, who would scorn the "instinct of Puritanism to control people for their own good...which burned the witches at Salem...[and] founded the Salvation Army" ("Mr. Stead and His Work," 5).

Actually, even as Frederic wrote, the American branch of the Salvation Army was involved in rescuing prostitutes.[25] Furthermore, a pamphlet version of the "Maiden Tribute" had scored a great American success days after its London publication. Stead himself, who would make an American tour in the 90's, was hailed by an organization soon to be called the American Purity Alliance.[26] In denial or ignorance of such developments, Frederic depicted an America where no reformer waited outside brothel doors to harass the prostitute or compel her redemption. Commending Englishmen who had "become like Americans" ("Mr. Stead and His Work," 5), he had an attitude one British colleague sarcastically described in this manner:

He was, of course, American, patriotically and flamboyantly so, and like a good American he was ever ready to point out our many faults and failings, and to contrast them with the full-fledged perfection of the other hemisphere.[27]

As an American abroad, Frederic could, like his imaginary clubman, point with contempt to the British puritans who hoped to suppress the sexual instinct. Evading the issue of American prostitution, he presented an idealized home country. There neither the social evil nor measures to suppress it were the questions of the hour they were in the Old World, as if America were the romanticized Utica of his youth.

How, then, did Frederic's London experience shape his ideas about the prostitute in the years before he became a novelist? Certainly the guises of the anonymous man-about-town and the American newsman critical of British puritanism enabled Frederic to discuss the prostitute sympathetically but with little risk to his reputation. Without condoning the behavior of the woman who "minister[ed] to the passions of the floating population" ("Saunterer," 22), he could explain that she did so for reasons society must understand. Save in the minority of cases, she should be an object of compassion. As such she could be helped not by evangelism but by letting her decide for herself if she wished to support herself in a better way.

These liberal sentiments, it should be remembered, did not prevent Frederic from viewing the prostitute as an anonymous member of an army of fallen women, without pasts or parentage, symbolic of the morality of large European cities. When Frederic came to write fiction, he remarked to an interviewer: "The pleasure of a novelist's life is living with his characters."[28] Given this philosophy of characterization, how well could he translate into fiction the ideas of the anonymous Saunterer and of the American reporter disgusted with British prudery? As *The Lawton Girl* would reveal, a journalistic tolerance of the sex trade in a foreign country was one thing. A novel under one's own name sympathetic to an American prostitute was quite another.

* * * * *

Despite his success as a foreign correspondent, freelance journalist for leading British and American periodicals, club and salon habitué, and intimate of London's leading literary men, Frederic intended to leave journalism and return home once his novels about life in upstate New York began to sell.[29] Accepted in the most sophisticated literary and political circles, on friendly terms with Shaw, James Barrie, the philanthropist Lady Jeune, and many English and Irish statesmen, he still presented himself, in the words of a British contemporary, as "the most thorough-going American who ever lived in the British Isles."[30] He would entertain society dinners by playing the American eccentric, roaring out spirituals, telling yarns, and, like Joaquin Miller before him, embroidering on the hardships and drama of his American boyhood.[31]

Exploring his Americanism in a more serious way, in 1886 he began a series of novels dating from the Revolution to his own time. His ambition was to present a panorama of his native Oneida County, in the words of a modern commentator, "a documentary summary of life in a little-chronicled corner of America."[32] Within two years of his arrival in England, he had published his first novel, *Seth's Brother's Wife* (1887), in which the as-yet-unrepentant prostitute Jessica Lawton is briefly introduced. His second and third works, the historical novel *In the Valley* and *The Lawton Girl*, his study of a reformed prostitute, appeared in 1890. Other work set in America followed: on the Civil War in *Marsena and Other Stories* (1893) and *The Copperhead* (1894), and *The Damnation of Theron Ware* (1896), which would become a best-seller and secure Frederic's reputation. Ironically such financial freedom would come too late. He never did return to settle in America, and died, only forty-two, but two years after *The Damnation*.

Frederic's New York State fiction drew on a rich understanding of the historical, social, ethnic, and political divisions of his home country. Such sweeping concerns are well summarized by Larzer Ziff:

Harold Frederic, sitting in London, detached from the immediate political maneuverings of upstate New York, brought into existence a fully articulated human community. The peculiar quality of rural brutality as well as rural speech, the way the political boss...ruled the countryside as well as the town, the relation of the best families to the processes of making public policy, the aldermanic view of responsibility, the contrasting social roles played by the Methodist and the Episcopal Churches, the Dutch resentment of the English settlers who had migrated from Massachusetts, and the code of the masculine small-town world as opposed to the public code of sexual morality....[33]

As important to Frederic as the lives of leading families, Methodist elders, and maneuvering politicians was the local Girl Who Went Wrong, represented by Jessica Lawton. Frederic had already conceived of this character by the time he wrote his first novel, *Seth's Brother's Wife*. There Seth Fairchild, an unsophisticated news reporter recently come to the fictional city of Tecumseh, reminiscent of Frederic's Utica, returns briefly to the farm. He reflects contemptuously about Jessica and her family:

The Lawtons were a low-down race, anyway. He had seen one of the girls at Tecumseh, a girl who had gone utterly to the bad....[34]

Details of Frederic's early journalistic life in Utica are sketchy. What is known is that, like his character Seth, he worked in a local newspaper "to chronicle day after day in the curtest form, fires, failures, crimes, disasters, death...."[35] Omitted from this crime-reporting repertoire is Frederic's knowledge of one Jessie, jailed for knife-wielding in a brothel, and made miserable by evangelical townswomen who come to her cell and exhort her to repent.[36] The hapless Jessie and her treatment may well have inspired his naming of Jessica and his vision of her Thessaly reception.

By the time Frederic began notes for *The Lawton Girl*, he seemed to share the autobiographical Seth Fairchild's low opinion of her. She seems not far removed from the lower class of London street women deplored by the Saunterer. Frederic's earliest page of notes, written in 1886 or early 1887, ends with this brief, unflattering mention:

The city Lawton girl returns—study of the harlot in a village, alleged husband.[37]

Cryptic as this is, the notation is suggestive. At this early stage of composition, Jessica still seems to fit the description in *Seth's Brother's Wife* of a girl "gone utterly to the bad." The use of the word harlot implies that, despite leaving the city, she is still in some way attached to her profession. And there is the equally daring idea of a prostitute's search for an "alleged husband."

Despite a glancing acquaintance with Utica's brothels and a later familiarity with the streetwalkers and bordellos of London, Frederic soon abandoned the idea of making a seasoned city harlot of Jessica Lawton.[38] How could he integrate such a character into the life of a central New York village? Or employ the same non-judgmental tone about active prostitutes as he had used in his *Pall Mall Gazette* articles?

Frederic's solution in the next stage of composition is to present Jessica as a reformed and guilt-ridden prostitute. As his notes indicate, she is a far cry even from the quiet London women of the *Gazette* essays who leave the trade without fanfare, as if simply changing jobs. Seeming surer of how to develop the new character than in his brief earlier notes, he now describes how Jessica will suffer when she returns home to her shiftless family and unwelcoming town:

The Lawton girl—after utter failure to live at home and more or less cruel rebuffs from "good women" of the town, finds [the] only patrons for her millinery dressmaking are factory girls. She makes friends with them—finally founds sort of a Club for them. She meets with much ingratitude, nasty sneers, coarse misapprehensions at outset, even from them.[39]

Gone is the earlier focus on the wayward woman who supposedly married and then left for a life of professional sin. Indeed there is nothing of the "harlot in a village" about the Lawton girl. Even from this brief description it is clear that, with an eye to audiences in censor Anthony Comstock's America, Frederic chose a more workable theme, the penitent's self-imposed punishment. It is as if the gentle, kindly middle-rung London prostitute of Frederic's Saunterer tours returned home to endure being forgiven.

At this stage of composition, Jessica was still not the central figure she would become in the finished version. A minor character, she was carefully censored. Her death scene was one of the first to be outlined in detail. Such a plot decision, so early in the composition of the novel, was a bow to "wages of sin" thinking and censorship. The final version also killed off Jessica and retained the deathbed scenario, which Frederic later acknowledged that he regretted. But he seemed unaware of the extent to which the death of Jessica resolved the difficulty of imagining her reintegration into small-town American society.

The first working title of the book, *Reuben Tracy's Partner,* referred to the amoral young lawyer Horace Boyce, the son of an old but declining family. Boyce plans to swindle the Minsters, Thessaly's rich manufacturing family, on whom the town is dependent for work, but will be caught by his honest partner Reuben Tracy. The Boyce-Tracy conflict is central to the final version, but in it Jessica will no longer be a minor character. Also, she will be befriended by Reuben Tracy, whom Frederic now casts as her old schoolteacher-turned-town lawyer. In the final version, Horace Boyce will add to his sins and become Jessica's ruin, as callously unconcerned with her fall as he is with her penitential return five years later.

Earlier versions relegated Jessica to a minor role. In the final one her moral ascent, contrasted to Horace's moral descent, will be a central concern. In her attempts to "live it down," she will hold a mirror up to the hypocrites who had cast her out.[40] Her courageous life and sad death will illustrate, in the words of the literary editor of the *Boston Globe*, who praised the novel when it appeared, "the obligation of overcoming wrong-doing by right living, with the certainty of victory."[41]

In its finished version, there are actually two main stories in *The Lawton Girl*. One is the sequel to *Seth's Brother's Wife*, which continues that novel's saga of social ambition, political division, and sexual hypocrisy in a manufacturing town. The opposition between innocence and cynical experience, which in *Seth's Brother's Wife* was personified by Seth and his brother Albert, are in *The Lawton Girl* embodied in Horace Boyce and Reuben Tracy. The virtuous Annie Fairchild and wayward Isabel Fairchild of *Seth* are paralleled by the virginal Kate Minster and the fallen Jessica. And as in *Seth*, though unlike *The Damnation of Theron Ware*, the generous young man triumphs, stilling town gossip about his friendship with Jessica and foiling Horace Boyce's plot to swindle the Minster family.

The other story in *The Lawton Girl*, to which many of the novel's period reviewers responded, is that of the Magdalen. Overlooking some obvious differences in the protagonists' sexual histories and historical periods, one favorable review found the story "similar to *The Scarlet Letter*."[42] The heroine is invested with "a pathetic interest," remarked the *Boston Commonwealth*.[43] A midwestern newspaper was moved by her story to say:

Jessica's repentance...should be noted by 'the Pharisees' who forget 'that repentance even at the eleventh hour is better than continuance in sin' and who force back into vice or to the grave unfortunate women such as Jessica.[44]

Boston's *Cambridge Tribune* lauded Jessica's resolve,[45] and the *Critic* concurred in praise of "an unfortunate girl...[who] returns to the scene of her disgrace with the determination to live it down."[46] Some expressed sympathy for girls like Jessica, the noted journal of social issues *Public Opinion* viewing her as unfortunate.[47] All employed euphemisms to describe prostitution: "the difficulties in the case," "the social question," "the existence of such people."[48] Despite Frederic's careful omission of any details of the trade, a number of reviewers found the subject matter "coarse," "seamy," "unpleasant," and, all in all, "rather dingy reading."[49]

Partly in deference to Frederic's reputation as a serious novelist, others read *The Lawton Girl*, in the words of the *New York Tribune*, as, "despite the title,...the story...[of] fraudulent conspiracy."[50] The *Philadelphia Public Ledger* found it a business story;[51] a story of "the modus operandi of monopoly and business dishonesty," agreed the *Philadelphia Times*.[52] William Dean Howells thought Horace Boyce, the protagonist, a "cheap young reprobate," but avoided any reference to Jessica.[53] Only a few seemed aware of the structural problem of the novel, that Jessica is the title character, but her story is for some reason subordinated to that of the villain.[54]

Modern critics have transformed this problem in structure into a dismissal of Jessica Lawton. The authors of a recognized study whose aim was to render "unhurried" judgments of Frederic's best-known fiction cannot bring themselves to refer to Jessica as a former prostitute. Borrowing Victorian terminology, they call her a woman who "returns to her village in courageous shame." They do not discuss her further except to dismiss her in a reference to the novel's "slightly daring overtones."[55] They see no connection between the atonement plot and what they term the real focus, the disruptive effects of the corrupt Social Darwinism of capitalists like Horace Boyce.

But why did Jessica sin in the first place? The novel acquires more unity if one traces her fall. A working girl from a poor family, bored with her limited life, she craves excitement. She is fair game for the slick new money man who casually seduces her, leaves her to a brothel fate, and goes off for an extended tour of the pleasures of the Continent. Viewing the novel as seduction fiction also clarifies the ironies of the opening scene in which Horace Boyce, filled with schemes for self-advancement, returns home on the same train carrying the penitent Jessica. She is, in effect, a symbol of his moral insensitivity. As the novel unfolds and she forgives Horace and even martyrs herself for him, she becomes the cause of his moral awakening.

One modern commentator, Austin Briggs, Jr., acknowledges Jessica's influential presence in the narrative. It puzzles him:

The really odd thing about Jessica, what makes her so unconventional in the role of fallen woman, is that most of the time she is just what one expects to find in a conventional blonde heroine.[56]

Briggs's puzzlement about Jessica, like other critics' dismissal or omission of her, obscures Frederic's goal, which was to place the "harlot" in the same "village" whose other moral, social, and economic divisions his novels dramatize. Certainly this purified ex-prostitute is out of place in a study of small-town society. Yet in her very "oddness," she illuminates Frederic's difficulties in presenting the prostitute to an American audience, difficulties which we shall now examine.

* * * * *

From the beginning of *The Lawton Girl,* it is clear that Jessica bears no hint of her recently discarded profession save remorse. The melancholy but resolute woman who returns home after five years of life in the city is garbed in black. Her face shows suffering; her handkerchief is at the ready to hide her tears. She chooses to return in winter, as if to add to the anticipated emotional chill of her reception.

Whatever her carnal knowledge, it has been obliterated by the desire for a life of self-imposed sacrifice. She has been cautioned by her friends Seth and Annie Fairchild—the same Seth who in an earlier novel had judged her so cruelly—to remain with them and do millinery work in the more welcoming city of Tecumseh. She is convinced that to undo her past means to face, as Frederic didactically describes it,

the ordeal which she had proposed to herself—the task of bearing, here in the daily presence of those among whom she had been reared, the burden of a hopelessly discredited life. (21)

Jessica's trials begin the moment she arrives in Thessaly. The railway clerk looks at her with an "offensive expression" (18). She must watch in mortified silence as her ex-lover, the affluent Horace Boyce, who, unknown to her, had traveled on the same train, alights and condescendingly gives orders to her shiftless father Ben Lawton. Boyce wastes no time in condemning her. Moments after he glimpses her at the station, he warns his good-hearted law partner and Jessica's former schoolmaster Reuben Tracy that she will return to prostitution within the month.

Her motives are questioned by rich and poor alike. The minister's wife ostentatiously snubs her. Other influential women gossip about her carriage ride in the company of kindly Reuben Tracy. Her own sister mistakes Jessica's offer of employment as brothel procurement. The young factory hands are half-convinced that her shop is a house of prostitution and they camp there and knock on her door after the shop has closed for the day. Worst of all, the factory girls she had hoped to help by providing a recreation room jeer, gawk, and like the rest, insult her.

Such mistreatment, bitter as it is to her, tests the mettle of this strong-minded young woman. Her reform is a religious conversion in secular terms. She wishes to make her life both a warning and model to the factory girls and bears their abuse to show her good will. As she tells the sympathetic Reuben,

I want to be a friend to other girls placed as I was when I went to your school, with miserable homes and aching to get away from it, no matter how; and I want to try and keep them from the pitch-hole I fell into. (85)

Jessica's aim is to found a Working Girls' Resting House where young factory workers otherwise tempted to waywardness by the boredom of their lives can find peace, comfort, and a place to reflect. That, rather improbably, Jessica's plan begins to work, Frederic ascribes to her self-imposed trial of the spirit. Suppressing the longing for excitement by reminding herself of the "memory of those...hours which dragged-

...gruesomely" in the brothel (192), she "exorcises" her yearnings by immuring herself in her house and shop. She practices humility, she teaches her sister Lucinda to sew, lets her childlike father warm himself by her fire. In a final effort to create a family, Frederic notes in passing as if embarrassed by the child, she sends for the young son she had not been able to keep with her in her brothel days.

Her greatest success is with the town's factory girls, who come to the clubroom behind her millinery shop. In this haven, they improve their sewing skills and distance themselves from the rowdy male factory hands who soon tire of beating on Jessica's door as if her place was a bordello. A sympathetic counselor and a vocational guide, she in effect creates one of those girls' clubs which were fixtures of settlement work in British and American cities in the 80's and 90's. The social settlement novelist Walter Besant's description of an East End club applies equally well to Jessica Lawton's:

> The girls came every night; they talked,...learned needlework, they were on terms of friendliness and personal affection with their leaders...[and] learning unconsciously lessons of self-respect and order.[57]

Jessica soon becomes an empowering employer who gives her young women piecework to do and whose shop anticipates the "model workroom" of Emmeline Pethick's Esperance Club in the early 90's.[58] The resentment against the bosses characterizing the town's factory workers is entirely absent in Jessica's workplace. She is on far better terms with her girls than was Frederic's mother, strong-willed Frances Frederick (sic) de Motte. A widow "as self-reliant as any woman" in the Mohawk valley, Mrs. de Motte ran a successful Utica vest-making business.[59] To the end of his life, Frederic recalled "the exceeding harshness of his mother's voice" above the noise of the sewing machines as she gave orders to her women.[60] While it is tantalizing to speculate on Frederic's motive for creating a reformed prostitute who combines enlightened sewing shop management with a quiet belief in social reform, the dearth of biographical material regarding Frederic's childhood makes such speculation unprofitable. What is clear is that Jessica's managerial and leadership talents would have been envied by the many women who entered the settlement movement at the end of the nineteenth century.

Frederic's vision of Jessica as a helper of young women was no doubt influenced by his observations of London's feminine philanthropy, which, given his appetite for the newsworthy, could not have escaped his notice as he was composing *The Lawton Girl* in the late 80's. Women were flocking to philanthropic work. Within a decade, some twenty thousand would be professionally employed in it, with twenty times that number in semi-professional and voluntary capacities. Frederic was also on cordial terms with Lady Jeune, a noted befriender of unwed mothers. She was an influential hostess as well, and he attended her political salons where the social issues of the day were discussed.[61] It would have been surprising had he not known of her advocacy of rescue homes. Finally, her articles in the *Fortnightly Review,* a journal to which Frederic also contributed, enjoined women to "hold out the hand of fellowship, and lead the fallen again to a pure life."[62]

Frederic had less tolerance for Ellice Hopkins, a Stead ally he mentioned sarcastically in one of his *Pall Mall Gazette* articles.[63] Hopkins, a tireless anti-prostitution crusader and founder of rescue homes and working girls' clubs, was a formidable figure. As part of her drive for a single standard of sexual morality, she spearheaded ladies' rescue committees and men's chastity leagues. Frederic's rather tolerant treatment of the seductive Horace Boyce would have appalled her. One of her main concerns was preventing girls like Jessica Lawton from falling. Of such girls, she wrote in 1880, the "original faults had been nothing greater than unruliness, idleness...and reckless love of fun..."[64] Throughout the 80's, Hopkins campaigned to establish local organizations to watch over those she termed the "friendless."

Nor could Frederic have been ignorant of the era's famous prostitute-turned-reformer, thirty-six-year-old Rebecca Jarrett, who had been converted by no less a person than the wife of the Salvation Army's founder, General Booth. Mrs. Booth sent Jarrett to Liverpool, where she stayed in the halfway house for prostitutes founded by their ardent befriender Josephine Butler. Soon Butler, convinced that Jarrett was "ready and able to help in the work of reclaiming others,"[65] purchased Hope Cottage as house of refuge so that Jarrett could begin missionary work among the kind of women she had once been. By all accounts Jarrett was quite successful, and the women she redeemed went on to reclaim others. As Butler described it, they "got their poor sisters to come home with them to their lodging, and gave them tea, and afterwards spoke to them about God."[66]

The *Pall Mall Gazette* editor W.T. Stead, who had heard of Jarrett through his evangelical connections, exhorted her to help him expose the corruption of the life she had left by aiding him. Jarrett, responding to Stead's suggestion-threat that if she was "really penitent," she could "make amends for [her]...crime" by procuring "not for ruin but for rescue," used her old underworld contacts to help him "purchase" thirteen-year-old Eliza Armstrong. The "Maiden Tribute" affair was launched. All was not success, however, for Jarrett was arrested and, like Stead, eventually imprisoned for her part in the affair.[67] Her aristocratic ally Josephine Butler steadfastly defended the ex-prostitute as a model rescuer:

She would stand in the midst of a den full of men and women of the lowest type, pray with them and for them, and teach them to pray; and when other persuasions failed, she related to them what she herself had been, and what God had done for her. (*Rebecca Jarrett*, 9)

Just as he found Ellice Hopkins loud and intrusive, Frederic would hardly have admired the rather self-promoting Jarrett, who sought out prostitutes, exhorting them on streets and in public houses.[68] Unlike Hopkins or Jarrett, middle-aged women who were professional orators, the much younger Jessica Lawton, despite her fairly public atonement, has a horror of calling attention to herself and elects to share her monastic seclusion with some needy girls. Her club is as much a refuge for her as for the young women of Thessaly. She is at best a mute critic of a society which judges the lower-class woman who falls while exculpating her upper-class lover. Nor is Jessica the only "womanly" reformer acceptable to Frederic is a way her real-life counterparts are not. The town heiress Kate Minster visits Jessica's shop and fleetingly interests herself in the club. A sheltered and self-involved young woman, she calls Jessica's project "a pet of mine" (396). She is quite incapable of nursing dying Liverpool prostitutes like Josephine Butler or, like Lady Jeune, writing essays on saving the fallen for a leading periodical. In Kate, Frederic reduces the philanthropic crusade to help poor women to the frivolities of wealthy ones. She soon loses interest in Jessica's plan when she realizes that marriage to the up-and-coming Reuben Tracy is her real mission.

However much the self-effacing female patient is Frederic's alternative to the aggressiveness of a Jarrett or a Hopkins, she still does not satisfy her creator's need for a purified ex-prostitute who, having renounced the world, is no further threat to it. For the hard-working Jessica proves as good a businesswoman as she is a social worker. There is even one amusing scene in which Jessica, who wishes the support of Kate Minster and her aunt for both the Home and the millinery shop, sequesters her down-and-out father and hoydenish sister because the proper ladies are coming to call, testimony that entrepreneurial shrewdness and self-interest are not dead in her.

With Jessica's new-found economic success, however, comes the interest in men which in his *Gazette* articles Frederic had defined as a by-product of feminine independence. We recall his predictions in "Musings on the Question of The Hour":

Even among women we must look for less rather than more self-denial in the future....When women possess a means of livelihood independent of marriage they are less chaste than a body of women looking to marriage as their sole means of support. (11)

What Frederic could state as fact in his *Gazette* essay he could not articulate in his fiction. Just at the point when Jessica (without, Frederic assures us, yet being aware of it) is beginning to entertain an affection for Reuben Tracy, her desire to be a secular Sister of Mercy begins to conflict with her awakening as a woman. The problem of acknowledging her sexual impulses Frederic evades altogether. To justify her return, he had presented her as one determined to be socially useful. Five years earlier in the *Gazette* articles he had toyed with the idea of the ex-prostitute as a woman living a full new life without guilt. Now he recoils from exploring that possibility in art. Jessica was for a time an acceptable social activist, a non-assertive alternative to the big-city woman reformer. But the birth of new ambitions trigger other yearnings as well, yearnings "to be less chaste than women looking to marriage as their sole means of support."

Frederic quickly transforms his lovesick ex-prostitute into an idealized penitent. She embarks on a mission to earn community respect which will end with sacrificing her life for her seducer. Well before the finale, Jessica engages in a series of saintly actions, the first of which is to offer maternal forgiveness to Horace Boyce. Horace's rapacity has finally defeated him. His marriage suit has been rejected, and he is faced with exposure. Indeed he is so taken up with his troubles that he cannot summon his usual sneer for Jessica when they meet by chance. In describing the scene as he had originally envisioned it, Frederic wrote:

I had prepared for her here a part of violent and bitter denunciation [of Horace], full of scornful epithets and merciless jibes...[yet] she relented at the first sight of his gray hair....[69]

This early impulse is certainly closer to the spirit of Jessica as the harlot in a village who confronts an alleged husband as in Frederic's earliest notations. Yet instead of permitting her to hurl those scornful epithets and merciless jibes, he turns Jessica into a model of compassion.

As her ex-seducer, sensing a kind presence, pours out his troubles to her, she repeatedly tells him how sorry she is. She listens to his catalogue of self-pity and tries to think how she can give her old lover the "incentive of her sympathy" (411). At no point in Horace's monologue does Jessica experience resentment for her considerably harsher life. Just as she has always protected her seducer from the knowledge and burden of his unwelcome child, she does not reproach him now. Instead she comforts him: "I've learned a host of bitter lessons since we were—young together, and I'm too much alone in the world to want to keep you as an enemy" (414). When he misunderstands and moves to embrace her, she caresses him with a "beaming countenance" (414) expressive of spirituality. She leaves him as impressed by her nobility as someone of his kind is capable of being.

In her forgiveness of her old lover and the altruistic acts that follow, Jessica joins both Hawthorne's Hester Prynne and the sentimentalized Magdalens who people British fallen woman fiction from the 1840's through the 70's.[70] The type has been described by one student of the form as "almost equal to the Madonna," "pure and inspirational."[71] Frederic admired *The Scarlet Letter,* and like Hester Prynne, Jessica, another unwed mother who now lives by her needle, Jessica both nobly refuses to name her seducer and becomes a spiritual guide to unhappy women. Yet in the important matter of social class, Jessica resembles the British model of the lower-class girl reduced to poverty and even prostitution by an aristocratic lover's deceit. In her hard city life and lack of bitterness toward her rakish seducer (Boyce is certainly no Arthur Dimmesdale), Frederic's Jessica is the sister of such mid-century title characters as Mrs. Trollope's Jessie Phillips and Mrs. Gaskell's Ruth. Mourned by their creators as saintly victims, these respective unwed mothers are saved the Lawton girl's brothel fate only to die, Jessie in a poorhouse, Ruth from a fever caught nursing the worthless father of her child back to health. Frederic's Jessica also calls up the remorseful sexual pariahs of popular writers like Mrs. Houstoun and Wilkie Collins. In Houstoun's *Recommended to Mercy* (1862), Helen Langton atones for her life as a kept woman by working with prostitutes. Jessica, in her attempts to prevent young factory girls from falling, might have received the Biblical compliment given Houstoun's heroine: those Helen Langton helped "called her blessed." Mercy Merrick, a prostitute become a counselor in a House of Refuge in Wilkie Collins's *The New Magdalen* (1872), takes a similar path to repentance, although with his characteristic daring, Collins marries her off to the clergyman who reformed her.[72]

Jessica Lawton is a compendium of these predecessors, compassionate to egotistic seducer and vulnerable factory girl alike. She outdoes the mid-century atoners in altruism; in her dying moments she urges Reuben Tracy, whom she secretly loves, to wed the virtuous Kate Minster. Significantly, earlier in the novel Frederic had subordinated Jessica's desire to "live it down" to her plans for a millinery business and girls' social club. The Jessica of that part of the novel was more than an American Magdalen: she looked forward to a new life, not back to a tarnished one. But the ambivalence a triumphant ex-prostitute created in Frederic led him to seek refuge in Magdalen convention. Because Jessica's success is disturbing, her eagerness for a moral life must become a desire to sacrifice that life altogether.

Thus, like Nancy, the prostitute-savior in Dickens, one of Frederic's favorite authors,[73] Jessica vows to rescue the innocent while protecting those whom her worthless lover would victimize. Soon after she comforts the querulous Horace, she leaves a winter sickbed to aid him for the last time. She learns that a mob is planning violence against the Minsters in the mistaken belief that it is they and not the culpable Horace Boyce who have swindled the town and closed the factory. With the fixed purpose and rhetorical intensity of Nancy, Jessica speaks of her resolve:

"It's got to be done," said Jessica, her eyes burning with eagerness, and her cheeks flushed. "If it killed me, it would have to be done." (404)

Kill her it will. She begins her determined progress in wretched weather, with "bowed head and a hurried, faltering step" (437). She is reminiscent too of Esther, the dying prostitute of Mrs. Gaskell's *Mary Barton* (1848), "all unfit to meet the pelting of [the] pitiless storm," or Dickens's ill-clad Martha in her quest for Little Emily.[74] In true Magdalen fashion, Jessica rushes to embrace the martyrdom she has imposed as the price of atonement.

In her work on the Dickensian fallen woman, Francoise Basch has remarked that his female sinner's desire for expiation and death culminates in a "calvary of redemption."[75] Nancy, a fairly willing scapegoat of the brutal Sikes, dies praying for redemption. As we have observed, another American novelist, Edgar Fawcett, imitated the Sikes-Nancy scene in his description of the murder-deliverance of Cora Strang. Frederic imagines a less violent death for Jessica, but one no less Dickensian. Her mission is all but accomplished. She has warned those she sought to protect, and her calvary now draws to its close. In delirium on her death-bed, she recalls her recent wanderings. She remembers that she had stopped on the way to Horace's house to rest:

It was under a lamp-post, she remembered; and when the vehement coughing was over, her mouth was full of blood, and there were terrifying crimson spatters on the snow....How strange it was—in the anguish of that moment she had moaned out, "O mother, mother!" and yet she had never seen that parent, and had scarcely thought of her memory even for many, many years.

Then she had blindly staggered on, sinking more than once from utter exhaustion, but still forcing herself forward, her wet feet weighing like leaden balls, and fierce agonies clutching her very heart. She had fallen in the snow at the very end of her journey; had dragged herself laboriously, painfully, up on to the steps, and had beaten feebly on the panels of the door [of Horace's house] with her numbed hands.... (464-465)

While Dickens might have tempered Frederic's graphic description of Jessica's blood on the snow, he might well have appreciated its dual metaphoric significance. The woman whose snowy purity had been sullied is now giving her life's blood to redeem herself. She is the quintessential Magdalen, groveling and penitent. In her delirious remembrance of the mother who did not live to guide her, furthermore, she is reminiscent of another dying prostitute, Alice Marwood in *Dombey and Son,* who forgives her own morally absent mother.

Into this conventional Victorian literary scene Frederic inserts a carefully moralistic description of the brothel in which Jessica worked. He outdoes W.T. Stead and Ellice Hopkins, the censorious evangelicals whom he had satirized in his *Pall Mall Gazette* articles:

Her sense wandered off, unbidden, unguided....[She saw] silk dresses, opened boldly at the throat, and with long trains tricked out with imitation garlands. They were worn now by older girls—hard-faced, jealous, cruel creatures—and these sat in a room with lace curtains and luxurious furniture. And some laughed with a ring like brass in their voices, and some wept furtively in corners, and some cursed their God and all living things; and there was the odor of wine and the uproar of the piano, and over all a great, ceaseless shame and terror. (465-466)

The sin of Jessica's bordello life is no sooner established than it is undercut by her horror at its recollection. Furthermore, only in her delirium can she remember her shame. Like her British predecessors Alice Marwood and Esther Barton, she imagines that her sinful life has been a dream. The scene thus embodies the same ambivalence about the prostitute's moral responsibility as does the novel itself. As a victim, she was not a willing participant in sin. As a sinner, she must atone by good works and death.

In her last moments Jessica reaches the end of her missionary quest. Heiress and factory girl weep at her bed while she teaches forgiveness and effects a reconciliation between Reuben Tracy and a sobbing Horace Boyce. She even extracts a promise that Horace live a better life and take care of their son. She chastens and possibly reforms him with the plea that the boy be taught "not to lie—ever—to any girl." To conclude this stylized scene of the moving death, Frederic has Jessica imagine herself a heavenly bride with flowers in her hair, beseeching entry into heaven. Guilt-ridden to the last, her final words are those of the novel: "I tell you I *have* lived it down!" (472).

While *The Lawton Girl* received a respectable amount of attention in England and America, its sales were hardly enough to help Frederic leave journalism and live on his earnings as a novelist. Some reviewers took the novel to task for its "unhealthy subject," but there may have been a quite different reason for its rapid descent to obscurity.[76] Even by the standards of what Frederic called the "polite fiction" of the previous decades,[77] Jessica was a predictable Magdalen. Had he reviewed the novel rather than written it, Frederic would have criticized the author for imposing on the fallen woman the censorship of a death scene. He disliked bowing to the censors and scoffed at those who denied spiritual regeneration to the woman of loose morals. A few years after *The Lawton Girl*, he lauded George Gissing's 1884 novel *The Unclassed* for its courage in dealing with the reformed prostitute. Gissing not only provides a detailed if idealized description of the streetwalker Ida Starr but exacts only a brief repentance. He then rewards her with an inheritance and a marriage to a man of culture. Not for him the ex-prostitute as masochistic atoner. In praising Gissing's approach to redemption, Frederic acknowledged that by the early 90's it could have been regarded an "added claim...to notice and popularity."[78] Not long after his positive review of Gissing, he deplored his own decision to "kill off Jessica—she who had not deserved or intended to die." It was, he conceded, a "false and cowardly thing to do."[79]

However much Frederic relied on an antiquated convention, the Jessica Lawton of the first part of his novel was not intended to be a copy of the British model. Frederic's working notes reveal that he discarded the original idea of the unrepentant harlot in a village in favor of a reformed prostitute. This courageous young woman would return and help the distressed factory girls thrown out of work when the local iron mill closed. He had even envisioned Jessica as a kind of activist who used her club as a meeting place for these young women. Although the novel does not develop these possibilities, Frederic refers admiringly to Jessica as a capable organizer. He describes her as one who "distinctly belonged to the managing division of the human race" (13). He applauds in her those qualities which "expressed anything rather than weakness": energy, optimism, practicality, independence. She is successfully battling the sadness brought on by memories of her unhappy past with "strength" and "resolution." Such descriptions of Jessica's resilience were consistent with Frederic's *Pall Mall Gazette* remark that, if she were not damned by public opinion, an ex-prostitute could successfully re-enter society. The chilly welcome Thessaly accords Jessica Lawton is not that American tolerance of moral difference of which Frederic boasted in his *Times* article on Stead's anti-vice campaign. But she is beginning to win the trust of the townspeople and the friendship of the powerful.

Furthermore, there is nothing in the novel which prepares or accounts for Jessica's precipitous descent from self-reliant shop and social settlement work to masochistic atonement. One of Frederic's strengths as a novelist is his ability to locate character within a believably American communal context.[80] When he attempts to impose saintliness on the village prodigal daughter who wishes to begin again, it seems extraneous to her story. Joaquin Miller, Edgar Fawcett, and Stephen Crane had featured the prostitute in a Bowery melodrama where, a hapless victim, she was doomed to pay for her sin. Frederic tried to place the ex-prostitute, a woman of greater strength than a Maggie or a Cora Strang, in a landscape of greater possibility, far from urban corruption, where she could express a characteristic American wish to defy time and start anew. Thus Jessica's plans for self- and social reform initially succeed. As a woman determined to renounce her past, to redeem her "wholly discredited life" (21), she is convincing enough at first. Yet when Frederic has to acknowledge her sexual past, he cannot sustain his belief in her optimistic American spirit.

Nor does he draw on the British models available to him in the late 80's. In his journalism he observed and praised the London prostitute, including the one who left her trade on her profits from it. If we cannot be certain that he read Gissing's *The Unclassed* prior to *The Lawton Girl*, he was very much aware of the new literary compassion for the fallen woman. Instead of trusting his own observations or the examples offered by recent fiction, he could only defend his prostitute, could only sanctify her, by killing her.

The death of Frederic's good prostitute issued from his inability to sustain a belief in the very goodness on which the novel had insisted. Describing his approach to characterization in *The Lawton Girl,* he explained that he allowed the protagonists to take matters "into their own hands," leaving him in the "posture of a spectator" ("Preface to a Uniform Edition," 4). Put another way, he was expressing a wish for verisimilitude: literary characters should act much as people do. Her creator's desire for realism may well account for Jessica's inability to be a living saint. In her wish to "live it down," she tries to isolate herself from men, but is still stirred by them. She may channel her continued interest in Horace Boyce into a supposedly asexual compassion, but she still has burgeoning feelings for Reuben Tracy:

The touch of his hand upon her shoulder had been more to Jessica than his words....And when he had ended with his exhortation of robust bravery, she was conscious of feeling weaker than for months before....[T]he nameless feminine yearnings for wardenship and shelter from life's battle took voice and pleaded in her heart. Ah, yes! he spoke of her being strong, and the very sound of his voice unnerved her. (86)

Jessica's susceptibility to men disquieted Frederic. He defended her by stressing that such feelings depressed her, made her ill, and caused her to endanger her life in a quest for absolution. Her suicidal heroics express his need to dominate her at a time when she threatens to become not an earthly saint but a woman with desires. Erasing her impurity in the name of sanctity was thus for Frederic more than slavish obedience to genteel convention or literary censorship. It became an urgency to cancel out the very sexuality which prompted her fall. While there was the counter-impulse to damn the unchaste woman, whether reformed or not, he buried that impulse in an insistence on her purity.

Frederic's decision to cover over female waywardness with a purity in which he could not fully believe can be better understood if we turn to his depiction of the coquette, a stock character in his early and late fiction. Satirizing the very woman whose virtue was superficial at best, Frederic was still reluctant to dissociate her sexuality from the purity he found so fraudulent.

* * * * *

The would-be temptresses of Frederic's novels and short fiction enjoy the respectability and financial security for which Jessica Lawton longed. Frederic criticizes them for a frivolity the economically hard-pressed Jessica could not afford and a hypocrisy she would have scorned. Vain, selfish, and bored, these women are dissatisfied with their leisured lives but unwilling to relinquish the luxury which keeps them so respectably at home. Isabel Fairchild (*Seth's Brother's Wife*), Julia Parmalee ("Marsena"), and Celia Madden (*The Damnation of Theron Ware*), who are related by birth or marriage to their town's leading family, channel their energies into a determination to live life theatrically—as long as they are not punished for it. They play at seduction only to retreat behind a seeming virtue, leaving their infatuated young men in confusion or despair.

If their deliberately short-lived flirtations suggest a covert rebellion against convention, they thrive on their own coquetry. A pampered young wife with a middle-aged husband, Isabel Fairchild escapes from what she sees as her "sad and sterile" small town life in fantasies of an affair with her impressionable brother-in-law Seth. In Frederic's Civil War tale, Julia Parmalee, though she engages in the showy patriotic philanthropy of the local ladies' committee which aids Northern soldiers, prefers the more amusing activity of playing off the eligible bachelors of the town against each other. The heiress Celia Madden devotes herself to Catholicism but finds time to toy with the affections of an unsophisticated Protestant minister.

However seductive these women are, they pretend to be pure. Here Isabel, who has finally arranged time alone with her unsuspecting brother-in-law, makes the most of her charms:

Seth brought a hassock for her feet, and her put his own chair alongside, where he could see her....The sunlight flared upon the white curtain above her, and its reflections glowed back again from her crown of golden braids, luminous against the azure of the chair....Seth found his mental vision fixed on that beautiful profile....[E]specially sweet was the portrait when the eyes were closed, and the lovely fullness above the lids, as in the face of a Madonna, was revealed in the wavering light. (208-209)

Isabel is touched by light, canopied in white, crowned with golden hair, and placed on a chair-throne whose azure color calls up associations with the blue worn by the Madonna. To all of this Seth responds: her face is that of the Virgin. What causes Isabel's seductive appeal, though, is not innocence but its appearance. Frederic ironically reminds the reader that Isabel is an artist in self-arrangement. What falls on her is not the steady light illuminating a saint but a wavering light which hides the truth of her morally unsteady nature. In her studied somnolence and posed vulnerability, Isabel inspires desire, not adoration.

As he gazes at her face, Seth cannot acknowledge that this flirtatious married woman stimulates him. He saves himself from such ungentlemanly thoughts by conjuring up a Madonna. He responds to her sexual appeal and the "lovely fullness above the lids" by convincing himself that it is her innocence he worships and not her body he craves. Only when in the novel's conclusion he comes to his senses just short of an affair can he see Isabel as a "siren" and "witch."

The less fortunate eponymous hero of Frederic's Civil War tale "Marsena," another of Frederic's ingenuous young men, is trapped by the theatrically angelic Julia Parmalee. She is the town beauty, he too smitten to take heed of the rumors that she has been engaged to four different men—a "remarkable young woman!" (186) is Frederic's satiric comment. Marsena is the town photographer and, lost in admiration for the innocence his photographs of Julia capture, he takes the image for the real thing. When she visits his darkroom he cannot disentangle her sorcery from her purity:

Here, in the close darkness beside him, was a sorceress, a siren, who had at a glance read his sore heart's deepest secret....It was like being shut up with an angel, who was also a beautiful woman. ("Marsena," 189)

Like Seth, Marsena represses the sexual responses to the siren Julia by idealizing her. He inhabits his fool's paradise well beyond that day when he was first, so to speak, in the dark. He woos her for weeks, escorting her to a stereopticon show of magazine photographs of the famous which he had arranged for the town. As the images parade before the assembly, the waggish operator interposes a photo of Julia and a handsome lieutenant, Dwight Ransom. The warning to Marsena is obvious, yet he keeps his delusion intact, oblivious to Frederic's irony that the show's only other picture of a woman is of the courtesan-adventuress Lola Montez. A *naif* almost to the last, Marsena joins the army hoping to impress the fickle Julia. Only when he is dying in a military hospital and this literally fatal woman pushes him out of bed to give it to Ransom does he learn—too late.

It takes even more credulity for the Reverend Theron Ware, the title character of Frederic's 1896 best-seller, to see the brilliantly red-haired, cigarette-smoking aesthete Celia Madden as a Madonna.[81] Yet, invited to her rooms to hear her play Chopin, Theron prefers to link her to the many pictures of the Virgin decorating her apartment than to the scantily clad classical statuary which also graces the room. He quickly explains away the unrobed statues and conjures up safer religious associations.

He looked from the [picture of the] Madonna to Celia....He could see the outline of her brow and cheek, the noble contour of her lifted chin....In the presence of such a face...there ceased to be any such thing as nudity....(202)

What Theron is lured by but cannot articulate is that Celia is both temptress and Virgin, sensualist and monastic. She concocts a fantasy world in which hedonism and the cult of the virgin, woman as free agent and woman on a pedestal, are supposed to proclaim her individuality.

Opposed to a future of marriage and motherhood, which she regards as traps, given to impromptu lectures on the history of ideas, a dilettante artist and a consummate self-dramatizer, Celia is a threat to Theron's naive notions of womanhood. Not for her the meek religiosity and calico dresses of his demure wife Alice. Celia's favored attire bespeaks what Frederic satirically terms her "intellectual attainments" (95). Her white Grecian gown and Madonna-blue headband are a sartorial version of a philosophy of the self which combines Matthew Arnold's Hellenism and her own brand of Mariolatry. With her statue of Venus and official credo of "obey my whim" (266), Celia considers herself an Arnoldian Greek. She is "one who worships art, beauty and freedom," disdains the "Jews" who lack "spontaneity of consciousness" and, in her freethinking interpretation, who wish to keep the "feminine element" out of religion. The irony is that Celia expresses her "Greek" belief in "[a]bsolute freedom from moral bugbears" (208) by associating herself with the Virgin Mary, in whose name she exhorts Theron to abandon male-centered religion and engage in "worship of the maternal idea" (206) in the person of the inspiring Celia herself. A self-appointed apostle of the eternal feminine, Celia sees herself as both Venus and Mary. What she lacks in intellectual rigor, she makes up for in conviction. She knows her beauty will inflame and her purity will insure she is adored but not violated. Her garments, if sexy, after all, are white. She confers one kiss on Theron and, soon after, casts him aside.

With Celia, Frederic's conflation of virgin and vamp is complete. As her last name suggests, she maddens men with her dual devotion to Venus and Virgin. This Catholic Circe reduces intellectual freedom to narcissistic flirtations with men who do not interest her. For all her vocal defense of woman's individuality, her sensuality, like that of Frederic's other *femmes fatales,* is never fully realized. She entices, then protects herself from sexual danger by spending time with malleable young men or reassuringly forbidden Catholic priests. She may lecture on the need for woman-centered religion, smoke cigarettes, and pound out mazurkas in her candle-lit rooms until dawn, but her sexy holiness is a mask for her need to control men rather than surrender to them.

Celia is thus a far more potent figure than Isabel Fairchild or Julia Parmalee. If her sexuality is troubled, it is no less powerful for that. And she is a wealthy man's daughter. Her economic self-sufficiency heightens her ability to dominate. While Celia is no democrat, she might well have applauded Jessica Lawton's philosophy of female liberty. Pleased with the success of her millinery shop and social experiment, Jessica reflects late in the novel that "she was now perfectly independent of...any man. She was her own master, and need ask favors from nobody" (412). Beneath Jessica's penitence is the desire to be free, not only from lifelong apologies for her past, but from the subordination to men which had characterized it. The impulse to independence is of course short-lived, for soon after re-encountering Horace Boyce Jessica renounces her new freedom in the name of self-sacrifice. Celia, too, always the object of Frederic's minimizing irony, will be reigned in by her creator in a sequel to *Theron Ware, The Marketplace* (1899).[82] Yet for a time both Celia and Jessica resemble the New Woman, that period social and literary type whom many, Frederic included, found so disturbing. As a social phenomenon the New Woman was most often associated with the college-bred professional in search of equality with men. In fiction, though, many took the lead of the socially concerned Jessica or the free-spirited Celia and "refused to conform to the traditional feminine role, challenged accepted ideals of marriage and maternity, chose to work for a living...or argued the feminist cause...and were firmly identified by readers and reviewers as New Women."[83]

The most controversial aspect of woman's new emancipation drive, Frederic realized, was her arrogation of male sexual privilege. In his *Pall Mall Gazette* articles, he uneasily remarked that self-supporting women of the lower classes, whose numbers were multiplying as industry's need for them increased, were no longer willing to be controlled by the sexual double standard. Such women annoyed him less than those who entered the professions, particularly his own field of journalism. They provoked a denigrating jest which revealed his charge that such women were unsexed by intellectual activity: "A lady journalist? No, she was too pretty for that" *(March Hares, 7)*. Frederic often ridiculed the woman writer who lacked the allure of her working-class sisters. It was as if work outside the home involving the professions produced "lone women with eccentric coiffures and startling costumes," who "emerge from heaven knows where" and, like a flock of unsightly birds, "mysteriously gather" in the British Museum to work up articles *(March Hares, 177)*.

In notes for his novel *Gloria Mundi*, Frederic called New Women "[h]ens who won't sit."[84] The crude remark suggests that Frederic's hostile insistence on the woman journalist's lack of femininity is simply resentment at her abdication of woman's biological role. The heroine of his novel *March Hares*, as we shall see, gives the lie to Frederic's defensive posture that New Women are unattractive to men. So too do the sexually active heroines of the era's New Woman fiction. One work which Frederic particularly disliked was Grant Allen's immensely popular *The Woman Who Did,* which went through twenty-one editions the year of its 1895 publication.[85] "What could be hoped," Frederic responded angrily late in the same year, of a public which took the Allen novel "as a serious performance, worthy of thought and discussion?" ("Gissing," 225). What Allen's Girton-educated protagonist Herminia Barton "did" was to take a lover and choose to combine her subsequent single motherhood with earning a living. An "animated compendium of every feminist idea in circulation," Herminia lectures men on the importance of sexual freedom and rejects her lover's marriage proposal as confining and old-fashioned.[86] *The Lawton Girl* demonstrated Frederic's ability to envision the sexual pariah as a heroine, provided she felt shame at her unwed motherhood and the prostitution in which she engaged to support her child. What outraged Frederic was that Allen's protagonist chose Fallen in the name of New Womanhood, proclaiming herself unrepentant and unwed. Ignoring the fact that Herminia lived a cloistered existence devoted to motherhood after the early death of her lover and was punished for her advanced views by a rejecting daughter who embraced traditionalism, Frederic deplored "the Grant Allen boom" and concluded that *The Woman Who Did* was a "dirty" book ("Gissing," 225).

Frederic's uncharacteristically heated condemnation seems hypocritical in terms of his own life with American-born Kate Lyon, whom he met in 1890 shortly after he completed *The Lawton Girl.* Already married, he could or would not wed her, though she would bear him three children. Perhaps his distaste for the Allen novel was less for the idea of the unwed mother, who at least was not a hen who wouldn't sit, than for the terms of Herminia Barton's sexual freedom. It was one thing for Frederic to choose not to marry the mother of his children; it was quite another for a woman to reject a marriage proposal from the father of her illegitimate child.

Irritated by novels in which women, whether mothers or not, sought lives free from marital convention, in an interview granted in 1896, the year *Theron Ware* was published, Frederic said he "refused to discuss the New Woman" at all.[88] That same year his novel *March Hares* had a good deal to say about the type, none of it complimentary. Frederic casts as his heroine an inept New Woman, who, down on her luck, is providentially rescued from streetwalking, and, as it turns out, from a return to her former work as a researcher, by marriage. In *Gloria Mundi,* published two years later, Frederic is still worrying at the issue. The self-supporting career woman Frances Bailey, whom he has nicknamed Frank to indicate her unnatural assault on the masculine world of work, initially refuses marriage to a duke so that she can run a flourishing typing business. As early as the mid-1880's, an estimated 80,000 Englishwomen were working as typists, and the view that typing would emancipate them by allowing them to achieve financial independence was commonly held.[89] Frederic, who took sections of his *Gloria Mundi* manuscript to an establishment similar to Frances Bailey's, would have been well aware of the popular association of typing and female emancipation.[90] Gissing's 1893 novel *The Odd Women,* a book with which Frederic was familiar, had already explored the idea. Frances Bailey was not as outspoken about the economic emancipation symbolized by the female typist as was Gissing's Rhoda Nunn, but she believed in the symbolic importance of the field. Predictably, Frederic is reluctant to grant her the New Womanly life that she seeks. She abandons her business and plans for an eventual career as a journalist to live at a ducal estate Frederic describes as a "mausoleum, a place of skulls" (297), penance for her unholy aspirations. Usually a careful delineator of motive, he provides no convincing reason for her decision to quit her career for a man she was willing to lecture on economics but showed little sign of admiring, let alone loving. Frederic summarily marries her off to wealthy Christian Tower and immures this now suitably idle helpmeet in a marital cloister.

As in Frederic's fiction with American settings, the chaste woman who seeks independence or dominance outside of marriage must become the obedient wife. The unchaste one has to be controlled in a more punitive way. Autonomy-seeking Jessica Lawton rather quickly becomes suicidal, viewing self-annihilation as preferable to self-reliance. In the posthumously published *The Marketplace,* Celia Madden is similarly punished, but, because her sexual sin was less grave, she is allowed to live out her atonement in an arid spinsterhood, which she perceives as just. Now regretting the pain she has caused men—"I spread trouble and misery about me" (190)—she renounces the life of the heartless flirt and by implication her sexuality as well. She now declares herself too guilt-ridden to marry, although she extolls "Marriage, a home, children," which, she sighs, are "great things to a [good] woman" (190). Like the reformed prostitute who can still pose a threat to the social order, Frederic's most dangerous coquette raises the twin specters of carnal knowledge and financial independence. Her nunlike repentance, like Jessica's, lays such ghosts to rest.

The fate of Frederic's unorthodox feminine protagonists reveals a literary strategy which controls woman's sexuality, linked to a will to power, and, in the case of Celia and Jessica Lawton, to the dangerous New Woman, through penance or a safely restricting marriage. Whether it is the Madonna-associated Isabel and Celia, Julia the Angel of Mercy, or Jessica the Magdalen, Frederic uses a rhetoric of purity to transform the temptress and restore her lost virtue. A brief discussion of a similar transformation of his mistress Kate Lyon, both in his life with her and his autobiographical novel *March Hares,* can add dimension to an understanding of Frederic's purifying imagination and the contradictions which characterized it.

* * * * *

Soon after he sent the manuscript of *The Lawton Girl* to his publishers, Frederic met and formed an extra-marital liaison with the American writer Kate Lyon which lasted until his death in 1898 at forty-two. He met Kate when she was working for a London publishing house as a writer and researcher. When she became his mistress, she ceased to be economically independent. If on one level she was a kept woman, however, Frederic took care to legitimize his relation to her in all save legal marriage. Despite the existence of his Methodist wife Grace, in 1891 Frederic established a household with Kate in London. In 1893 he moved with her and their two children to Surrey. Throughout the 90's, he maintained the two households, though he spent increasingly more time in his second one.[91]

Kate seemed suited enough to this arrangement. Though when she and Frederic moved to Surrey she began to call herself Mrs. Frederic, what scanty evidence exists suggests that she did not press for marriage. Her son Barry saw her as a woman contented with her place in Frederic's life.[92] Unlike the heroine of *The Woman Who Did,* Kate seemed to see herself as a wife rather than a mistress or an unwed mother. Friends visiting Frederic's second family remarked on the strongly domestic quality of her relationship with him. Though a professional writer, Kate published very little during her years with Frederic and apparently preferred her identity as "wife" to that of self-supporting author.[93] When he died suddenly in 1898, Kate waited for her share of Frederic's estate, i.e. for her what she trusted her "husband" had done for his widow and second family. In need of money, she refused payment for research work done for her friend and Surrey neighbor Stephen Crane. Only when her legal hopes were dashed did she take up the role of the single working mother. Commenting on Kate's relationship to Frederic, Ruth, his daughter by his wife Grace, summed Kate up as a "yes, yes woman."[94] Whatever its negative suggestion of flattery and feminine wiles, the remark also suggests that she presented and possibly viewed herself as the deferential helpmeet. She was worlds away from Grant Allen's Herminia Barton.

However much Kate Lyon imposed domestic convention on her unconventional living arrangements, she received a predictable amount of social ostracism. Kate might have experienced the kind of social chill felt by Amy Catherine Robins, the mistress of Frederic's club friend H.G.

Wells. Although Wells soon divorced and married Miss Robins, for whom he had left his wife, one biography described their situation in London during the time they were living together: "Until they were married, it was not possible for them to go about together socially except to visit close friends, and when Wells accepted invitations Jane often had to stay behind."[95] Frederic too continued to move in society, often taking his daughter Ruth on theater outings. Kate, with whom he did not dine out, simply was not received. Ruth, who had to withdraw from a fashionable school because of her father's liaison, continued on close terms with him.[96] Like the many who disapproved of Frederic's two households, she reserved her scorn for Kate.

Like "Kate Frederic," Wells's mistress called herself wife. When a series of London landladies discovered Miss Robins's status, Wells later ruefully recalled, the neighbors built a "gardenwall of insults and slights" to demonstrate the "unsoundness of our position." "We dropped our disavowal of the Institution of Marriage," he remarked, "and married, as soon as I was free to do so, in 1895."[97] By the late 90's it was rumored that Frederic was about to follow Wells's example. Yet for years he seemed contented to engage in what friends euphemistically dubbed his "ignoring [of] social conventions."[98] His domestic version of illicit sexuality, the wife-mistress and the wife, suggests that had he been familiar with his club acquaintance George Bernard Shaw's dictum, "a man with two addresses is a libertine," Frederic would certainly have disagreed. He apparently believed in the propriety of spending part of the week with his legal wife and children and the rest with Kate Lyon and his second family. Furthermore, whatever discomfort was occasioned Grace Frederic and her household by this decision, Frederic's own mind was "calm, his conscience clear," wrote a close friend, "for he felt that his marital relations [with Kate] were pure, his children [by her] growing up in an atmosphere of love."[99]

In life as in art, Frederic seemed to need to convince himself that the mistress was as pure as the wife. There is some scholarly speculation that the strait-laced Grace Frederic consistently refused a divorce, which suggests that Frederic saw Kate Frederic not as the Other Woman but as the one he longed to make his wife. Such a view, nevertheless, cannot account for why Frederic continued to live in husbandly fashion with both women and play the Victorian paterfamilias in two such different arenas. Whatever Grace Frederic's part in this triangle, his dual need to question his traditional marriage and to cosmetize his illicit one reveals the kind of fascinated distrust of woman as sexual free agent which informs his fiction, particularly that on the prostitute.

In 1896, six years after Frederic began to live with Kate, he published *March Hares,* a light romance reportedly inspired by his first meeting with her in the British Museum reading room.[100] The novel is a comic tale of a successful writer who falls in love with a hapless career woman about to enter prostitution. Under cover of romantic comedy, the novel would allow Frederic both to acknowledge and defend his mistress against charges of immorality. Before analyzing *March Hares* in light of his relationship with Kate, however, it is important to study the work as another of Frederic's conflicted discussions of saving the prostitute.

In the novel's opening, the sometime writer, university intellectual, and man-about-town David Mosscrop is returning from a riotous London evening. He is "sick with disgust" (37) with himself for a night which may well have included a visit to a brothel called "Savoy Street," for later in the novel, coming upon the building which houses it, he gazes knowingly at the first floor windows. As if representing its occupants, the brothel sign has "caught his eye" (140), and there is no doubt he is familiar with the red-light haunt. By then, a man in love, Mosscrop resists entering.

Well before this self-tempting activity, as he moodily walks home accompanied by thoughts of his morally dubious evening, he is still intrigued enough by London's Available Womanhood to notice an attractive girl out walking suspiciously early on Westminster Bridge. Because her dress is "of an almost flaring order" (7), he smiles squarely at her. Just as he is about to make a suggestive comment, he realizes that this potential pick-up is another kind of professional entirely, a young researcher for whom he has taken down heavy volumes in the British Museum reading room. His impulse to protect rather than hire her established, Mosscrop strikes up a conversation with Vestalia Peaussier. Whereas before she had inspired quite other feelings, she now enlists his gentlemanly sympathies. She tells her tale of straitened circumstances and impresses him with her "air of shyness" (20) and "maidenly reserve" (19). He whisks her off to dinner, new clothes, and lodgings—for herself alone—with the conviction that she is his "special providence" (185). Saving her from poverty, without expecting sexual favors in return, will ensure his moral rejuvenation.

So it does, after two hundred pages of comic complications involving her disappearance, a subplot concerning an aristocrat in love with an heiress, mistaken identities, and the discovery that Vestalia is a millionaire's lost niece. Mosscrop finally takes the certifiably chaste Vestalia as his wife, but not before Frederic has employed this gently ironic tale of star-crossed lovers to play with the difference between the respectable woman and the fallen one. As their romance first unfolds, Vestalia confides that she had just decided to become a streetwalker when she met Mosscrop. In the course of an idyllic London day, she proceeds to accept meals and gifts from him with, Frederic stresses, childlike enjoyment. In reality she is at the mercy of Mosscrop's purse, and, her "innocent fearlessness" (54) aside, is well aware of it. He too knows his bargaining power over this garishly clad girl and, in Frederic's satiric thrust at the London man-about-town, even fears being recognized in her possibly compromising company. The narrative plays coyly with a serious theme, the illicit possibilities a woman's destitution suggests. Is Vestalia to be a kept woman or to remain the vestal virgin which her name connotes?

Frederic soon provides the answer. Unlike the "Saunterer" essays or *The Lawton Girl, March Hares* was written in a comic vein, with Frederic questioning his own familiar contention that innocence is a pose of the seductress. Now seductiveness itself is the pose. Vestalia, seeming the streetwalker, is actually the virgin. No sooner does Mosscrop chivalrously befriend her than, her confidence restored, and with some *deus ex machina* help from rich relations, she gains her rightful place in society.

If, in her fairy-tale escape from the street, Vestalia is more fortunate than the Jessica Lawtons or London streetwalkers she was about to join, it is not because she has been educated to be a New Woman. Careerism has, after all, reduced her to poverty in the first place. Rather it is that, for all his past misconduct, when Mosscrop meets her on Westminster Bridge he does not act like a Horace Boyce or a London rake. Belying Frederic's view that poverty pushes women to prostitution is one potentially more upsetting: female independence is allied to sexual waywardness. Vestalia's initial inability to survive as a New Woman suggests that if a woman wishes to earn her living, particularly as a writer in competition with men, she must be willing to contemplate a less savory profession. Furthermore, Vestalia's willingness to become a prostitute, a fate averted in the comic world of the narrative, is hardly a tribute to the professional woman or her economic self-reliance.

Quite apart from the novel as another of Frederic's ironic deflations of the emancipated woman, its autobiographical overtones are intriguing. Austin Briggs, Jr., argues convincingly that the worldly Mosscrop is a version of Frederic himself.[101] Briggs contends that Mosscrop, whom Vestalia and the reader encounter returning from an evening in dubious company, is based on the younger Frederic of his Saunterer period, the Frederic who wandered in and possibly experienced the red-light lures of London's "labyrinth." The vision of Frederic as a brothel patron, discreetly hinted at by a number of commentators, does overlook the fact that Frederic deplored those friends who pretended to be respectable and shamelessly patronized prostitutes. He called them hypocrites and found them "not such good fellows after all."[102] Or was Frederic himself being disingenuous? The truth of his acquaintance with prostitutes will no doubt remain elusive. What is clear is that he gives Mosscrop some of his own characteristics (both are brilliant talkers and possess an encyclopedic knowledge) and life experiences (each has a fateful British

Museum meeting). It is thus noteworthy that he also depicts Mosscrop as a patron of prostitutes only to undermine that portrayal. Mosscrop may think nothing of picking up an attractive street girl, but, unlike Frederic's harlot-seeking friends, he is a good fellow. When he discovers that the woman he had encountered is no Haymarket denizen but an unemployed lady researcher down on her luck, he is chivalry—and indeed rescue—itself.

The defense of Mosscrop is Frederic's argument for the moral worth of a masculine *bon vivant* much like himself. Such a stance, his negative comments about male patrons of prostitutes notwithstanding, occasions Frederic far less ambivalence than the defense of Jessica Lawton or even Vestalia Peaussier. In contrast to Jessica, whose salvation is hard-won and ultimately fatal, Mosscrop experiences a rapid and painless reform by saving a woman from prostitution. However much she is worth saving, then, for the prostitute to be saved, she must like Vestalia be rescued before the act—or, like Jessica, die, as it were, after it.

In terms of Frederic's relationship with Kate Lyon, *March Hares* is particularly revealing. Like Mosscrop, who rescued Vestalia, Frederic in effect married Kate in all but law and transformed her into a wifely figure and mother. He protected her from the financial perils of a writer's career, a feminine vocation of which he disapproved. But why was such protection needed? The comic fantasy of a rather foolish New Woman compelled to solicit on Westminster Bridge covers over Frederic's fear that New Women might be loose women as well. Much like Vestalia, Kate was changed from independent woman to wife.

Here of course art provided a more convincing transformation than life. Despite Kate's adoption of the name "Mrs. Frederic" and his insistence on the domesticity of his life with her, Frederic either would or could not approve of her change from mistress to wife, from sexually unconventional to redeemed. Hence, perhaps, the vision in *March Hares* of the Prostitute Who Was Not.

Quite apart from its correspondence to Frederic's life, his art unleashed the fears generated by the twin threats of woman's sexual and economic independence. Despite Frederic's insistence on Jessica Lawton as an economic victim forced to enter the brothel to support her illegitimate child, the prostitute could, as Frederic's "Saunterer" essays acknowledged, save money while in the trade. Jessica's hat shop could well grant her further independence. Thus the prostitute and the independent woman briefly merge. Jessica threatens to be a New Woman; New Woman Vestalia Peaussier "chooses" prostitution. Yet neither is permitted to maintain her economic independence nor, in the world of her respective novel, to continue in the sex trade. The women's association with paid promiscuity permits Frederic to denigrate their quest for independence, then to render the prostitute powerless, reduced to the dying saint or the misguided career girl who craves husbandly guidance. However, as Frederic's last novel to touch on the prostitute would reveal, his doubts about her redemption had not been quieted.

In 1898, a few weeks after Frederic's career ended so prematurely, his novel *Gloria Mundi,* which contained a debate about saving the prostitute, appeared. Briefly, the novel centers on the idealistic Christian Tower, who has been elevated from obscurity to a dukedom. With the contrasting but equally unattractive examples of aristocratic self-indulgence and rigidly utopian communalism provided by the two branches of his family before him, Tower engages in a long quest for a better use of his new wealth. On an eye-opening tour of West End places frequented by prostitutes, he feels a rush of compassion for those "unhappy and dishonored" women (306). He later confides to his hard-headed relative Cora Torr:

Tonight I went to the Empire [vaudeville theater], is it not? And the sight of the young women there—it terribly affected me. I wanted to shout out that they were all my sisters—that I would protect them all—that they would never be forced by poverty and want to face that miserable humiliation again. (323)

Christian Tower proves true to his names, for he combines a Jesus-like desire to aid the wretched with an ivory tower remoteness from the complexity of social problems. His fuzzy idealism is promptly met by Cora's counter-vision. "These girls are lazy, greedy, good-for-nothing hussies....They haven't an idea in their empty painted heads except to wheedle or steal money from drunken fools" (323). Christian's idealism had already received a check when another worldly friend told him the story of one Slingsby Chetwynd, who, in a characteristic Frederic slap at affluent do-gooders, embraces reform for a "whole week" (298)—shades of Kate Minster—and becomes passionate about settlement work among the fallen. For his dubious pains an aggressively unregenerate woman "smashes his hat in," and someone throws him into a cellar. *Sic transit* moral reformers.

Heeding such warnings about the moral irreclaimability of the loose woman, Christian reduces his planned benevolence to a facile and rather futile act of charity. He more or less hires a policeman to hand out roast potatoes to a handful of "poorly dressed, fagged, bold-faced, furtive-eyed women" (351) concluding their evening shifts in Piccadilly and Leicester Square. He buys off his own conscience as well when he delegates contact with these "lurking figures" (350) to policemen and potato sellers. Soon he finds a more manageable female type to reform. He weds the sometime New Woman, Frances Bailey, and immures her in a monied life remote from either the harlots of Haymarket, or the typists she employed in earlier days.

The conversion of a male *naif* to the impossibility of saving the prostitute suggests that Frederic's ironic attitude toward W.T. Stead and the *Gazette* editor's female philanthropist allies had not altered during the decade and a half since the Maiden Tribute affair. Frederic still perceives those who would rescue the streetwalker as fools out of touch with the economic realities of the trade. Lillian Gilkes suggests a related source for the Tower portrait in Stephen Crane. Frederic had befriended Crane when the young author arrived in England with "Mrs. Crane," Cora Howorth Stewart, in 1897. Christian may well be in part a satiric response to the chivalric philosophy of his new friend.[103] It seems more than a coincidence too that Frederic's novel features a youthful savior of prostitutes arguing with a seasoned female observer possibly reminiscent of Cora Crane. As a former madam, Crane's common-law wife may well have shared Cora Torr's pragmatic view of the prostitute. There is an added irony in the fact that, like Crane, Frederic's protagonist abandons his talk of salvation as he becomes accustomed to the amenities of London life: belief in redemption as phase rather than conviction.

Compared to Frederic's fairly forgiving philosophy of middle-rung prostitution in the "Saunterer" essays, Cora Torr's view is a harsh one, though more convincing than the sentimentality of Christian Tower. Still, *Gloria Mundi* is an odd postscript to *The Lawton Girl*, not to mention *March Hares*. On a deeper level, this interchange between the prostitute's friend and foe suggests that to the end of his artistic life Frederic needed to imagine the prostitute longing for rebirth only to deny her the possibility. Jessica Lawton's success as a more palatable social worker than her real-life counterparts notwithstanding, Frederic had to transform her from a power in the community to a death-seeking Dickensian Magdalen. Although in her search for a new independence he linked her to the era's reformist ex-prostitutes, professional settlement workers, and burgeoning New Woman, Frederic could only defend her by sanctifying and killing her off.

His admitted adherence to genteel convention dictated the Magdalen's death only up to a point. Jessica, who wished for a purity she was too divided to attain, issued from Frederic's own mixed feelings about her redemption. Had he explored this opposition in her nature, his penitent would have transcended stereotype and been complex and even tragic. Instead he glorified her sacrifice, which issued not from the ambitious New Woman she was becoming, but from his need to control her as he had the power-seeking seductresses of his other fiction.

The apparent worldliness of Frederic's journalism on the London prostitute was belied by his Saunterer's belief in the hardened prostitute as would-be escapee. So too the unorthodoxy of his taking Kate Lyon as a mistress was undercut by his insistence on her wifely and maternal roles. His fiction buried alarm at the sexual activity of women in a series of similarly purifying transformations. They ranged from Jessica Lawton's settlement house life and holy death to the Mary-worshipping Celia Madden's penitential spinsterhood to the safely limiting marriages of the still-respectable Isabel Fairchild and Vestalia Peaussier. The unregenerate West End prostitutes of his expatriate sauntering become in his American art Women Who Went Right. His American coquettes, for all their comic wantonness, remain virginal. But because woman's sexuality provoked the dual fear of her promiscuity and her drive to power, Frederic distrusted the very women he had purified. Nowhere was this distrust more evident than in imagining the prostitute. Like Joaquin Miller, Edgar Fawcett, and Stephen Crane, Frederic found the cost of redemption too high.

Pictures

The Seduced Innocent—the protagonist of fiction about the prostitute from the mid-century urban thriller to the Progressive novel—here pictured in the *Police Gazette* of November 19, 1892.

A titillating vision of the Ruined Virtue tale told by Miller, Fawcett, and Crane, from James Buel's *Mysteries and Miseries of America's Great Cities*, 1883.

An unrepentant prostitute—a far cry from Frederic's sorrowful Magdalen or Kauffman's exploited white slave—from Buel's guidebook.

Crane's account of the Dora Clark arrest, with illustrations of a very proper Dora, in the *New York Journal* of September 20, 1896.

The underclass and its "degraded women," images explored from Miller through Phillips, from Helen Campbell's 1897 guidebook, *Darkness and Daylight.*

"The Story of Susan Lenox, Her Fall and Rise"
by David Graham Phillips

"This great novel, having read it in manuscript, its spirit and purpose have not passed from my memory. The heroine is depicted as an illegitimate child, and the purpose of the fiction is to show the blight that attaches to innocent illegitimacy.

"It is one of those fictions that has a meaning, the only kind of fiction that moral and intelligent people have any right to spend their time over or give their thought to."

A girl beautiful, intelligent, unhappily born, cursed with the cruel stigma of illegitimacy, fights against the world. Phillips tells of her journeys down the hill, the cruel selfishness of relations, pushing their own daughter ahead of her. The marriage forced upon an inexperienced child. The horrible revelations of what false marriage really is. The curse of a union without love on the woman's part, without refinement or kindness on the part of the husband. The flight of the girl hating immoral marriage more than any risk in life.

Then the story the public will read with breathless interest, the struggle against hunger, cold, anxiety, and the last, worse danger that threatens helpless women.

It is indeed, as Dr. Parkhurst says, fiction "that has a meaning, the only kind of fiction that moral, intelligent people should read." With his extraordinary power fully developed, David Graham Phillips tells of the fall that could not be avoided, and then of the spirit conquering, of the rise of the soul, the end of a struggle. The story of Susan Lenox is the story of cruelty inflicted by cold civilization upon helpless girls—a story of beauty and of horror. It is a lesson in powerful literary work, a lesson of true moral teaching.

No story but this wonderful narrative of the fall and the rise of a beautiful, unhappy spirit, will be discussed in this country, as long as the reading of the story lasts.

A Few More Reasons Why You'll Want Hearst's:

W. W. Jacobs' New Novel, "The Castaways"; Rex Beach's Novel, "Rainbow's End"; New Series by Robert W. Chambers; George Randolph Chester; Stories by E. Phillips Oppenheim, Angela Morgan, Arthur Stringer, Larry Evans, "Mr. Dooley" (F. P. Dunne); Illustrations by W. D. Stevens, Henry Hutt, Howard Chandler Christy, James Montgomery Flagg, etc.

Get this story and save 33⅓%

So great is the demand for this story that each issue of Hearst's is sold out immediately upon publication. Make sure of your copy for the next 10 months by sending $1 with the coupon opposite. This very special offer saves you 33⅓%. Act now!

Tear Off, Mail Today!

Hearst's Magazine, 119 W. 40th Street, New York. Gentlemen: For the enclosed $1 please enter my name to receive Hearst's Magazine for the next 10 months.

Name....................................

....

Street....................................

City......................................

State................................Feb. H.

—the heroine Susan Lenox

Drawings by Howard Chandler Christy

Hearst's Magazine
119 W. 40th Street, New York

© Hearst's Magazine

On Sale At All Newsstands

A ladylike Susan in a sermonic advertisement for the Phillips novel from the June 1916 issue of *Hearst's Magazine*.

The reluctant prostitute, Susan Lenox, as described by Phillips and illustrated for the January 1916 installment of *Hearst's* in Howard Chandler Christy.

Chapter Five
Reginald Wright Kauffman and Progressive Era Truth

Newsman Reginald Wright Kauffman was the author of the 1910 best-seller *The House of Bondage*,[1] widely considered "*the* novel of prostitution" of the decade and a half prior to World War I.[2] Typically Progressive in his desire to inspire social reform by the publication of muckraking exposés, Kauffman found many who agreed that American fiction could now permit the prostitute to speak. He was thus challenging both lingering genteel tradition and his nineteenth-century literary predecessors, who felt that her working life had to be left unexamined, and her voice unheard. Novelists Stephen Crane and Harold Frederic, and to an extent Edgar Fawcett and Joaquin Miller, had paved the way by imagining the American prostitute. Yet, unlike Kauffman, they did not depict her relationships with her pimp, madam, clients, and colleagues; present her attitudes about the trade; catalogue her wages; or describe her bouts with venereal disease. These writers lacked the motivation or interest to gather such data, the belief that fact-gathering of this nature was central to the creation of a sympathetic portrait, and the confidence that fiction purporting to present actual conditions would be published.

Crane had impressionistically sought information about prostitutes in ambiguous Tenderloin evenings and random interviews. Frederic had sauntered casually through London's better brothels. Fawcett and Miller had relied on the conventions of mid-century "wicked city" fiction. Kauffman, in contrast, had amassed his data in a thorough and fairly systematic manner. His novel was the product of ten years of interviews in the vice districts of major American cities and an extensive knowledge of local and national reports on the "social evil." Maintaining a nominal residence elsewhere, he and his newswoman wife Ruth Hammitt lived in rundown neighborhoods, gained the confidence of the prostitutes they interviewed, and "pursued [their] researches in a living medium."[3]

To enhance the public perception of him as a truth-telling novelist, Kauffman frequently described himself as a reformer rather than an artist.[4] In *The Girl That Goes Wrong*, a book of sketches published shortly after *The House of Bondage*, he explained that he had studied the problem of prostitution in all its phases—in houses, flats, tenements, and in the darkened streets and doorways; from the places patronized by clubmen to those patronized by sailors, peddlers, and thugs...in puritan Boston and hypocritical Philadelphia, in Chicago, Minneapolis, Baltimore, Washington, and Denver as well as New York...in scores of our larger cities and smaller towns. (7)

This posture encouraged the identification of Kauffman's recent best-seller with his investigative work. He had already capitalized on such an association in his preface to *The House of Bondage:*

[It] is the truth only that I have told. Throughout this narrative there is no incident that is not a daily commonplace in the life of the underworld of every large city.... I have written only what I have myself seen and myself heard.... ("Caveat Emptor," n.p.)

To further establish the authenticity of the novel, he appended to it the influential 1910 Rockefeller Grand Jury Report on prostitution in New York City.[5] An editor's note carefully instructed the reader that Kauffman's facts could be "duplicated indefinitely" in reports such as Rockefeller's (467).

Given the difficulty which reformist turn-of-the-century novelists had encountered in envisioning the prostitute, how true, though, were Kauffman's claims of verisimilitude in *The House of Bondage?* To some degree his novel was indebted to his years of investigation and research. Yet the tension between acknowledgment and denial of the prostitute's sexual activity which characterized the fiction of his late-nineteenth-century predecessors was just as present in his own work. Like Crane, Frederic, and their contemporaries, Kauffman could only resolve the conflict between compassion and condemnation by creating a sanitized prostitute. His white slave heroine Mary Denbigh joins the jilted Maggies, bloodless Nells, and saintly Jessicas of late-nineteenth-century writers. Kauffman's blameless brothel captive is not the herald of a new sociological realism about prostitution which Kauffman claimed. Rather, she suggests her creator's "solution" to the disturbing problem of the prostitute's carnality, a solution which Kauffman found in the ideology of the Progressive era itself.

Kauffman's other work in which the prostitute and *femme fatale* appear demonstrates that he was nagged by doubts about the very truth that *The House of Bondage* helped to popularize. However much he presented a Progressive defense of the streetwalker and brothel dweller, he could not rid himself of the conviction that prostitutes were predators, not victims. As such they were carnally culpable, not spiritually innocent. Like those before him, Kauffman's literary resolution is thus an uneasy one, covering over his conflict about the very nature of feminine sexuality itself. Before studying what his texts reveal of tensions central to the early-twentieth-century novel of prostitution, however, one should place Kauffman in a Progressive era context.

* * * * *

The Progressive era, dating roughly from the beginning of the century until the First World War, when the focus shifted from national to global problems, was so termed because of a dedication to progress in correcting social ills. Many of those who advocated stricter control over big business and improved living conditions for the poor believed in an assault on the red-light districts corrupting the moral fiber of America's cities. The rescue of the prostitute, a woman perceived as exploited by vice interests, would follow from investigation and exposure of her oppression. Social critic Anna Garlin wrote:

The Scarlet Woman is at last...admitted to human rights. Society is no longer content to let her be the scapegoat for the sins of the people.... She shall be studied and cared for as one upon whom has been unjustly visited the results of a permitted system growing out of a cherished indulgence of man....This new abolition movement is nothing less than a crusade to destroy the traffic in womanhood, to wipe out the commercialized brothel which demands that traffic, and to bring all the moral and educational forces of society to bear upon the suppression of the social evil.[6]

Spencer's ideas were representative: a heightened interest in saving the prostitute, viewed as a victim of capitalist greed and masculine lust; a belief that analysis of her life would fuel the campaign to restore her to society; and a conviction that the prostitute was an entirely unwilling part of the vice trade.

Such emphases were not entirely new. In 1893, the same year that Crane's privately printed *Maggie: A Girl of The Streets* went unnoticed, visiting British anti-prostitution crusader W.T. Stead published a tract which purported to include interviews with brothel inmates.[7] Like the many Progressive reformers who followed him, Stead argued that these women were driven to prostitution and were too demoralized to leave it. Throughout the 90's, Stead-inspired Social Purity forces called for a national commission to investigate prostitution, particularly white slavery, or the forcible procurement of women. Yet most Americans still viewed the social evil as a necessary one, a conviction that lurks beneath even the chivalry of a Stephen Crane or a Harold Frederic. National interest in eradicating prostitution by battling tolerated vice districts, by eliminating the venereal disease associated with prostitutes, and by destroying the alleged white slave trade, came only with the Progressive era.[8]

In detailing the experiences of a woman in the brothel and on the street as well as in the underpaid domestic work which propels her back to "the life," Kauffman was riding the crest of a wave of social scientific interest in the prostitute's life. To study commercialized vice now meant to interview the woman who was both victim of and witness to it. By the 1910's virtually every major American city had set up vice commissions. Instead of Stead's sensational interviews with vengeful prostitutes rhetorically cursing existence, these committees conducted extensive investigations in which red-light women were asked batteries of questions. Investigators elicited information regarding a woman's first sexual encounter prior to prostitution, marital and maternal status, previous employment, number of daily and weekly clients, and spending habits. The 1911 Chicago Vice Commission report, among the most important of its day, even included facsimiles of account books used by Chicago madams listing "credit to inmates for services rendered."[9]

To present what one 1913 vice commission termed "reliable information...systematically corroborated,"[10] surveys listed the profits the prostitute derived from her activities. Yet reformers minimized the prostitute's financial gains, pointing to the enormous revenues she earned for her keeper or madam and the commercial interests to which these people were allied. The Syracuse Vice Commission, one of the better-known of its time, offered as representative an account book kept by a city prostitute which listed large debts incurred to the madam for board and clothing. "From this it appears that the inmate's real purchasing power...is a third or nearly a quarter of her gross receipts, while the madam is enriched accordingly," the report concluded. The Chicago Vice Commission buried the fact of seventy-dollar weekly profits of prostitutes in one typical "50-cent house" in a wealth of data about the prostitute's "capitalized value" to the house.[11]

Deploring such exploitation, Progressives also contended that economic need had driven women to prostitution in the first place. "Is it any wonder," one commission asked, "that a girl who receives only six dollars per week working with her hands sells her body for twenty-five?"[12] Tenderloin women brought before one state commission testified that they had entered the life because they were unable to live on their weekly wages of $3 to $5.[13] Economist Elizabeth Butler, preparing a massive survey of women workers, received similar stories:

She had a mother and two sisters dependent upon her, and her mother was always urging her for more money. She began while still in the store to 'make money on the side.' The management discovered this and dismissed her. She...went into a house of prostitution...from which she sends her mother money.[14]

Rheta Childe Dorr, a defender of the factory girl and a colleague whose influence Kauffman would acknowledge in his preface to *The House of Bondage*, melodramatically concluded that there was only one course for many young women to take.[15]

In addition to economic need, whether the result of poor wages, family pressures, or both, Progressive vice commissions and other concerned inquirers acknowledged a variety of lesser reasons for a woman's downfall, including unwholesome neighborhood influences, psychological maladjustment, and the desire for excitement or fancy dress. *The House of Bondage* would echo such views. Yet Kauffman was far more interested in presenting a scenario of economic enslavement than in dramatizing the causes, many of them volitional, for a woman's entry into a potentially profitable trade.

While it found no evidence of vice syndicates or an organized traffic in women, the Rockefeller Commission report did argue that prostitution was forced activity. The Report so impressed Kauffman that he appended it to his novel. Journalist George Kibbe Turner, whose muckraking *McClure's* articles helped inspire both the Rockefeller investigation and the opening scene of *The House of Bondage*, went further. Convinced that "cadets" from vice organizations were scouring small-town America, he wrote:

The men in the business made trips into the industrial towns of New England and Pennsylvania, where they obtained supplies from the large numbers of poorly paid mill girls....[16]

Turner painted an alarming picture of the Jewish and Italian runners sent by shadowy vice organizations to stalk the girlhood of America. Whether the victim was a village innocent, a bewildered immigrant, or a malleable slum dweller, to Turner the new recruit was a girl rather than a woman. Presenting commercialized vice as a business for procuring and selling teenage girls, he boldly claimed that a young woman could "always be sold profitably either on the streets or in the houses [brothels] of American cities."[17] Such allegations produced widespread anxiety. The phrase "girl who disappeared"—presumably into the maw of the corrupting city—became a familiar one. National anti-slavery agitation soon resulted in the 1910 passage of the Mann Act forbidding interstate transportation of women for immoral purposes. Perhaps as important in terms of Progressive thought, Turner and other white slave theorists popularized the idea that whether a woman had been abducted, manipulated, or made desperate by poverty, she was easy prey for the procurers "watching and hunting [her] out at amusements and places of work."[18]

The Progressive vision of the prostitute as Woman Coerced had a certain basis in fact. The more reliable contemporary evidence suggests that an unknown number of women were drawn into the trade by poverty or procurement and exploited once in it. Reformers had more difficulty explaining why a woman chose to become a prostitute. There was little attempt, for instance, to account for the results of one 1914 study of the women's former occupations which revealed that it was the highest rather than the lowest paid saleswomen who turned to prostitution. As for the existence of white slavery, over a thousand white slavers were prosecuted between 1910 and 1918 under the Mann Act and—a less reliable statistic—about seven percent of some six thousand prostitutes interviewed in one study listed white slavery or "extreme coercion" as causes.[19] But, as Turner's articles suggest, facts about the prevalence of forced prostitution were often stretched and incidents sensationalized. With little or no proof, white slave narrators argued that over half of American prostitutes were white slaves. Soon after the passage of the Mann Act, Turner himself admitted that he had no first-hand evidence for his *McClure's* assertions.[20]

Kauffman, too, blurred the distinction between fact and *idée fixe*. To exculpate the prostitute, *The House of Bondage* drew on the Progressive belief in her economic victimization and essential innocence— at least of moral responsibility for her trade. Kauffman's literary strategy transformed the experienced woman of the streets into the outraged white slave. Her abduction and brothel incarceration seemed to exist only to provide her with muckraking material. Thus distanced from her own involvement in sexual activity, she became an orator who roused social indignation by offering the "facts" of the traffic in women.

Significantly, Kauffman's sanitizing insistence on the sexless prostitute was a reversal of his earlier conviction regarding her sinful carnal knowledge. His first novel, preceding *The House of Bondage* by almost a decade, condemned the prostitute as well as any woman who engaged in wayward sexuality. Despite his celebrated defense of the prostitute in his most famous novel, his early Victorianism revealed a conflict about Progressive truth which he would never resolve.

* * * * *

A man whose goal, like a character in one of his early novels, was to "mould public opinion in the larger affairs of life,"[21] Reginald Wright Kauffman was born in 1877 in Columbia, Pennsylvania, to a family which on his lawyer father's side had been in America from pre-Revolutionary days. Educated at St. Paul's School, Kauffman entered Harvard in 1896. He only stayed a year, leaving to become a reporter for the *Philadelphia Press*. As he later recalled, he became interested in prostitution at that time, curious to learn more about the women he saw soliciting on Philadelphia streets.[22] By 1900 he was an editorial writer for the *Press,* commenting on the topical concerns of the day. More importantly, he completed *Jarvis of Harvard* (1901), a novel which drew on his observations of Philadelphia streetwalkers and of Cambridge prostitutes frequented by young Harvard men.

Looking back on his earliest period as a newsman and novelist, Kauffman cast himself as one whose attitude toward prostitutes was that of "simple human fellowship" (*The Girl That Goes Wrong*, 5). He claimed compassion for these pathetic women, who were compelled to seek customers in the most inclement weather and whom hardship would soon age. Yet his novel *Jarvis of Harvard* is a condemnation of the prostitute. Equating feminine moral worth with chastity, Kauffman deplores the fact that women who lose or cast away their virtue can only do harm to themselves and, what is far worse, the young patricians who encounter them.

Whether or not Kauffman was acquainted with Harvard classmate Frank Norris and his *Vandover and the Brute*, an 1894 apprentice novel linking masculine personality degeneration to the prostitute, there are a number of similarities between *Vandover* and Kauffman's work.[21] Both warn affluent young men of the dangers of what Norris terms the "other lower side of...life that began after midnight in the private rooms of fast cafés" (27). Like Vandover, Richard Jarvis is lured by the tainted charms of prostitutes. Yet Kauffman makes far more of his protagonist's will to resist the corruption that such women produce. Vandover, unable to control the proverbial Victorian beast in his nature, becomes a kind of animal, losing his fortune and ending as a handyman for a former acquaintance more prudent about consorting with women of the town. Kauffman's Jarvis, in contrast, is so tormented by tavern evenings in the company of prostitutes and casual affairs with other unchaste women that there is little doubt he will atone in marriage to pure young Cambridge socialite Peggy Bartol. Jarvis conquers sin by renouncing the evil desires aroused by the prostitutes he so guiltily frequents. As the novel closes, he plans to marry the ladylike Peggy, whose very innocence of sexuality, Kauffman assures the reader, will mean Jarvis's redemption.

Instead of taking to task a class of men who divide women into paragons or prostitutes, the novel, in its emphasis on the inspiring power of Pure Womanhood, subscribes to the very thinking it claims to deplore. In his preface to *Jarvis*, Kauffman argued that his book was an indictment of the sexual double standard which permitted young collegians to consort with prostitutes, then marry respectable women while covering up or continuing illicit undergraduate practices. In *Jarvis*, however, what matters is the saving of its young protagonist, not of the street women who might need saving as well. At best, Kauffman displays judgmental pity for the flashy or bedraggled women who earn their livings from Harvard men. No Vice Society censor would have objected to these depictions: "They were frail-looking creatures on the face of one or two of whom the finger of death had already set its unmistakable mark," or their "shabby hats [were] unable to hide the bright, tired eyes, tinged

with the royal purple of suffering" (286). Throughout the novel the
women are described briefly and rather obliquely. There is certainly no
attempt to probe their lives or feelings. Nor does Kauffman argue that
they deserve better fates that those suggested by their misery and weakened
health. Whatever insights Kauffman's conversations with prostitutes had
provided him, there is nothing in *Jarvis* which could not have been
found in any late-Victorian work on the female sexual sinner.

Furthermore, though they are unappealing and pathetic, these
prostitutes are far from the economic slaves who would later become
the objects of Kauffman's compassion. No ruthless "cadet" has entrapped
them. No avaricious pimp or madam demands their profits. These
difficulties—if they exist—are not important enough to discuss. Instead
the novel is caught up in the efforts of young Richard Jarvis to subdue
the animal in his nature and "be worthy of a pure woman's love" (181).

In the portrait of heiress Mary Braddock, who briefly traps the
conflicted Jarvis in an affair, Kauffman further reveals his disgust at
feminine sexuality, whether hired or not. A spiritual sister of the tawdry
"casual sweethearts" of Jarvis's café wanderings, Mary garbs herself in
gauzy black costumes which conjure up both seduction and sorcery. Jarvis
himself attributes his desire to her sinister powers rather than his own
impulses. She reminds him of the "relentless occult priestess of some
forgotten heathen god" (181). Her "low, wise laugh" at Jarvis's taunt
that she is like an animal reinforces his fear that he may never be free
of her, "that [his] destruction was unavoidable and complete" (278). In
one scene, looking on him as "Semiramis must have looked on a comely,
new-bought slave" (274), Mary moves to embrace him. The narrative
applauds Jarvis's wild resolution to kill her and be free. Instead of
condemning Jarvis's murderous desire, Kauffman defends it as the
momentary madness produced by the dangers of the temptress. Jarvis
comes to his gentlemanly senses and resists his upper-crust Semiramis.
But the implication is that, whether a town prostitute or a Cambridge
heiress, the woman who abandons her chastity is a frightening menace.

A few years after *Jarvis*, Kauffman became associate editor of the
Saturday Evening Post. Under the editorship of George Horace Lorimer,
the *Post* became, in the words of Frank Luther Mott, one of the chief
popular magazines of the "ambitious young men of the great middle-
class American public."[24] When this business-oriented, conservative
readership was not poring over articles extolling the virtue and success
of the millionaire or suggesting the promise of democracy for the
American worker, it sought entertainment in adventure stories or
sentimental romances.[25] Kauffman's paragon Peggy Bartol, with her
absence of sensuality and her redemptive effect on an errant patrician,
could well have figured in a *Post* story, although, like many of the Boston

reviewers of *Jarvis*,[26] Lorimer would have balked at fiction discussing the impure women from whom Jarvis was saved.

However much his four years at the *Post* fired Kauffman's ambition for popular success, they did not provide an environment for developing a deeper understanding of the economic inequities in American life or the oppression of social outcasts like the prostitute. As if in reaction to the *Post*'s conservatism and his own, in 1907 Kauffman took over the associate editorship of the *Delineator*, a journal critical of social and economic conditions. Under its new editor Theodore Dreiser, the former women's fashion magazine was beginning to question traditional ideas of womanhood. Articles on divorce and women's suffrage appeared. While the topic of prostitution was too provocative for a journal with a quasi-genteel orientation, the magazine did accept advertisements from journals publicizing their articles on prostitution and white slavery.[27]

By 1909 Kauffman had become seriously interested in the ills of American society, among them the economic mistreatment of women symbolized by prostitution. His earlier revulsion at feminine licentiousness seemed to have entirely disappeared. He became managing editor of *Hampton's*, the muckraking journal which Dreiser had also edited for a time, and whose articles attacked "power trusts," Wall Street, and economic and sexual double standards. *Hampton's* contributor Charles Edward Russell, who argued that it was not governmental but a combination of important business interests that controlled America, helped shape Kauffman's thinking.[28] *The House of Bondage,* soon to be published, would underscore Russell's anti-trust theorizing by depicting a shadowy and powerful political boss who controlled the brothel in which the abducted heroine Mary Denbigh was forced to work.

During Kauffman's time at *Hampton's,* his views on the prostitute were particularly influenced by his colleague Rheta Childe Dorr, who had interviewed many slum women considering prostitution. Dorr concluded that low wages and unhealthy influences like the dance hall and the saloon forced them into the trade.[29] Kauffman's preface would also acknowledge the influence of Dorr's friend Maude Miner, the founder of Waverley House, a reform home for young prostitutes, and an advocate of more humane anti-solicitation laws.[30]

A decade after *Jarvis of Harvard,* Kauffman had moved from a moralistically Victorian to a compassionately Progressive view of the prostitute. The virgin heroine of his *Jarvis* period was replaced by the compelling brothel victim whose purity had been violated. Kauffman could now argue that the same system which protected the virtue of the respectable woman left her lower-class counterpart vulnerable. By the time he wrote *The House of Bondage,* he was convinced that the prostitute was an exploited worker in an underworld sweatshop. The novelistic methods he employed to dramatize her oppression and repudiate her Victorian condemners would capture the spirit of his age. He would earn international approval, and, for a time, still his own doubts about the disturbing sexuality of the wayward woman.

* * * * *

Nothing in Reginald Wright Kauffman's life approached his success in *The House of Bondage*.[31] The *New York Times* commended the novel for "attacking and exposing one of the crying evils of our day," which, at least in terms of its popular success, was an understatement.[32] The book was the first American best-seller to focus on the prostitute and one of the earliest works of American fiction to tackle the subject of forced prostitution or white slavery. Kauffman called the book's success amazing, and credited it with launching anti-prostitution investigations and legislation.[33] It certainly went through printing after printing, was translated into French, German, Swedish, Finnish, and Japanese, and was still selling well three years after it first appeared.[34] It even won praise from anarchist Emma Goldman, who applauded what she termed its unsentimental explanation of the forces driving women to prostitution.[35]

Some questioned Kauffman's reformist motives and agreed with the *Current Opinion* reviewer who contended that Kauffman had exploited his subject, "making capital out of the victims of Mrs. Warren's profession."[36] But this was distinctly a minority view. Even Anthony Comstock's Society for the Suppression of Vice, which would engage in a successful campaign to censor David Graham Phillips's *Susan Lenox: Her Fall and Rise* (1917), the subject of the next chapter, found nothing sensational in Kauffman's book.[37] Indeed *The House of Bondage* prudently avoided censorship by omitting the references to prostitutes' solicitation comments, high profits, and escapist activities which had prohibited so sober a document as the 1911 Chicago Vice Commission report from being mailed.[38] Yet the larger reason for the novel's popularity must be found in an analysis of Kauffman's manipulation of the truth of his day.

If Kauffman was mindful of censorship when he chose to omit descriptions of the services provided by his supposedly passive prostitute heroine, fear of Comstock's ire does not account for his vision of her as an innocent who can only acquire knowledge of her situation by questioning others. In the work of Crane and his contemporaries the prostitute fled sexual knowledge through atonement, hysteria, or suicide. Kauffman's protagonist seeks awareness by gathering information about what has befallen her. But Kauffman's decision to turn her into an investigative reporter who interviews inmates and customers alike evades the reality of her immersion in sexual activity as much as any romanticized nineteenth-century scenario. He masks the truth of his prostitute's activity for himself and his reader. Both his earlier fiction and his work following *The House of Bondage* reveal his disapproval of prostitution as unnatural feminine conduct, deviation from the chastity characteristic of the moral woman. Yet when he defends the prostitute, he cannot acknowledge the kind of sexuality which, if admitted, would force him to condemn the very prostitute he wished to defend. Instead he presents his prostitute heroine as a researcher and her colleagues as orators who lecture her on the evils of the brothel. He thus resolves his conflict between condemnation of the sexualized prostitute and compassion for the victimized one.

The House of Bondage opens with sixteen-year-old Mary Denigh, a small-town girl from Pennsylvania dissatisfied with the brutality of her father, the demands of her overworked mother, and the monotony of the chores the family's straitened circumstances require of her. She encounters Max Crossman, a flashy German Jew who is actually a runner for a New York brothel. At first frightened, she soon believes his claim that he is a prosperous travelling salesman. Much as Fawcett's Cora responded to Caspar Drummond or Crane's Maggie to Pete, Mary agrees to meet Crossman for an evening. Spotted by her censorious older sister, she fears her father's Draconian wrath and leaves with Crossman for New York. He has promised: "ve get married righd avay. Nor more school, nor dishvashin', nor scoldin' " (25). The ingenuous girl is easily persuaded.

While Crossman is as slick as any nineteenth-century seducer, his thick accent and foreignness signal a more sinister purpose. Once in the city, he takes Mary to a place where, too gullible to understand the perils of crimson-walled rooms with nude sculptures, she imagines they will be married. She is plied with the drugged drink of Fawcett's nineteenth-century seduction scenario and meets her fate unconscious in both senses of the word. Her fall is more brutal than that of Fawcett's Cora Strang. Fawcett's naive heroine at least cared for the seductive Caspar Drummond. In Kauffman's white slave version, coercion and violation are parts of a business transaction. Mary is signed over to her purchasers, her defloration sealing the bargain. In effect there is no seducer, no villain to reproach or flee. There is only an anonymous customer supplied by the madam, herself the agent of faceless business interests and corrupt politicos.

Mary awakes the next morning to find that she has begun what Kauffman, evading censorship, didactically calls her "descent to hell" (62). She discovers that her clothes are gone, replaced by the badges of her new profession, a crimson kimono, high-heeled shoes, and black silk stockings "slashed with red" (57). Her room is locked and she will not be permitted out of it until she "consents" to her new life. For Mary, unlike her nineteenth-century sisters, there has been no descent from jilted, broken-spirited girl to streetwalker or brothel inmate. Overnight, her bondage has begun.

Although to modern readers this seems a stereotyped and sensational beginning for a novel claiming documentary truth, Kauffman was not faulted for choosing a white slave heroine rather than one driven by economic need. A *New York Times* reviewer spoke for the many who found Mary "typical enough" in believing the "usual promises of marriage."[39] Hutchins Hapgood in the *Bookman* complained that the narrative became monotonous but found the book in every other respect "lucidly conceived."[40] In his preface to the 1911 English edition, future poet laureate John Masefield provided the most confident appraisal of the novel's truth. "There is nothing sensational in his account, and nothing unusual...," he remarked.[41] Masefield went on to claim that English girls as well were tricked into the trade in the way Kauffman had described.

Disgusted that people preferred to ignore the facts, reformer Brand Whitlock ridiculed the kind of story in which "some poor girl had been abducted, borne off the brothel, ruined...and never heard of more."[42] Sociologist Walter Reckless even tackled the Bible of the movement, Chicago prosecutor Clifford Roe's *Panders and Their White Slaves* (1909),[43] a tract cited approvingly in a publisher's note following *The House of Bondage.* Reckless found that Roe had transformed prostitutes' statements and altered their stated reasons for entry into the trade. The Reckless book contains one girl's matter-of-fact description of her sexual relations with a number of men and an interview with the madam who had recruited her. Asked by the madam if she would like to make money, the girl simply says she would. In Roe's story, and the many variations which comprised his five-hundred page narrative, the same girl is coerced and blameless.

Like Kauffman, Roe is fixated on the Abduction and Rescue plot. All of his former prostitutes claim that they were white slaves. All of his procurers express penitence for having lured innocent girls into houses of prostitution. Roe's pseudonymous Mabels, Fannys and Mildreds tell the same exculpatory tale. It is one which, except for its inclusion of a brothel imprisonment scene, is the "wicked city" story of the previous century. While to leave the quiet village is to become a prodigal daughter, Roe's women often manage to escape the brothel and, with such a story, probable criminal prosecution as well. Sisters of Kauffman's Mary Denbigh, all claim to have "trembled at the thought of becoming a bad woman" (62). They allege nostalgia for the girlhood from which they had been wrested and vow to return to the village now that they have been "rescued from bondage" (50).

Though he builds on Roe's story of the tarnished ingenue and describes her eventual attempt to return home, Kauffman's novel transcends the white slave tract. Mary Denbigh quickly moves from a bewildered white slave to a woman initiated into the economics of the brothel. Once Mary, renamed Violet to make her more marketable, gives into the threats of the madam, she begins to learn how very meager are the wages of sin. At first, Violet is offstage, experiencing the "infamy" and "torture" of her new life, while Kauffman is onstage providing the meaning of her experiences. Violet's customers, he explains, are purchasing a commodity. Their money is a "certificate of qualification" which constitutes their right to what "the house of Rose Legere was maintained to sell" (67-68).

When Violet begins her life in the brothel, she is viewed as an innocent requiring enlightenment, not as a woman whom life in the sex trade inevitably educates. Her own customers seem eager to impart knowledge. One anonymous client, depicted without irony as her "sagest adviser" (76), points out that once a woman has been a prostitute, it is impossible for her to find work as anything else. Another customer, playboy Philip Beekman, who will appear repeatedly in the novel, lectures Violet on her situation, telling her she is really in an economic prison. From Beekman she learns that the "yid" Max Crossman is only one of an army of those who make a business of procuring women for brothels.

Still ingenuous after weeks in the brothel, Violet marvels that "men make money that way" (79), but determines to discover how the rest of the brothel money is allocated. She knows she is impossibly in debt to the madam, Rose Legere, for high room and board, but comes to a deeper understanding of this indebtedness when she observes Legere paying bribes to the police. From this woman Violet requests and receives a lesson on the "regular system with...regular prices" (76) which means paying off the crooked district boss O'Malley and his police minions on the beat. Violet's probing questions to house servants and her eavesdropping supply further facts. The madam gives much of her money to her parasitic Italian "fancy man," who in turn treats her little better than the customers do the girls.

It is from the other inmates that Violet receives the most information. As if she were a one-woman vice commission and they testifiers before it, these seasoned prostitutes give her the kind of interview that figured in the reports of vice commissions and probation officers like Maude Miner. From the German girl Fritzie, a representative of the immigrant women widely though erroneously believed to dominate the ranks of prostitutes, Violet learns that the life at Rose Legere's is better than that of an exploited domestic worker. A little later in her stay at the brothel, Violet receives a different opinion from one English Evelyn. Typically, Kauffman moves back and forth from melodrama to reportage.

As the cries of an unwilling initiate echo in their ears, the women realize a new slave has been brought to the house. In response to the screams of the new victim, Violet asks her new colleague the facts of the case. The voice of sociological experience, Evelyn analyzes the forces which dragged the screaming girl to her present fate. She describes the crowded tenement with its dubious lodgers and imagines the bad company the unnamed girl encountered in the dance-halls, then widely believed to be a recruiting ground for Max Crossman and his kind. Indeed, in the phrase of Kauffman's *Hampton's* colleague Rheta Childe Dorr, the dance-hall was "the veritable forcing ground of vice and crime in every city in the United States."[44] As convinced as Mrs. Dorr and other Progressive reformers that a girl is forced into the life by bad environment and worse company, Kauffman's Evelyn offers a series of other stories, including her own, for Violet's edification.

Evelyn is a Progressive orator, yet the story of her own life is pure nineteenth-century Seduction and Abandonment. Like Cora in Edgar Fawcett's *The Evil That Men Do*, Evelyn had been cast off by a wealthy man and despondently descended to the brothel life. However, unlike Fawcett's broken heroine, who abhorred the life to which she had become wedded, Evelyn sounds as if "her only interest in it were economic" (143).

"It's a business, then, ain't it?" Violet asked. "A regular business," nodded Evelyn— "fifty cents up... There are hundreds of young chaps all over the country who make their living by selling girls to places like this—and worse than this; and there are more who make better livings by making one, two or even three girls walk the street for them. Just now, in New York, the street's the main thing." (143)

Evelyn continues in this vein for nine pages. She lectures on everything from make-believe employment agencies which "catch the girls by regiments" to the red-light districts of large American cities:

She talked of Denver, with its two-room houses in which the front seemed one large window where the sole inmate displayed her wares; of Chicago with the curtained doors through which was thrust only a hand to receive the varying price of admission, even a quarter of a dollar sufficing: of the same city's infamous clubs maintained by politicians for their own debauches... She said that young girls unsoiled would sometimes fetch their owners fifty dollars for their initial destruction, but that, as a rule the sums were relatively small. (143-144)

It is not difficult to see why as a novelist Kauffman had the reputation of the reformer, not the artist.[45] There is some attempt at characterization. Evelyn's flat recital suggests a world-weariness quite different from the ingenuousness which prompts Violet to press the older woman for details and ask how such things are allowed to happen. Nevertheless, this is hardly a convincing conversation between a seasoned prostitute and a tyro. These are the official truths unearthed by commissions of inquiry.

Evelyn is the professional researcher, committed to an implausibly scientific analysis of her chosen profession. While to some extent her speech is a report of actual conditions, she omits any concerns of greater importance to her. There is no discussion of her ways of dealing with the pressures of the life, types of clients, and profits.

The Chicago Vice Commission, which began gathering data a few months after the Kauffman novel, filtered its tome of testimony through the perception that the "language used by the girls and their men acquaintances is unprintable."[46] If Kauffman's own interviews did not lead him to a similar conclusion, it was probably because the women did not trust him enough to speak freely. Furthermore, even in terms of the bowdlerized presentation of information which characterized the interviews with the Florences, Lillys, and Bessies cited in the Chicago vice report, Kauffman's Evelyn and Violet discuss their lack of financial gain from prostitution with startling disinterestedness.

Furthermore, unlike Kauffman's women, a fair number of the real-life Chicago prostitutes expressed satisfaction with their trade and wages. "There is more money and pleasure in being a sport," one former factory girl told an investigator. Though this was not a majority opinion, others were quoted as choosing prostitution because they were "tired of drudgery," did not want to be "kicked around as servant[s]," were "born with the devil in [them]," or saw prostitution as "easier than working,"[47] all ideas which Kauffman either discounts or omits entirely. Although, as historian Ruth Rosen observes, many women tended to give unreliable information or selected answers from a set of those supplied by investigators, no doubt some of the information about volition was supplied by the women themselves.[48] With due allowance for their own possible lack of authenticity, *Madeleine* (1919) and *Nell Kimball* (written in 1932), memoirs of Progressive era prostitutes, suggest that prostitutes spent much of their free time in casual conversation, often ridiculing the sexual practices of their customers.[49]

In *The House of Bondage* Kauffman presents prostitutes who, though supposedly in the life, were really outside of it, commentators on the exploitation of women. Many of Kauffman's interviews with the real-life counterparts of English Evelyn and Mary/Violet centered on the women's bitter sexual experiences and pragmatic acceptance of their lives.[50] Whatever his knowledge of their experiences and the colloquial or profane language the women used to express themselves, in his art Kauffman could not seem to envision a prostitute other than as an oratorical victim of social injustice. For however brief a time, he found this safely sanitized woman a comforting alternative to the tainted creatures of his *Jarvis* period.

Kauffman was not the only novelist claiming to present the facts of prostitution who depicted the prostitute as an oratorical authority on a corrupt system. Walter Hurt's *The Scarlet Shadow* (1907) is a novel loosely based on the 1903-1904 Colorado mining wars between owners and the Western Federation of Miners. It includes a brothel scene in which prostitute Marguerite Howard, incensed that a group of reformers has come to convert the inmates of a brothel called the Palace of Pleasure, decides to lecture them.[51] She tells the respectable citizens of Denver that they are accountable. She exhorts them to understand that "the commercial courtesan, whose vice is not voluntary," is victimized by the hypocrisy of those who go to church but collect huge rentals from the brothhels they own. "Give to woman economic independence," she contends, "and there'll be never a harlot in the land" (272). She peppers her speech with Socialist rhetoric, Biblical references, classical allusions, and even quotations from Charlotte Brontë. She is so little the scarlet woman and so much the enlightened orator that a silent and rather crestfallen lot of crusaders, jolted by her eloquence, files out of the brothel to ponder her speech. Soon giving up her new role as an activist, Marguerite succumbs to despair and poisons herself. Rhetorical to the last, she leaves behind an eight-stanza poem lamenting lost virtue and scorning the money which had purchased her.

Based on a Socialist pamphlet on the social evil, Estelle Baker's novel about a San Francisco brothel of that name, *The Rose Door* (1911) has ex-inmate Grace Howells lecture the respectable Mrs. Thompson on the life histories of the girls at the brothel.[52] Much as Kauffman's English Evelyn responds to Violet's catechism, Grace answers Mrs. Thompson's questions about the brothel women. To Grace, the girls are trapped in an "occupation fostered by the state" (177) which exploits the impoverished to protect the virtue of more privileged women. Grace's allusive ability is almost as impressive as that of Marguerite Howard:

And when the breaking of one half of its daughters that the other half may live, is pronounced by the nation Expediency, its dying ones deserve to rank with the soldier—the patriot who fights and dies for his 'boarding house,' as Ingersoll has put it. (177)

Though Grace has exchanged prostitution for a career convincing virtuous women to save the fallen, Baker makes clear that eloquence will save neither the debilitated Grace nor her sisters still in the life.

Death after the "fate worse that death" is also the lot of the white slave in social worker Virginia Brooks's novel *Little Lost Sister* (1914).[53] As with Kauffman's protagonist, Elsie Welcome receives a brief political initiation from Lou, a more experienced woman. Like Violet, Elsie cannot believe that the man she thought had married her (it was a mock ceremony, she discovers) was a white slaver. The alcoholic and embittered Lou replies rhetorically: "It's hard for anyone who is decent to believe that men can fall so low. Why, nobody believes it! The men who run the city government don't believe it, the law makers don't believe it, the vice commission doesn't believe it" (225).

Writers like Brooks, Hurt, and Baker joined Kauffman in projecting their opposition to prostitution onto the unlikely figure of the prostitute herself. Her outrage if hardened, her incredulity if new to the trade, are aspects of her creator's indignation. There is none of the profane and matter-of-fact defense of the life which so alarmed vice commission investigators that they bowdlerized such supposedly shocking testimony. The vice reports, in recording the pragmatism of the money-making prostitutes, at least acknowledged this attitude existed. In Progressive fiction the prostitute becomes instead a muckraking reporter, disgusted by greed, uninterested in profit. One has the feeling that were she to appear before a Rockefeller Commission, she would have posed the questions and then responded to them.

Kauffman carries the idea of the prostitute as muckraker farther than his contemporaries, who give their characters the podium or seat in the lecture hall only to consign them soon after to oblivion. Violet, in contrast, acquires more and more information as the narrative proceeds. Her development as a character is pictured less as a series of increasingly sordid experiences than as her effort to "learn so's I can see it—see it all" (256). Soon after her fact-gathering session with Evelyn, she gains freedom from the brothel by promising to testify against Rose Legere at a white slavery hearing. The hearing will be initiated by a customer bearing a grudge against Rose and seeking to establish his reputation as a reformer—a possible Kauffman slap at "disinterested public prosecutors." Violet is soon safely installed in a tenement room shared by two young working girls and rechristens herself Mary. She immediately receives tutelage from a young Socialist, Herman Hoffmann. His last name is perhaps deliberately reminiscent of his creator's. Like Kauffman, the young man has facts and statistics at the ready. A successor to Evelyn, he too lectures Mary on commercialized vice.

At first this scene seems little more than another compendium of statistics on the number of urban prostitutes, a catalogue of their previous poorly paid jobs, and a "shame of the cities" critique of widespread poverty and the corrupt political organizations which garner huge profits from prostitution. We recall that Kauffman typically described himself as one who had "studied the problem...in all its phases...in scores of our larger cities and smaller towns" (*The Girl That Goes Wrong*, 7). On one level Hoffmann does little but present Kauffman's conclusions. If one views him as Kauffman's working class alter ego, however, the scene becomes emblematic. The author outside of the prostitute's life tells her what her own experience has been.

Kauffman does emphasize that Mary has been aged by her life; she looks twenty-five, not sixteen. A few weeks in the brothel have etched experience on her face. Despite this, she is presented not as a sexually experienced woman but as a truth-seeker, a guise which enables her to remain admirable despite the degradation to which she has been subjected. As a theorist, Kauffman believed that a prostitute's activity was far less important than the system which fostered it. As a novelist defending the prostitute, he applied this theory with a literary sleight-of-hand. Mary cannot be said to have lived as a prostitute because she has not yet understood the oppression which placed her in that life.

With unconscious irony, Kauffman observes, "clearly or deeply she could never think without help from a stronger and better mind" (253). Such a statement reveals Kauffman's own conflict about imagining the sexually active woman. Were a prostitute to think clearly, she would recall her experience. Kauffman would then have to acknowledge her sexual activity. Of course the logic of the novel requires that Mary eventually achieve enlightenment. Kauffman will then have to employ rhetorical strategies which undercut her knowledge. His condescending characterization of her at this point in the novel reveals his fear she will achieve the very clarity which he claims that she seeks.

Kauffman's "better mind" continues teaching Mary by the very narrative ordering of subsequent events. A succession of scenes bombards her with the experiences believed to drive women to prostitution in the first place. She finds work as a servant but is underpaid and overworked by a series of conscienceless female employers. She is then rejected by an aristocratic settlement house worker who had first recommended housework because it was healthier and safer for slum girls than the factory. These women are a far cry from concerned professionals like Kauffman's *Hampton's* period colleagues Rheta Childe Dorr and Maude Miner. The men turn out to be false rescuers as well. The would-be prosecutor who effected Mary's escape cements an alliance with madam Rose Legere and now intimidates Mary so that she will not testify. Another former customer, Philip Beekman, recognizes her when she becomes a servant in his home and orders her out. Whatever they lack in credibility, these plot twists insure that Mary's return to the trade will be no more her choice than was her initial entry.

Kauffman typically emphasizes acquisition of knowledge rather than the sexual activity associated with it. When, defeated and alienated, Mary returns to prostitution, this time as a streetwalker, she is still a girl acquiring an understanding of corruption rather than a now-embittered professional immersed in it. Calling herself Violet again, she seeks instruction from a young saloon prostitute. She learns what rates to charge customers, where to lodge, what streetwalking territory is safest from harassment from police and pimps. She moves from learner to expert. Soon she can haggle with customers and conceal evidence of illness from them, bribe policemen on the beat, and dull herself with drink.

In keeping with the activism that an awareness of injustice can inspire, Violet becomes the only kind of avenger possible. In protest against her victimization, she exacts retribution by seeking out her abductor Max Crossman and infecting him with venereal disease. Brushing aside the fact that she also infects the other men whom she solicits, Kauffman presents her mission of retribution as a kind of martyrdom. "Her physical sufferings mattered little to her," he explains, because she "had accomplished her great work, she had achieved her mission" (414). She then descends to fetid opium dens and the ultimate degradation of the waterfront brothel, where she again encounters Philip Beekman. When he offers an apology for having reduced her to working in such places, she completes her martyrdom and forgives him.

Kauffman then transforms her briefly into the Prodigal Daughter. A sailor who wants Voilet's services kills Beekman in drunken rage, and Violet flees possible consequences in a return home to Pennsylvania. Her frightened mother, though pitying her, will not take her in. When she returns to the city which has ruined her, she reacts to her recent experiences in this fashion:

Out of the bitterness of her own heart, out of the abysses of her knowledge of things as they are, she saw much of the truth...No rescue of a slave could put an end to the slavery. She knew only that, down the years, wherever walked the great god Poverty, that great god led Prostitution by the hand. (465)

Mary receives her final tutorial at the place of her initial one, Rose Legere's, where she has returned to beg admission. She is refused. A student to the end, she asks why. The last words of the novel both instruct Violet and pronounce her death sentence: "The life's got you, Violet," intones Rose. "You're all in" (466).

In *The House of Bondage* Kauffman claims he has endowed the prostitute with the right to tell the truth about her experience. Yet his way of directing attention to her as a witness to painfully learned lessons is to present her as an investigator or an orator, a desexualized figure. More than any of his contemporaries, Kauffman was able to transform the prostitute from the silent, incoherent, or impossibly saintly figure of the nineteenth-century imagination into an expert on the corrupt city. This artistic choice brought with it a corresponding insistence on the prostitute as an urban social conscience. Whatever sexual activity she engages in offstage, onstage she is first and foremost a theorist. But in her very ability to theorize about economic cause and effect, to analyze rigorously and apportion blame, the prostitute is insured a distance from the very world in which she is submerged.

Rather than accuse the author of *The House of Bondage* of a failure of imagination compounded by careful avoidance of the censors, it is important to understand what Kauffman attempted to achieve by placing the prostitute on a soapbox. Violet discovers from her underclass associates and working-class friends what Kauffman himself had learned about the business of prostitution. His refusal to separate Violet's enlightenment from his own becomes an affirmation of Progressive ideology. That the ignorant country girl and the sophisticated newsman reach an identical conclusion about prostitution reasserts the truth of her supposed victimization. In so doing, it reinforces Kauffman's sanitized vision of the prostitute.

In the works following *The House of Bondage,* how conscious was Kauffman of his rejection of the literary strategy he had so recently and effectively employed? How willing was he to admit that his most celebrated novel had imposed a truth rather than arrived at it? His later works suggest doubts about the very ideas *The House of Bondage* had affirmed. The prostitute becomes a threatening figure, mercenary and unclean, a frightening reminder of the potential waywardness of all women. A brief review of this work reveals Kauffman's doubts about the white slave myth he had been so instrumental in popularizing.

* * * * *

An advertisement for *The Girl That Goes Wrong* capitalized on Kauffman's reputation by claiming that his new book was a truthful account of the "inexpressible conditions of human bondage of many young girls and women in our cities..."[54] Kauffman himself claimed that his sketches, though they used the composite to represent the individual, were absolutely truthful, indeed "not fiction at all" (1). With titles like "The Girl That Was Poor," "The Woman That Succeeded," and "The Girl That Wanted Ermine," the sketches seem more like moral fables than factual accounts. What is more important than its genre is the fact that *The Girl That Goes Wrong* includes a number of women who have not been coerced into prostitution or into wayward behavior, such as adultery or promiscuity, which Kauffman saw as little better that prostitution.

The preface to *The Girl That Goes Wrong* outlines the very ideology of the prostitute's sexlessness that many of the actual sketches will undercut. Kauffman describes one meeting in the early 1900's with a Wilkes-Barre prostitute, the first supposed white slave he had ever met. The anonymous woman responds to his request that she describe her life by refusing to say anything more than "it's worse than they can say, because there's a lot in it that there ain't no words for" (7). With the replacement of anybody for they, this is the speech Kauffman gives Mary after her escape from Rose Legere's. Whether Kauffman took an authentic statement and placed it in the mouth of his fictional character or used the same invented speech twice, he obviously found it a significant one. In its brevity and deliberate ambiguity the speech suggests a reluctance to discuss what is sordid about the prostitute's experience. Eloquent in its way, it implies both moral outrage and humiliation. Because she disapproves of her own life, Kauffman's prostitute is another sympathetic Mary Denbigh.

The preface contains other sources for *The House of Bondage*. A teenage prostitute from Philadelphia explains that she and her friends are too afraid of their pimps to quit the life. One Chicago "victim" adds that girls like her are "too broken down to do any other sort" of work (8). An older woman, with rouged face and red mouth, belies her hard appearance by telling a white slave tale similar to Mary Denbigh's. She was forced to become a streetwalker by a man who used false promises to lure her from a country town. She continued as a prostitute because she needed "some more money on [the] kid's boarding school bill" (4). The woman agreed never to see the child again, but, she told Kauffman, she was paying the bills.

Of the sketches in *The Girl That Goes Wrong*, a number do present the same exculpatory tales told by the encountered or invented women of Kauffman's preface. "The Girl That Was Hungry" and "The Women That Serve" narrate the woes of susceptible tenement girls. One former domestic servant with a little boy to support is the virtuous Nada, The Girl That Was Poor. She is haunted by the whimpers of the hungry children of her family and is about to become a streetwalker. Like a "virgin led to the Minotaur" (120), she finds dubious salvation in a department store job. It is only a matter of time until there too a supervisor or customer will coerce her. All of this is by now vintage Kauffman, familiar enough. Yet, significantly, to the stories of women tempted, jilted, and impoverished, he adds tales of women who *preferred* to go wrong. Spoiled Letty Dowling, The Girl That Wanted Ermine, admires the kept woman in her upper-crust apartment building and decides to emulate her. Another girl of good family, curious about the city's opium dens, "went to see," and shames her family by her fall into debauchery and, presumably, prostitution to support her drug habit. The actress-turned-courtesan in "The Woman That Succeeded" enjoys the comfort, celebrity, and supposedly reduced workload of her new life. Almost as culpable is Martha Dominic, the Bohemian woman who specializes in corrupting young girls by introducing them to her fast set, or the Parisian art student who lives in sin and later, a married woman, lies about her past.

Like the factory girls, domestic servants, and other slum dwellers trapped in prostitution whose stories comprise much of *The Girl That Goes Wrong*, these women end in poverty or disgrace. Nevertheless they represent a disturbingly willed sexuality which belies Kauffman's insistence on forced prostitution. While he makes the point that those eager to prostitute themselves are not pressed by need, he also suggests that the women are not capricious or perverse. He turns defensively to traditional explanations such as laziness or love of sin. But the sketches evidence a tension between Kauffman's need to reassure himself that these women meet the same fate as their blameless sisters and his awareness that volitional fallen women are in a different category from hopeless victims. Significantly, Kauffman places the unnamed Parisian art student-turned-wife and the heedless Mrs. Dominic, women who are only wayward, in a collection of sketches about the prostitute. The implication is that by their depraved behavior they have earned the label. In their calculation and flirtatiousness these women are reminiscent of Mary Braddock, the *femme fatale* of Kauffman's early novel *Jarvis of Harvard*.

Kauffman's alarm at the determined immorality he describes in *The Girl That Goes Wrong* is even more apparent in *The Sentence of Silence* (1912). The novel returns to the Jarvis character, the young patrician both drawn to and repelled by the predatory prostitute of the American metropolis. Kauffman argues that Dan Barnes is compelled to visit red-light districts. He is suffering the effects of a sentence of silence to which parents who believe children "don't need to know" had condemned him. Dan's childhood was in a representative small town named Americus where his parents plaster their walls with scriptural quotations and set their lips firmly at the mention of some wayward youth or ruined girl. He is taught that the way to avoid temptation is not to think about it. Soon curiosity about the sex act makes him secretive and ends by "warping his whole moral fiber" with "impure thoughts" (66). As the novel proceeds, Dan cannot resolve the conflict that "made his mind want purity and his body want purity's antithesis" (398).

The prostitutes he frequents, particularly the materialistic Cora, whom he takes as his mistress, signal his uneasy rebellion against small-town morality. Like his predecessor Jarvis, Dan equates prostitution with sin. He longs to redeem himself by marriage to the "holy, clear-seeing purity" (387) he believes is symbolized by Judith Kent, a high school sweetheart whom he encounters again in the city. After contracting venereal disease from Cora or one of her sisters in the trade, Dan cures himself of the disease and of his need to see prostitutes. He marries Judith, the woman whose chastity he is sure will inspire his own, only to find to his fury that the sentence of silence had destroyed her virtue as well. Judith has become a threatening figure. She believes in sexual freedom and has even had lovers. Dan's fury provokes her feminism. The novel concludes with her retaliatory defense: "What have I been? Nothing you've not been. What right have *you* to ask?" (411).

What is striking about *The Sentence of Silence* is the way its prostitute characters give the lie to Kauffman's claim to be an advocate of sexual freedom and a single sexual standard. In a preface defending the book for having an impure heroine like Judith Kent, Kauffman wrote that his novel was an argument for the feminine right to the same kind of sexual experience that men have. He went on to criticize men for "imposing upon our daughters an abstinence from which we absolve our sons" (ix), including himself in this criticism of male repressiveness. Yet Kauffman seems unaware of the extent to which his novel, purporting to criticize masculine sexual ideology, embodies it. He claims to disapprove of the hypocritical notion that "men that took any woman's body they could get were horrified at the notion of any woman sharing their liberty" (ix). Yet his plea for an enlightened attitude toward the sexually active, even promiscuous woman, is contradicted by his novel's increasingly dark vision of the prostitute. The fact that he blackens the character of the prostitute while he maintains the feminine right to sexual fulfillment suggests that his earlier fears about the fundamental impurity of prostitutes—fears suppressed in *The House of Bondage*—have resurfaced and now extend to respectable women as well.

* * * * *

The House of Bondage presents a world in which men take advantage of women's ignorance. Kauffman excoriates the male need to transform rural girls into brothel dwellers. Even as a free agent, no longer in the brothel or chained to a pimp, a prostitute like Mary Denbigh is exploited by customers who cheat or refuse to pay her. Had she been properly instructed in her small-town setting, Mary, like Dan Barnes, might have warded off the Max Crossmans and Rose Legeres. It is all the more surprising that in *The Sentence of Silence* this vision of entrapment is entirely inapplicable to the manipulative prostitutes who lure Dan Barnes. Now it is the women who stalk their prey, waylaying men like Dan on darkened streets, inveigling them to their rooms. Kauffman's masculine innocent is surprised and disgusted that a woman, jesting coarsely, asks him for money. He concludes that she is "a terrible woman" (173). In this Kauffman novel, the man is the one poised to "turn and flee," the one who comes "reluctantly forward" (169) when a bright-eyed prostitute asks him if he is "out for a good time" (169).

Cora, the woman Dan, along with other men, is keeping as a mistress, is the quintessential mercenary. She attracts his attention with a transparently phony tale of having lost her money. In a calculating way, she accepts Dan's visits as long as his money can support her. She spins no seduction tale. She is not at death's door, but is contented with her life. Far from being defenseless when attacked by Dan as money-hungry, she can threaten "as if a sewer-pipe had burst," loosing all the "vile thoughts that her life had bred in her" (326). Cora the survivor has replaced Mary Denbigh, the ideologue of social injustice.

In *The Spider's Web* (1913), the prostitute has traveled so far from the innocent Mary Denbigh that she is in the willing employ of the political machine which plots the destruction of the idealist out to expose it. To blacken the reputation of young attorney Luke Huber, the Municipal League's candidate for mayor, underworld connections of the "Spider" capitalist send Luke a prostitute with a Joan of Arc face and a luring voice. Her innocence is all appearance. It barely conceals her "sordidness, and "frigidity" (195). Sizing up her prey, she tries to lure him to a brothel by telling the same kind of white slave tale Kauffman himself had claimed to hear so many times. In this case the woman's sister has been taken away "an' she's straight—and I know she's not here in Pearl's Six' Av'nue place" (223). Luke, too virtuous and suspicious to take the bait, escapes her and her white slavery lies.

In his work after *The House of Bondage*, Kauffman views as a ruse the white slave truth he had believed in only a few years earlier. Gone is his defense of the prostitute's economic motives. These women's ability to emerge unscathed from their mercenary encounters has disqualified them as victims and made them suspects rather than witnesses. Without endowing their offstage sexual dealings with verisimilitude, Kauffman plays on the same image of the prostitute as polluter that he had employed in his earliest fiction. Here the anguished Dan Barnes delivers the novel's judgment of the prostitute:

He must give it up, this life of dirtiness. He passionately wanted to give it up. There was no romance about it. You could in no wise approach it without, sooner or later, being soiled. He wanted the clean [woman], and he wanted to know that he was not irretrievably besmirched. (327).

The references to dirt and soil are to the venereal disease Dan has contracted and the sin in which he has engaged. Now, as in his *Jarvis* days, Kauffman is concerned with imperilled male virtue. But the threats are no longer restricted to the prostitute or self-styled *femme fatale*. In this darker vision of feminine behavior, even the apparently pure small-town sweetheart conceals a woman of the world. To the beast in man has been added the beast in woman. The young rake seeking to "be loved by a woman pure in body and in mind" (328) wakes up to find that he has married a woman who has not, as he imagined, "remained aloof from his lower desires and above them" (398).

One of the last scenes in *The Spider's Web* reveals the fears and fantasies generated by the idea of the respectable woman as lustful being. Crusading Luke Huber has been defeated by the stratagems of a J.P. Morgan-like Spider. He is ousted from the nomination for mayor of New York by a reform league fearful of the Spider's power. Luke rather improbably finds himself defending the Forbes factory, owned by the father of the girl he loves, and in which he has invested all of his money, against violent strikers. Caught up in the violent mood of the moment, Luke and Betty Forbes find shelter from the fray to enact a sexual war of their own.

What occurs is nothing less than a period fantasy about the underside of feminine respectability. The bloodshed that Betty has witnessed strips her of civilization for a moment. She undergoes a metamorphosis into a woman of the streets. Her cheeks are, in Kauffman's word, scarlet, a literal and figurative association with the prostitute. She becomes provocative, her teeth suggestively biting "deep into the vermilion of her lower lip" (386). She has even torn open her dress, but, for the censors' sake, only at the throat.

Like the prostitute who can infect and wound, Betty, a sexual menace, is associated with the capacity to do violence. She stands, revolver in hand, ready to ward off the very men she entices. As Bellona, she defends her father's factory. As seductress, she can lure men to their death. The virtuous Luke is reduced to bestiality before her. He lunges toward her, in a scene worth quoting at length:

He put out his arms. He wrenched her to him. His right arm clutched her about the supple shoulders, the fingers of his right hand sinking into her firm left breast. With his left hand he shoved her face upwards...[H]is opened mouth closed upon hers.

He heard the revolver clatter to the floor. She writhed in his embrace. He had expected the perfect response. Meeting an abrupt refusal, he was taken off his guard, and she escaped from him.

She staggered into a corner. The devil that possessed him had lost its power over her. She had reverted to her natural being. She did not cry, but she stood there with her hands pressed tight against her breast, the fingers mechanically busied with repairing the opening blouse. Her face all horror at the thing she had been .

"What must you think of me?" she was moaning— "I don't know what came over me. What must you think of me?"

He thought nothing. He could think nothing. He could realize only that he was again to be robbed. Twice to-night the cheat that played with men at the game of life had given him the winning hand, only to sweep the stakes from the board just as Luke reached for what he had won. The blood lust changed its form; it assumed an ungovernable fury. Something crackled in his brain as if he had seen imperfect feedwires at the touch of a trolley-wheel. The crimson veil fluttered again before his eyes.

He turned and bolted the door. He turned again and ran to her. His face was wet with sweat, black with powder, terrible.

She understood. She lowered her head and tried to dodge past him. She cried out.

His strong fingers caught her hair. The hair streamed down. Her forward lurch brought it taut. He jerked at it; she fell toward him. His free hand caught her throat and stopped her fall. He tossed her against the table; her feet brushed the floor, but he pressed her shoulders tight to the table's top. He bent over her, one hand at her throat, the other raised to stop her mouth, his beating breath on her face.

She was wholly in his power now. The outside world was impotent because the outside world could not have heeded her appeal; the woman herself was helpless because her captor's was the strongest body. Again came to Luke the frightful sense of Power, again the dizzy knowledge that he could do whatever he chose. At that instant the madness fell from him. (388-389)

The scene crystallizes Kauffman's thinking about feminine solicitation and masculine lust. On one level Betty's violation by Luke is the same kind experienced by the white slave Mary Denbigh. Luke is the captor, Betty the virgin nervously trying to cover her exposed flesh. Like a Mary Denbigh, Betty seeks escape from the evil-faced violator. Luke, his face satanically dark, "black with powder," surges toward her. The kind of Apache dance which Luke forces her to do is akin to the procurer or anonymous customer breaking in a recalcitrant captive. Luke wishes Betty's submission so that she will be "wholly in his power."

Male violence has inspired Betty's seductiveness, her inflaming behavior. But on a deeper level Kauffman suggests that this is not without a certain provocation. Betty is in a sense the aggressor, enacting the same role as did Cambridge prostitutes with Jarvis, hard-boiled Cora with Dan Barnes, even vengeful Mary Denbigh with Crossman. Betty, after all, first lures; only later does she writhe in the embrace of the man whose lust she has inspired and whom she now abhors. Beneath the fantasy of the beast in man is a more troubling one: the beast in woman, the pure woman as prostitute.

Fear of woman's sexual power had been present in Kauffman's fiction from the beginning. In *Jarvis* it is not only the sickly lower-class streetwalker who threatens the health and virtue of young American manhood. The corrupting temptation posed by the carnally knowing woman is present in the women of Jarvis's own class. Mary Braddock is no down-and-out Cambridge streetwalker, propelled by material need. Although the novel defuses her seductive force by marrying Jarvis off to her chaste antithesis Peggy Bartol, it is to avoid the unsettling implications. If a Mary Braddock can be impure, why not a Peggy Bartol? Certainly the feared scenario of the respectable girl throwing off the mask of virtue is finally realized in the closing scene between Judith Kent and Dan Barnes in *The Sentence of Silence*.

Fear of feminine sexuality, however, generates denial of that fear. Just as *The House of Bondage* insists on the essential innocence of the lowliest streetwalker, *The Spider's Web* must undo the frightening vision of a respectable woman now debased. Kauffman casts out fear by asserting that Betty's is not natural behavior for the virtuous woman and by implication all women. Reversing his earlier identification of nature with Betty's animalistic behavior, he insists that it is natural for Betty to be in "horror at the thing she had been," much like Mary Denbigh was the day she woke up in a brothel. When Betty fights off Luke's advances until he comes to his civilized senses, she assumes her more suitable role as a moral inspiration, a curb on unregulated masculine desire.

In a very real sense, the scene in *The Spider's Web* offers a vision of unregulated and thus illicit sexual behavior. It is a vision which, in *The House of Bondage*, Kauffman avoids at all costs. There he focuses on the profits corrupt pimps and madams earn from selling prostitution—not the lust which fuels the prostitute's customer. But the acknowledged truth of *The House of Bondage* is, if only for a short time, made evident in *The Spider's Web*. It is not money but sexuality, "bloodlust," which is at the heart of human behavior. And sexuality is ugly: part barroom brawl, part visitation of the devil.

* * * * *

In the years immediately following *The House of Bondage*, a novel which "capsuled the popular image of white slavery,"[56] its author questioned the Progressive era truth on which his novel was based. He had, after all, rendered that truth acceptable, both to himself and his readers, by blurring the distinction between the prostitute and the fact-finding, speech-making reformer. Saddling a passive teenage victim or a detached brothel professional with such oratory did not produce convincing art, but it did provide a sympathetic figure, and one recognizable in its time.

Reginald Wright Kauffman, like Stephen Crane and Harold Frederic before him, tried to conquer his fear of the prostitute and the female sexual aggression she symbolized. Like these imaginers of the prostitute, he resolved the problem of sympathy for so threatening a figure at great cost. His was a Progressive solution: to document the prostitute's life and deny that she was sexually knowing. Kauffman's fallen woman could now speak from experience—but it was only to mouth official truths. And, almost immediately after he had envisioned the desexualized prostitute, his conflict about her other, truer self reappeared, raising old fears about woman's nature and creating new ones.

The House of Bondage had shown Americans that the prostitute could be heroic. Yet Mary Denbigh is a heroine her own creator soon came to question. Eunice Lipton has aptly defined "ideology" as the "selective redefinition of given elements of the conditions of life."[57] What Kauffman provides in *The House of Bondage* is the ideological prostitute. His work of a few years later, in its negation of white slave thinking, suggests a repudiation of Progressive ideology. In place of Mary Denbigh is a shamelessly pragmatic prostitute, at once the seductress and the professional. This repellent woman is the bane of the muckraking ideologue who argues that she is oppressed, and of the patrician trying to live purely. It is no wonder that she is relegated to secondary status in Kauffman's literary world. Unlike a Mary Denbigh, a hardened prostitute did not merit a novel about her life in the trade. Only fellow Progressive David Graham Phillips's *Susan Lenox: Her Fall and Rise* would dare to make a heroine of the unrepentant streetwalker. In so doing, Phillips would inherit the conflict about feminine carnality which characterizes the work of Kauffman and his predecessors.

Chapter Six
David Graham Phillips and the American Heroine

In Reginald Wright Kauffman's blockbuster, *The House of Bondage,*
the escaped white slave Mary Denbigh, in ill health and defeated by
a judgmental society unwilling to aid her in a new life, crawls back
to the brothel she had once fled in horror. No longer a valuable sexual
commodity, she is refused work by the very madam who had helped
entrap her. Soon Mary's will be the deadly fate of the girls who trod
the mean streets of nineteenth-century fiction. At the novel's end, though,
Mary has not been killed off—a conclusion symbolic of the Progressive
unwillingness to blame the victim. She must live on, at least long enough
to bear witness to the savageries of commercialized vice. As we have
observed, Kauffman and his contemporaries used the oratorical prostitute
as a distancing device to evade the issue of her moral taint. But as in
the standard nineteenth-century scenario, she was a victim to the last.
Her status as a heroine still depended on the irreversibility of her fall,
not on her ability to survive, much less prosper.

Only one prominent Progressive novelist, David Graham Phillips,
imagined a woman who both profited and escaped from the sex trade.
Phillips is best remembered for his attacks on the plutocracy in articles
blasting corporate wealth for the betrayal of the American people.[1] His
biting 1906 *Cosmopolitan* magazine series, "The Treason of the Senate,"
denounced this governing group, already satirically known as the
"Millionaire's Club," for peddling influence to "the interests."[2] Phillips
called for direct election of Senators, a suggestion implemented in 1913
by the passage of the Seventeenth Amendment. What is less well
remembered is that, after producing social problem fiction that muckraked
big business fraud and political bossism, he became a tireless if
misogynistic critic of the fashionable American woman and an analyst
of feminine economic dependence, whether in the upper-class marriage,
the mass labor market, or the vice trade. Prostitution, and the need for
a fresh view of the woman who entered it, came to concern him more
and more. In 1911, he completed the massive *Susan Lenox: Her Fall
and Rise,*[3] a novel whose very title indicates an approach to the prostitute
distinct from that of other Progressives.

Whereas Kauffman's hapless Mary Denbigh succumbs, Phillips's title character prevails over a life of poverty, drug and alcohol addiction, pimps, and soliciting to become a celebrated actress. Not the least of her successes is that she escapes retribution. An incensed Society for the Suppression of Vice, which had remained silent about *The House of Bondage,* demanded that Phillips's publisher, Appleton and Company, ban his offending book. "As there is no attempt to point a moral," stormed Anthony Comstock's successor, John S. Sumner, it is "unfit for publication and distribution..."[4] In a growing assault on literary prudery, others voiced support for the novel and its protagonist's "victorious will...."[5] Legal battles ensued; Appleton offered a compromise and Sumner agreed to an expurgated version. In 1917, a few months after the original edition had appeared and been withdrawn, a bowdlerized *Susan Lenox* was published. Although the version would not have pleased Phillips, who died in 1911 only weeks after completing the manuscript, Susan's success story remained more or less intact. Those who tried to use her suffer and fail. She alone achieves triumph, lifted "high above the storms that tortured her girlhood and early youth" (II, 558).

In 1890, some years before he began *Susan Lenox,* Phillips, then twenty-two and fresh from crime reporting in Cincinnati, covered the Night Court beat for the *New York Sun* and had an excellent opportunity to find out what those storms were. His early *Harper's* and *Saturday Evening Post* pieces came to what would soon be familiar Progressive conclusions about women's sweated labor and forced entry into prostitution. The thousand pages of *Susan Lenox* would be peppered with such observations as this representative example:

No place did...[Susan] find offering more than four dollars a week...Everywhere women's wages were based upon the assumption that women either lived at home or made the principal part of their incomes by prostitution, either disguised or frank. (II, 63)

In its documentary emphasis, the passage would not be out of place in Kauffman's fiction. There are resemblances in narrative event as well. Like Mary Denbigh, Susan is inveigled into prostitution by a relentless pimp and escapes, only to fall into "freelance" streetwalking, drugs, and drink.

There, though, the resemblances between the two characters—and between their creators' approaches to characterization—end. Phillips's biographer remarked of *Susan Lenox* that "nothing like it had ever before been projected in American fiction."[6] Out of the economic and psychological debasement of the prostitute, Phillips sought, in the words of an admiring period reviewer, to create "as epic of feminine courage."[7] After four years of the trade, Susan emerges strengthened from the experiences, which in contrast had stolen Mary Denbigh's youth and health. A great admirer of manliness, which he equated with courage, Phillips conceived of Susan's Tenderloin life as one that would have destroyed her had she not possessed masculine endurance. Instead, and at no cost to her innocent and hopeful nature, she becomes a successful urban warrior. Her survival and eventual fame as an actress are thus linked to her heroism rather than to the sexual manipulation of the woman of the streets.

Phillips's work is distinct from that of the other imaginers we have studied not only because he elevates a prostitute to success, but because he refuses to moralize about her life. Viewed within the context of his journalistic pieces, magazine articles, and more than twenty novels, *Susan Lenox* is Phillips's only work to fully articulate a philosophy of feminine self-reliance. In her ability to climb to fame, Susan is far superior to the husband-hunting debutantes and shallow society wives of his other fiction. In her defiance of convention she also transcends the short-lived rebellions of his New Woman characters, who enter traditional marriage and relinquish the very freedom they had claimed to seek.

In our time, Phillips has been confused with a middle-of-the-road feminist.[8] His own era more correctly characterized him as one with contempt for American women, and a typical response to his work was that such portraits of women "would not make friends for the artist."[9] A number of his novels do juxtapose the wife, frustrated by her aimless life and subordinate position, with the professional woman who at first happily disdains such lack of purpose and marital subordination. What modern critics forget is that, like Harold Frederic before him, Phillips carefully undermines virtually all his New Women by relegating them to society marriages. His philosophy of women is further complicated by the fact that although he wrote a two-volume novel glorifying a prostitute, he constantly denigrates woman for a seductivenesses born of what he termed her "slavish and shameful position" as man's "cajoler and dependent."[10]

All of Phillips's works exhibit a split between a belief in female moral inferiority and a longing for a manly heroine who could transcend woman's limitations. Paradoxically, the prostitute emerges as that heroine. He identifies her not with the coquettish subservience he ascribes to most women, respectable or fallen, but with what he considers the masculine desire to dominate life. Susan Lenox becomes his masterful woman, her mettle tested but her innocence miraculously untouched by the vice trade. Inevitably such manliness in a prostitute calls forth the very liberated sexuality that defeminizing her was designed to undercut, and Phillips retreats into an inconsistent evocation of Susan as an old-fashioned girl. His female hero has conquered life, but she has done it untouched by the carnal: ideally male in strength, ideally female in chastity.

More than any other author studied here, Phillips romanticized the prostitute. Rather than acknowledge in her what he saw as the sex trickery of all women, he depicted his streetwalking protagonist as a strangely asexual mixture of femininity and masculinity, although he stopped short of recognizing the androgynous implications of such a character. Still, *Susan Lenox: Her Fall and Rise* remains a radical attempt to transcend late-Victorian assumptions about male dominance and female subservience, about the respectable woman as chaste and the fallen one as sinful. To properly understand how a prostitute became Phillips's American heroine, however, one must view his novel as the culmination of a literary quest for the female hero dating from his earliest days as a journalist and novelist.

* * * * *

David Graham Phillips was raised in midwestern comfort far removed from the seamy and impoverished urban settings of his most ambitious novel. He was born in Madison, Indiana, in 1867 to a banker father and a mother descended from the Revolutionary War hero Light-Horse Harry Lee. First a student at Indiana's DePauw University, he soon transferred to Princeton, from which he graduated in 1887. After apprentice stints on two Cincinnati newspapers, he went East again in 1890 to further his journalistic career. There, covering the Police Court beat for the *New York Sun*, he extended the study of the lower depths he had begun as a crime reporter in Cincinnati.[11]

In 1893, as London correspondent for the *New York World*, Phillips scored a success with his coverage of the sinking of the British battleship *Victoria* showing a resourcefulness which Harold Frederic, his rival London correspondent at the *Times*, must have admired. (Strangely, there is no evidence that the enterprising newsmen ever met.) By 1896, coincidentally not long after the *World* joined other metropolitan papers to carry front-page headlines about Stephen Crane's rescue of the morally dubious Dora Clark, Phillips had become an editorial writer for the daily. In 1902, he was able to leave journalism for freelance work and fiction. By then, he had clearly established himself as a versatile and prolific observer of the metropolitan scene. He was a well-versed, to quote some sample titles, in "The Bowery at Night" and "The City's Back Yard" as in "David Hill's Up-to Date Career in Purely Machine Politics" and "The Men Who Made the Steel Trust."

Among his earliest journalistic pieces, written years before *Susan Lenox* presented as its heroine the working girl who takes up streetwalking, was "The Union of Sixth Avenue and Broadway," published in *Harper's Weekly* in 1891 when Phillips was twenty-four.[12] Written in homage to the young women of "doubtful respectability" who passed him on the sidewalks of New York, the sketches steer clear of the censor by focusing on chorines and actresses, but Phillips slips in allusions to the prostitute in his mention of girls who are " 'about town' people" (302). He has only admiration for all of these attractive young women, who walk so jauntily past the corner of Sixth Avenue and Broadway in the Thirties. It is a locale he prudently refrains from further identifying for a proper *Harper's* audience. It is the heart of the Tenderloin—and the very place where Dora Clark would be arrested in the mid-90's.

Phillips was never known as a prose stylist, but this setting certainly inspires some of his best writing. He passes over the dinginess of Sixth Avenue to concentrate on Broadway, with its "electric lights flashing and gleaming, each with a luminous mist about it." The "yellow eye[d] carriages" contain "women in handsome evening bravery" (302) and cabmen who call out to the pretty pedestrians moving rapidly past. Phillips paints a word picture of the rushed activity of the evening cityscape in a way which anticipates the visual artistry of John Sloan. In 1907, the great Ash Can Group artist would create his own *Sixth Avenue and Thirtieth Street,* a painting which leaves no doubt that the laughing women passing the Sixth Avenue Elevated are prostitutes.

In "The Union of Sixth Avenue and Broadway" Phillips is the wondering observer of urban mores rather than the acerbic critic he would soon become. The men and women he sees hurrying by seem "strange, interesting people" willing to "steady their barks on the uncertain sea of adventure" (302). In his fantasy the men are mysteriously romantic figures who sport diamonds, wear fine clothes, and live on the edge. (Later on, he will be more critical of the type when he depicts Freddie Palmer, the sharklike gangster-pimp who lures Susan Lenox.) Susan's precursors receive even more praise:

The girls have short curly hair generally, and bright, keen eyes and ready tongues. They range *all the way in both directions from doubtful respectability;* they are *self-reliant* and *man-like* in many ways; they have learned not to be bashful in *asking things of an inattentive world.* (302) (emphasis added)

Earlier Phillips had admired the "handsome evening bravery" of the women in passing carriages. The sketch as a whole conflates feminine attractiveness and masculine self-confidence. The working girls' short hair even suggests that they have streamlined themselves for urban combat. These are the women who must be tough but alluring. Their livings depend on the patrons of music halls, variety theaters, and less respectable places where men hunt for feminine entertainment. Self-marketing becomes an emblem of womanly independence. Theirs, Phillips observes, is a typically American quest:

[T]o live in their own flat, is their dream; loss of youth and poverty is their horror. Sometimes they realize the dream; the horror they never miss. But some of them manage to stave it off a good while. They are always laughing loudly, gayly, in the streets; the smiles never leave their faces, and their ranks never decrease. (302)

Despite this rather lyrical vision of the fast city woman as a valiant optimist, it would be two decades before *Susan Lenox* resurrected the kind of manly heroine encountered in this youthful sketch. Certainly Phillips's early fiction, of which more will be said later, makes no attempt to do so. *The Great God Success* (1901), his first novel, centers on a working girl down on her luck who becomes the mistress of a successful newsman.[13] Rather than profit from her improved living standard, she develops a pathetic dependence on him which hastens her Camille-like death. Nor does a flirtatious secondary character in his next novel, *A Woman Ventures* (1902), reap the rewards of her burgeoning career as an actress and companion of men-about-town. She marries one of her admirers, whom she makes miserable by her capriciousness, and destroys herself through cocaine addiction.

A very early piece, "Foolish Girls Who Rouge," written in 1890 for the *Cincinnati Times-Star,* illuminates the ambivalence about sexual womanhood which prompted Phillips to create such morally weak characters.[14] A commentary on cosmetics, the essay anticipates Phillips's later denunciations of women's armament of sex charms, from their corsets and perfumes which improve on nature to their falsely passionate glances which beckon so seductively. In a way reminiscent of discussions of the urban predator in mid-century "wicked city" fiction, Phillips dwells with Swiftian misogyny on the hollow cheeks and ravages of age that the "sham element" (76) of rouge is meant to efface. Men must detect the deception, Phillips instructs, lest they fall into the toils of these metropolitan temptresses. To see "what is the matter" (77), they need only determine if the fine growth of down on a woman's face looks unnaturally red, and Woman as Deceiver will have no power to seduce.

In her useful history of American attitudes toward beauty, Lois Banner notes that as late as the 1930's there was a lingering nineteenth-century belief that the use of cosmetics identified the wearer as a prostitute.[15] Decades before the 30's Phillips is both playing on the association of cosmetics and female promiscuity and issuing the warning that woman is not what she appears. While it is not clear whether the rouged foolishness of woman consists of her flouting morality or of her illusion that man cannot penetrate her facade or both, the young Phillips clearly distrusts what his earliest novel terms "painted women." Might not the attractive and self-reliant girl appearing so "courageous" in her "evening bravery" turn out to be an urban parasite—and homely at that?

Viewed against the many novels on feminine conduct that he was soon to produce, Phillips's early journalism reveals a mind divided. He admired the real-life predecessors of Susan Lenox, attractive, hard-pressed girls who confidently engaged in the difficult pursuit of city success. Such admiration, however, warred with his greater suspicion that woman by nature preferred sexual manipulation to the manly virtue of hard work. In the next phase of his career, works like *A Woman Ventures*, *Old Wives for New* (1907), and the posthumous *The Price She Paid* (1912) explored the conditions under which women placed in compromising situations could attempt to surmount them.[16] During these years, Phillips worked secretly on the novel which would be his most forceful statement about woman's ability to transcend the limits of her sex and to emerge from the urban sexual battlefield strong rather that weak, innocent rather than corrupt. For years he wrote and rewrote *Susan Lenox*, searching for his ideal woman, part warrior, part ingenue. At the same time his fiction muckraked the affluent American woman, whom he charged was debased by chicanery and flawed by subservience.

Phillips's mythifying vision placed Susan Lenox beyond what he saw as the feminine need to be mastered by men. His decision to transform a prostitute in this way, particularly given his disapproval of feminine wiles, must be seen in the context of theories of masculinity and femininity articulated throughout his career in fiction and essays. We now turn to representative examples of each.

* * * * *

Shortly after he began *Susan Lenox*, Phillips published a 1905 article, appropriately enough in *Success* magazine, which offered a characteristic definition of heroism.[17] It was one which many in the Progressive period, aptly described by historian James R. McGovern as a time of "exaggerated concern with manliness and its conventional concomitants power and activity,"[18] would have applauded. The object of Phillips's praise was his DePauw fraternity brother Albert J. Beveridge, who had recently become an Indiana State Senator. Beveridge was one of the few politicians whom Phillips did not find treasonous to the Senate or the American people. What most impressed him was this exemplar's strength and endurance. Phillips employs the phrase twice in tribute to this manliest of men, so "easily a leader both in the mental and the manual" (526). Used to the conquest of adversity through force of will from his earliest days in a grueling logging camp, the future Indiana politician not only survived its hazards but rose to prominence.

Phillips's art extended his praise of Beveridge, who inspired the portrait of Hampton Scarborough, the reform legislator who becomes President in the 1905 novel *The Plum Tree*. Actually there is some of Beveridge in Phillips's many politicos and captains of industry, who combine a Rooseveltian adherence to the strenuous life with the conviction that "strength equals moral power."[19] Inevitably these apostles of maleness make their own rules and possess a cynical contempt for the masses which Phillips details in good muckraking fashion. Yet, like Frank Norris and Theodore Dreiser, fellow novelists of big business, Phillips cannot restrain his admiration for these Nietzschean men of power.[20] As Joshua Craig, one of the "real men" protagonists schooled in the "cold, wet hardship" of the Beveridgian wilderness, observes, "dealing with men as individuals, I make them do what I want, and make 'em like me as I am."[21]

If, put simply, maleness is strength, femaleness is succumbing to it, a philosophy of sexual polarization amply demonstrated in *The Fashionable Adventures of Joshua Craig* (1909). Written at the height of his career, the book cost Phillips his life. A biting portrait of the "grasping woman of fashion,"[22] it inspired a crazed man who took a central character, the money-hungry narcissist Margaret Severence, to be a portrait of his sister. He shot Phillips down on a New York street and then took his own life. As the book critic Annie Nathan Meyer acidly quipped soon after the murder, given Phillips's vision of women, it was surprising that the "shot which ended his career was fired by a man."[23] Certainly Joshua Craig sees women as acquisitions, badges of his worldly success. Intrigued by the over-refined Margaret, who presides over her Washington salon as a "social ornament," he reflects: "She has some brains—the woman kind of brains...I could develop her into a real woman [who would provide] love and sympathy and children" (88).

In scene after scene with Margaret, whose inability to find a purpose in life is matched by her parade of husband-trapping wiles, this "wild man," suggesting the "rude, fierce figurehead of a Viking galley" (3), tries to bend her to his will. To the ambition possessed by Phillips's other superheroes, he adds a ferocity which borders on physical menace. He is used to commanding women with a "look that was primeval" (144), and Margaret is no exception. After a resistance which Phillips deplores as the result of her false training in coquetry, Margaret, alternately drawn and repelled by Craig's "savage arms," finds herself "shrinking and burning and trembling under his caresses" (144). Her passion, however, is less sensuality that compliance, for having titillated the reader, Phillips distances himself from the discussion of sexual conquest. He insists that what Craig has taught the once-haughty Margaret is the "wisdom" of woman's submission to man. He even reverses the kind of Victorian scenario employed by Reginald Wright Kauffman in his early novel *Jarvis of Harvard,* that of the flawed male rescued by the innately virtuous female. By teaching Margaret where woman's true fulfillment lies, Phillips emphasizes, Craig has saved her from narcissistic beauty regimens, soulless intrigues, and Washington affectation.

Those who did not so highly prize the redemptive effect of the cult of manliness echoed the *Nation's* contemptuous comment that Craig was "a boor as well as a bear,"[24] but the novel insists that Margaret will cleanse her nature through wifely obedience. At the novel's close, then, the new Mrs. Craig follows her man to a presumably uncorrupted midwest.

The triumph of masculine force over feminine passivity occurs repeatedly in Phillips's fiction. *The Grain of Dust* (1911), one of his strangest novels, concerns a wealthy lawyer's obsessive pursuit of a resisting employee.[25] Here the prey is an obscure typist, a figure Phillips usually found more sympathetic than the Margaret Severence type. But young Dorothea Hallowell exists in this novel only to demonstrate the power of the relentless Fred Norman, whose philosophy of marriage is to "treat her as the warrior must ever treat his entire domestic establishment from wife to pet dog or cat or baby" (370). In *Old Wives for New*, a somewhat more palatable hero, the plutocrat Charles Murdock, reflects on the rightness of conquering the independent Juliet Raeburn: "No woman really wants to win...If [man]...lets her win, he thinks he's even weaker that she...and so he is, by God!" (124).

Female subservience as the natural order of things seems an odd philosophy for one opposed to the exploitation of women in the labor market and vice trade. Yet with the exception of *Susan Lenox*, Phillips's novels typically concern the affluent male's attempt to curb the spoiled women of his own class. Nor is the victory easily won. Even the masterful Joshua Craig takes hundreds of pages to win the coquettish Margaret over to a respect for life outside the false glitter of the social whirl. Her less malleable counterparts in other novels often dominate through sexual manipulation, extracting money from husbands unable to prevent their wives' worship of fashion and social advancement. The tale of woe told by Godfrey Loring, the sufferer of *The Husband's Story*, chronicles his struggle to curb his wife Edna's vanity, laziness, and passion for parasiteism (sic)" (315). The very inactivity of the well-off female, the "cozener and milker of man" (*Old Wives for New,* 315), so incensed Phillips that he frequently exhorted her to practice a domesticity that would fix her mind on loving instead of exploiting her husband.[26]

For all his conviction that man ruled woman by gender right, Phillips feared her sexual potency. In a 1911 *Delineator* article sermonically entitled "What Is a Successful Wife?" he warned: "If you rule through the sex charm, you will weaken...[your husband] as a force in the world." No sooner is his anxiety voiced that he reasserts the "fact" of male dominance: "the chances are that your attempt to rule him in that crude, lazy way will soon end in humiliation for yourself" (265).

Novels like *Old Wives for New* and *The Husband's Story* make good on his threat and punish unsuccessful wives with adultery and divorce, but Phillips's fiction abounds with women who rule, at least for a time, through the sex charm, prompting his charge that they are little better than prostitutes. As one of his success-driven young men, exasperated by the machinations of a debutante wishing to move from a rich father to him, chides: "every one of you is either an odalisque or trying to get hold of some man with enough money to make her one."[27] Other references to the society woman as prostitute are less polite. From the marriage-seeking heroine who endures the repellent caresses of a millionaire fiancé in *A Woman Ventures* to a minor character in *Old Wives for New* who loathes her plutocratic mate, the bargain is the same: feminine sexual favors for masculine wealth. One husband who analyzes his wife's code might as well be discussing that of his mistress: "Us old fellows realize perfectly that it's all a matter of money with the lady—that she has hard work to conceal her dislike. But damn it, she *does* conceal it" (*Old Wives for New*, 49). There is an even blunter use of the image in one of Phillips's last works, *The Price She Paid*, the story of the well-bred Mildred Siddall, who allows her youth and beauty to be sold in wedlock to an aged rake.[28] As she ruefully acknowledges, "at all times she must be fit and ready for any and every sybaritic idea that might enter her husband's head—and other purpose she had none" (88). Although love for Joshua Craig may save Margaret Severence from thinking of herself in this way, she is willing enough to enter a marriage that may make her a man's "plaything" (*Joshua Craig*, 108).

Phillips's negative attitude toward the corrupt values of the leisured woman was a fairly common one. It was shared by some of the most respected writers of the day. Abe C. Ravitz has pointed out that no class of women was more criticized in newspapers and magazines during the first decade of the twentieth century.[29] The Progressive-minded *Outlook* magazine, for example, rang with denunciations of her. The scourge of Standard Oil, Phillips's fellow muckraker Ida Tarbell, satirically found in the woman who saw herself as a "partner in an undertaking where her function is spending" a creature of indolent uselessness.[30] So did the social and economic theorist Charlotte Perkins Gilman, among her era's most important feminist thinkers, and Anna Garlin Spencer, the noted defender of the slum girl tempted to prostitution.[31] Unlike Phillips, however, most of those who denounced the idle woman saw her as betraying woman's innate moral superiority. Whether they exhorted her to abandon the false god of social success and return to the domestic arena or to enter social service as a volunteer or professional, they retained the nineteenth-century belief in woman's instinctual "nurturant ability" and "ethical insight."[32]

Phillips, in contrast, attacked the leisured women not for betraying the feminine nature but for demonstrating it. Still, he could both deplore woman as "servant of man's appetites...and pander to them" and search for a higher feminine type. Two representative novels, one from the early and the other from the mature phase of Phillips's career, test the premise that woman can "be man's equal, make her own happiness, work out her own salvation" (*A Woman Ventures*, 41).

These words of journalist Emily Bromfield, the heroine of *A Woman Ventures*, are echoed by Juliet Raeburn, the dress shop proprietor of *Old Wives for New*, who, like Emily, typifies "the new order in women" (97). They have carved their careers very differently. Compelled to support herself after her debt-ridden father's death and her rejection by a rich fiancé, Emily has groped her way to taking up newspaper work as a last resort. In contrast, the wealthy and confident Juliet had always embraced the independence of single life, and to that end invested shrewdly in fashion shops. Yet each woman possesses the qualities Phillips found so admirable in Senator Beveridge. Emily's "keen and courageous mind" (39) enables her to scoop her male rivals who are covering a bloody Pennsylvania mining strike. When one of her colleagues warns, "This is no place for a woman," she counters, "it's just the place for a reporter" (97). Juliet Raeburn enters only a slightly more welcoming profession, that of the entrepreneur. Her chief enterprise, a Fifth Avenue dress salon, is a monument to Gilded Age opulence, complete with marble fountains and—an emblem of her own business acumen—a fresco of Minerva, the goddess of wisdom. Juliet markets femininity, but she is clearly not immersed in it; she relaxes like a Joshua Craig, journeying to the mountains in search of the grizzly bears she downs on the first shot.

These women are further associated with what Emily terms the "masculine quality" (84) by their scorn of those who barter themselves in marriage. In the voice of Phillips himself, Juliet acerbically remarks that the married woman is too "lazy" to work, but not to "hire herself permanently to the same appetite" (471). While Juliet shuns emotional involvement on principle, Emily reverses the marital gender roles. She informs Marlowe, the malleable newsman whom she has wed, "I don't want you as my husband. I want you to be my lover" (118). She further insures her freedom by ordering him to keep the marriage a secret. When he acts much like a neglected wife and petulantly throws his infidelities up at her, she promptly divorces him.

What undercuts these New Women, as Phillips rather melodramatically proves, is a Real Man. No sooner does the ambitious Emily achieve professional success than she becomes smitten with her editor, Stilson, who had been her mentor and whose dark marital past lends him a Gothic mysteriousness. Emily soon succumbs to the electrifying presence of this Gilded Age Orson Welles. Responding much like

Margaret Severence to Joshua Craig, she reflects, "This is the man of all men...[B]y myself I am nothing" (221,223). As if erasing her former accomplishments, she refuses a lucrative job away from Stilson and thinks only of being "ruled" by him. Juliet Raeburn too becomes a convert to the religion of womanly duty. At first reluctant to enter into an affair with the unhappily married and magnetic Charles Murdock, she abandons the management of her dress business to nurse him through a serious illness. Transformed overnight from a resourceful businesswoman to an angel of the sickroom, she so exemplifies the womanly sacrifice Phillips advocated in "What Is A Successful Wife?" that Murdock's decision to divorce his indolent, useless wife and marry Juliet is presented as a moral act. Juliet's former independence is as nothing to the lesson she mouths: "When a real woman finds her master, she follows him" (495).

As his New Woman characters initially demonstrate, Phillips measures feminine self-reliance by invoking the masculine. Yet for him, as for many traditionalists of the time, the manly heroine is a contradiction in terms, for her heroism conflicts with her duty as a wife.[33] Thus when the Emily Bromfields and Juliet Raeburns find the men who can dominate them, they revert, as a vanquished Emily phrases it, to "only women after all" *(A Woman Ventures,* 285). Unable to envision the New Woman's marital equality, Phillips sends his once-manly heroines back to the domestic arena. There, "with no shadow or taint of pecuniary interest" *(The Reign of Gilt,* 272), they will practice the enlightened subservience he had urged for all women.

Ironically, in being among the few to meet Phillips's standard of submissive womanhood, these reformed New Women failed his greater test, that of manliness. He continued to search for a woman who could pass it. Perhaps because by the nature of her trade the prostitute was, in Joanna Russ's word, "unowned,"[34] she became the one woman whom Phillips did not relegate to the Victorian separate sphere of the hearth. In allying the prostitute with the male role, Phillips would give her his highest compliment, one he refused to pay the more conventional women of his other works. In *Susan Lenox,* the prostitute would become an American heroine, though, as in the other writers under scrutiny, the denial of sexuality which shaped her portrait would result in weakening it.

Phillips's misogynistic treatment of American women did not prevent him from being regarded as one of the most promising writers of the day.[35] If there is not enough evidence to support Alfred Kazin's contention that Phillips was *the* social novelist of his time, he was certainly widely read. His novels, many of them serialized in leading magazines, routinely sold an impressive 100,000 copies.[36] He was admired by Upton Sinclair and George Bernard Shaw. H.L. Mencken, who particularly admired *The Husband's Story,* for a time considered him the "leading American novelist."[37] Phillips's foes decried his penchant for the thesis novel, his shallow characters, and artless style.[38] Well before *Susan Lenox*, he was decidedly challenging genteel convention. Thus, his many portraits of well-to-do adulterers and courtesan wives provoked charges of his "disregard for decency and virtue," "vulgarity," and "absolutely needless coarseness."[39] Defenders like the influential muckraker C.E. Russell pointed out that Phillips was a reporter, "faithful to conditions as they exist."[40] Even one of his harshest critics, *The New York Times*, though dubious about his ability to portray women, conceded that his novels contained "some very truthful pictures and point[ed] a useful moral" about modern marriage.[41]

Two years after his death in 1911, Phillips was still important—or controversial—enough for his publisher, D. Appleton and Company, to bring out three of his posthumous works criticizing the idle American wife. But Appleton balked at publishing *Susan Lenox*. It was, after all, a prostitution novel whose central character was unrepentant and unpunished and whose scenes with pimps and clients made *The House of Bondage* seem tame. Shortly before his death, anticipating his publisher's fear of legal action from censors, Phillips met with Appleton's editor, J.H. Sears, and convinced him to publish the book.[42] The tortuous publishing history of *Susan Lenox*, which Phillips did not live to witness, would have disgusted him.

The first installment of *Susan Lenox: Her Fall and Rise*, trumpeted as the "greatest American novel," was published in the widely read *Hearst's Magazine*, known for its timely fiction and fine illustrations.[43] The serialization began in 1915, four years after an assassin ended Phillips's life. His sister, Caroline Frevert, had contracted for serial publication soon after his death, but Hearst Publications, like Appleton and Company, feared the Society for the Suppression of Vice and delayed. Such fears were not groundless. When the work was finally serialized, censors passed over the initial installments dealing with Susan's Indiana girlhood, her forced marriage to a backwoods farmer, and her flights to Cincinnati and then New York, all episodes which *Hearst's* had carefully bowdlerized. The May 1916 installment was a sanitized version of the episode in which Susan, now a cloak model, receives advances from a buyer whose account her employer craves. Anthony Comstock's successor, John S. Sumner, promptly reacted by taking the magazine to court on obscenity.[44] As it turned out, *Hearst's* had deleted the episode in which Susan, bowing to pressure from her employer, sleeps with a client. The magazine in its self-censorship had done its work well. The obscenity case was dismissed, and the remainder of the precensored installments comprising the novel ran until January 1917.[45]

In addition to excising all references to Susan's soliciting men, accompanying them to hotels, and indulging in violent or reckless behavior, *Hearst's* further attempted to cleanse Susan's conduct. Each installment was prefaced by Jesus's forgiveness of the adulteress: "Neither do I condemn thee, go, and sin no more." The famous Howard Chandler Christy contributed illustrations which gave Susan an added innocence.[46] To disassociate her from the stereotypical seductress, Christy lightened the hair which Phillips had described as dark. Christy's Susan is a classic beauty, by turns demure and soulful. She is the wistful ingenue warily navigating the sea of life, never the woman of the town immersed in it. In one of her early encounters with a man she picks up in a Cincinnati park, Phillips's description, which *Hearst's* printed beneath one Christy drawing, reads: "Susan observed him, saw that he was watching her, but she pretended not to notice him." In the magazine version, she accepts a friendly meal and they part, chastely.

The Christy illustration may well have titillated *Hearst's* readership with a less-than-ingenuous Susan. Her lovely features assume a studied obliviousness to the man she has "noticed." Still, she remains the ingenue in a situation fraught with sexual peril. It is the young man, eyeing her as she plays the modest maiden, who is the aggressor. Christy embroiders on the Phillips text by placing another woman nearby, most likely a professional in quest of customers. In contrast to her, Susan is indeed the reluctant prostitute.

Whether the readership accepted Susan's innocence or not, *Susan Lenox*, F.L. Mott informs us in his authoritative history of American magazines, was *Hearst's* greatest box office success.[47] To prevent a similar triumph for Phillips's publisher, Appleton and Company, Sumner's Vice Society again tried to use the courts to block publication. Some New York booksellers fearfully anticipated the outcome of the proceedings against Appleton and removed the novel from their shelves. *Publishers' Weekly* praised their act and pontificated, "Mr. Sumner deserves the thanks of the retail book trade."[48] In such a climate, Caroline Phillips Frevert, frightened by what she was as the adverse publicity of a second obscenity case, came to a compromise with the Vice Society. In it Appleton withdrew the original, uncensored edition, which had been published three months before in February of 1917. Sumner then excised one hundred passages of references to the prostitution activity of Susan and her sisters in the trade, and the original edition was withdrawn. [49]

The effectiveness of the censors in obliterating all trace of Phillips's intended version can be measured by the fact that when a university press reissued the altered novel in 1977, complete with an afterword by an important critic, a note erroneously claimed that the edition was the original one.[50] What will be analyzed here, however, is the real *Susan Lenox*. To analyze the novel properly must be to discuss the original version and restore the excisions which robbed the protagonist of the very experiences which had constituted her heroism.

Susan Lenox appeared after the white slave agitation had passed; by then the public regarded the prostitute as a venereally diseased menace to the troops about to fight a world war. Perhaps that is why the novel never attained the international celebrity of Kauffman's earlier best-seller. There is no doubt, though, that its sales were boosted by what one student of American censorship has termed the notoriety which is the standard side effect of anti-obscenity proceedings.[51] Isaac Marcosson, one of the few keepers of the Phillips flame, alleged that the novel was the "book sensation of the year."[52] If such was the case, interest cooled with the issuing of the censored version.

Critical response to the novel in its original form ranged from condemnation of its obscenity to praise for Susan as a noble heroine in a realistically drawn underclass setting. Opponents of the uncensored novel objected the most to its idealization of a prostitute. The *New York Times*, which had not reproached *The House of Bondage*, wrote of *Susan Lenox* that it "would have been much better for Mr. Phillips's reputation and the repute of American letters if it had never been published." Sounding like John S. Sumner himself, the *Times's* reviewer concluded by blasting the book as "revolting filth."[53] James Gerould of the midwestern *Bellman* swelled the anti-Phillips ranks. He expressed outrage that a woman "so sodden with vice...should escape all physical penalties" and, thus, the retribution he felt that her life merited.[54]

The tide, however, was gradually turning against the censors. The recently founded, liberal *New Republic*, for instance, reflected the loosening of attitudes about sex. While acknowledging the book's romantic view of prostitution, it found nothing of the pornographic. Rather, Phillips had "sought to relate his notion of [Susan's]...heroism to his horror of woman's debased economic condition."[55] Predictably, *Hearst's* extolled Susan's stoicism as if she were Hester Prynne, to whom a *Current Literature* reviewer also likened her.[56] The *Minneapolis Journal* went even farther, comparing her to the great fallen heroines of nineteenth-century Russian and British literature, Anna Karenina and Tess of the D'Urbervilles:

[T]his Susan Lenox redeems herself as one of those sisters of her could; and one knows that, howsoever the body of her has been victimized, the soul of her is great...She was made nobler by the suffering she passed through, by the efforts she put forth, and by her victorious will.[57]

Like most novels of prostitution by American authors, *Susan Lenox* has attracted minimal notice from scholars. Those few who have tried to resurrect it have split along much the same lines as commentators in Phillips's day. In the debate about whether a woman could emerge unscathed from her sordid experiences, they bow to modernism only by replacing the genteel charge of vulgarity with that of bad art.[58] Phillips's modern proponents extoll Susan's "fortitude and purpose" and her ability to keep her personality intact in the most desperate situations.[59] If she inspires her detractors' dismissive scorn by seeming utterly implausible, she impresses her admirers by her iconoclasm and individuality.[60] Only Elizabeth Janeway, although she did not have the benefit of the original edition, noted in passing that Phillips grafted the masculine personality onto his heroine.[61] This idea is well worth exploring at length. In all of his other fiction, Phillips, bound by his own distrust of woman's ability to escape her gender, had not been able to create a woman hero. Only the prostitute would free him from these restrictions and reconcile his conflict between a belief in feminine self-abnegation and self-reliance, between domestic woman and the woman of experience.

* * * * *

For Susan Lenox, the manly struggle for survival in a hostile environment begins at birth. She is born in Sutherland, Indiana, the illegitimate daughter of a woman who refuses to name the father and who dies in childbirth. Her entry into the world is commemorated by a nurse's dour pronouncements, "The child's dead" (I, 1), and "Everybody'll be glad" (I, 3). Revived by a physician who comments on her amazing constitution—the first of many references to her endurance—Susan will need all of her powers. Life soon enough becomes a battle against her relatives' vengeful disapproval. They fear the town's conviction that she will repeat her mother's sins, and, when she blossoms into a teenaged beauty, wrongly assume that she has seduced a town youth. Jilted by her affluent, if hardly courageous, young man when he discovers that she is illegitimate, Susan attempts to flee her family's control. She is tracked down and married off to an atavistic farmer, Jeb Ferguson. Phillips admired Samuel Richardson's great seduction novel *Clarissa,* and the assaults on her virtue and pride Susan endures from Ferguson are reminiscent of it. He is no Lovelace, but Susan, like the innocent Clarissa, is raped, and held against her wishes. Like Richardson's heroine, Susan, through force of will, remains spiritually undefiled.

Still, her marriage is the worst prostitution in which she will engage. Ferguson is both a customer and a folk version of a pimp: "That's the way to get along with me and get nice clothes—do what I say. With them that crosses me I'm mighty ugly. But you ain't a-goin' to cross me" (I, 149). Unlike Clarissa, Susan wishes to live. She escapes the morning after the rape, and lives in the forest on raw eggs pilfered from an outlying farm. With the help of Rob Spenser, a young newspaperman she comes upon in the woods and whom later she will more than help in kind, she escapes her husband's pursuit. In the first of the rather contrived series of reversals Phillips employs in the novel to heighten her difficulties, she loses track of him. She changes her name to Lorna Sackville, and fends for herself by joining a riverboat acting troupe. After a fire destroys the boat, she goes to Cincinnati. There, in one of the "offending" episodes omitted from *Hearst's* serialization and the censored novel, she sells herself for the first time to support her ailing manager-friend, Burlingham.

Burlingham's death marks the beginning of Susan's period as a young woman alone in the city, a frequent theme of period writers, many of whom took Phillips's position that with few skills a woman soon had to consider prostituting herself. Susan confronts this economic dilemma for much of the lengthy novel. She does not become a full-time prostitute, however, until she experiences sweatshop life and even helps support an impoverished family she befriends. She then alleviates her own poverty with a brief encounter with an affluent man, and goes off to New York as the mistress of Rod Spenser, to whom she has once again appealed for help.

Susan's is not the standard Phillips story of the woman dependent on a male provider, for she soon leaves Spenser to test her strength again. In Kauffmanesque fashion, Phillips interweaves the narrative of her subsequent trials and her struggle to keep "straight" with tales of her co-workers and neighbors, stories of hunger, ill health and the lure of the fast life. Attempting, like Kauffman, to create a documentary effect, Phillips includes statistics on women's labor and points to Susan's poorly paid respectable work—$3 at the paper box factory, $4 as a hat trimmer, and only tips and board as a saloon singer.

Unlike writers before him, though, Phillips presents Susan's decision to enter prostitution in earnest (sporadic encounters to supplement her meager income had dotted her life since Cincinnati) as a plausible strategy for survival. Her attitude toward the trade is markedly different from the desperation of Crane's street waif, the resignation of Frederic's unwed mother, the capitulation of Kauffman's brothel slave. After respectable work can no longer sustain her, she simply accepts the fact that "the woman alone...must make the bargain she could and accept the world's terms" (II, 104). For her prostitution is a tough urban apprenticeship, one in which she can "get over being a woman" (II, 192).

Ironically, her mentor in what he terms "living like a man" (II, 173), the slick procurer Freddie Palmer, is her greatest enemy. At first their encounter is straight out of Reginald Wright Kauffman's white slave novel. Palmer lures Susan to a place where he drugs and rapes her. When she wakes the next day, he gives her a new name, Queenie Brown, and attempts to control her through threats and blows. What happens instead is that, although for a time she does walk the street for Palmer, she learns from his sadistic "lessons in manliness" (II, 143) to harden her will and suppress the feminine longing for protection.

The narrative moves quickly to Susan's success in overcoming her exploiter. In one scene excised from the censored edition, she strikes and threatens to kill Palmer if he ever brutalizes her again, taunting him that she prefers to be free. She further enrages him by refusing the more lucrative customers he suggests, behavior far more likely to render her a police blotter statistic than a free woman. Yet central to Phillips's myth of the prostitute as Amazon is that she thrives on adversity. Thus in another scene which understandably shocked the period censors, Susan bests Palmer by reversing their gender roles. As he tries to subdue her by brute force, it is she who knocks him unconscious. She escapes to another part of the city and begins work as a freelance prostitute.

The Tenderloin which had claimed the lives of her literary predecessors only toughens Susan Lenox. She tests her strength in the urban wilderness much as an Albert Beveridge or a Joshua Craig first tested theirs in a natural one. Where Kauffman's Mary Denbigh had failed, Phillips's iron heroine succeeds. No venereal disease afflicts her; she avoids illness and unwanted pregnancy alike. The alcohol she constantly drinks, later joined to the opium she takes in seamy Chinatown dens, magically act to brace this woman with the constitution of a man.

On the sociological level, Susan is the hard-pressed working woman rather than the manly heroine. Phillips emphasizes that her decision to remain a prostitute after leaving her pimp demonstrates the truth of the Progressive assertion that lower-paying respectable work could "degrade her more that his life" (II, 224). Susan's disdain for impoverished respectability also echoes the sentiments of Margaret von Staden, a San Francisco streetwalker in the early 1900's, and Maimie Pinzer, who plied the trade in Philadelphia around the same time. Von Staden's memoir and Pinzer's letters to a benefactor bear out a modern historian's contention that prostitution seemed to some working girls to promise upward mobility.[62] Susan Lenox herself finds an undefeated economic climber in the prostitute Ida Driscoll, whom she meets before being taken over by Freddie Palmer. Ida balances regular clients, part-time brothel work, and romances with men to whom she presents herself as a respectable woman. Her plan to start a business on her savings seems feasible enough. Susan is not as well-established as Ida, but when she is free of Palmer, she does acquire a clean tenement room and a measure of financial freedom.

On a mythic level, however, the Susan who escapes Freddie's exploitation is an Amazonian figure of iron strength and manly ability. Mary Denbigh's customers, pitying her used look, educated her about the system which had enchained her. In contrast, a man whom the youthful-looking Susan solicits (changed in the censored version to a doctor she visits for a check-up) is so awed by a healthfulness greater that his own that he predicts she will have a long life and even concludes, "I envy you" (II, 167). Phillips's acknowledgment that the average prostitute was no Susan Lenox is often buried in a hymn of praise to his heroine. He argues repeatedly that the self-reliance which had enabled her to live on raw eggs, to reject a life as Rod Spenser's kept woman, and to vanquish Freddie Palmer characterizes her prostitution activity as well. She certainly lacks the sense of shame which plagued her nineteenth-century sisters.

What Phillips refuses to explore is the sexual defiance that Susan's street life suggested. The modern critics who have likened Susan to Moll Flanders or Tom Jones have not recognized that in Phillips's vision she is not a sexual adventurer.[63] Rather, she is the eternal optimist, who, encountering perils to her selfhood, sloughs off the pain of experience, "unaffected," Phillips writes, "by what she had been forced to undergo" (II, 242). Her dealings with men are not real sexual encounters but "buffetings" and "rude contacts" (II, 289), much as if she were Huck Finn making her way down an urban Mississippi.

To characterize the heroic ideal of nineteenth-century American literature, R.W.B. Lewis coined the now-famous term American Adam. Lewis's Adamic hero stood alone, "self-reliant and self-propelling, ready to confront whatever awaited him with the aid of his own unique and inherent resources."[64] As the exemplar of an American myth which "saw life and history as just beginning," this character, in Leslie Fiedler's phrase, was dedicated to the "dream of an escape from culture and a renewal of youth."[65] Far as Susan Lenox might seem from the "fair unfallen Adam" of classic American literature,[66] Phillips allies her to him. In one representative passage, for example, she is far more reminiscent of the boyish innocent who lights out for the territory than of the streetwalker who escapes her pimp:

In so much wandering she had acquired the habit of closing up an episode of life as a traveler puts behind him the railway journey at its end. She was less that half an hour from her life in the Tenderloin; it was as completely her past as it would ever be. The cards had been shuffled; a new deal was on. (II, 197)

The defender of Susan Lenox transforms her prostitution from feminine seduction to masculine endurance. Transcending the sins of Eve, she becomes a hero with elements of the time-defying American Adam. Phillips's masculinizing strategy lifts her out of the category of panders to male appetites in which Phillips placed other women. In a truly androgynous vision of the prostitute, such manly qualities would be balanced with those of the "whore with the heart of gold," Bret Harte's Miggles of 1870's western fame: gentleness, nurturing, compassion.[67] The dominant male in Susan would then co-exist with the comfort-giving female. Phillips, however, convinced as he was of female inferiority, did not associate women with such maternal qualities. Therefore, when he acknowledges the womanly element in his heroine, the ideal Susan represents is that of purity, i.e. the moral antithesis of sexual duplicity. For all that she has endured, she is the same sweet girl who fled the brutality of a drunken backwoodsman. However inconsistent in one supposedly so toughened by life, she joins innate refinement to girlish innocence. Even her loutish customers resentfully admit that they are in the presence of a lady. Freddie Palmer recognizes in her the same refinement which had impressed her sweatshop and tenement acquaintances. He taunts her with being "Sunday-schoolish" and sees in her face a woman "on the right side of the line" (II, 289)), the same images which Howard Chandler Christy explored in his *Hearst's* drawings of her.

Susan's finest qualities, however, issue from her maleness. When she leaves prostitution, it is not as the rescued penitent but as the savior of a man defeated by the kind of hardships which have invigorated her. After four years on the street, Susan encounters Rod Spenser, now a Bowery alcoholic. In the hands of a Bret Harte, the prostitute's decision to help the man who once aided her would be sentimentally depicted as feminine altruism. To Phillips Susan is merely astute enough to see that a reformed Rod could help her in the theater, which in fact comes to pass. She thus cares for him, supports him until he is working again as a playwright, and inspires him to the recognition that "I ought to have been the woman and you the man" (II, 271).

Susan moves swiftly from his benefactor to his mistress to the globetrotting companion of a now-smitten Freddie Palmer, in love with the only woman he could never conquer. What Phillips scorned in his previous fiction, the woman paid for by men, here he does not. Nor does the fact that Susan allows herself to be taken in hand by a spiritual father, the playwright and director Robert Brent, whom she had met through Spenser. Brent becomes a mentor, drawing out her acting talent and helping her establish a Broadway career. Interestingly, Susan is indirectly responsible for his death, for a jealous Palmer has him murdered. Oblivious to the *femme fatale* implications of this plot episode, Phillips employs it as a melodramatic way out for Susan. She is left Brent's heir, free of the domination of men at last. As a suitable ending to a fairy tale of prostitution, a beaten and womanized Freddie Palmer sobbingly tells her that she has "pull[ed] through everything and anything—and come out stronger and better looking and better off" (II, 542).

In describing *Susan Lenox* to a hesitant Appleton and Company, Phillips had initially termed it a sociological discussion of the city.[68] The novel illuminates this ambiguous reference, for it describes prostitution as the work of a group of women who prefer it to the sweatshop, factory, or sales jobs of their peers or of their own past lives. However, Phillips subordinates a documentary interest in conditions driving women to streetwalking to Susan's paid sexual activity. He visualizes it as the supreme test for one so "courageous for adventure—any adventure" (II, 135). Long before he envisioned Susan Lenox, he was in quest of a woman who could triumph over oppressive circumstance. Reigned in by his own distrust of women, he found in the unlikely figure of the prostitute an individual who could achieve autonomy.

Nevertheless, in his emphasis on Susan as a member of an aristocracy of talent and will, Phillips refused to explore the ways in which prostitution constituted a trial by fire. Nor, although he implied it, did he examine how prostitution had provided her with a life free from the social tyrannies which had led her to flee a repressive family and a grotesque marriage. A brief survey of writers whose work presents alternate approaches to the prostitute survivor can illuminate Phillips's reluctance to keep Susan Lenox in the very life which had defined her ability to endure.

* * * * *

Between 1911, when *Susan Lenox* was completed at the height of Progressive interest in the prostitute, and 1917, when the American entry into the First World War diverted national attention from her life, a number of writers joined Phillips in depicting a woman who lived rather than died from the trade. Among the most notable of those opposed to Reginald Kauffman's vision of the doomed white slave were the reformer Brand Whitlock, the cultural and political radical John Reed and his fellow contributors to the Socialist journal *The Masses,* and the Greenwich Village poet Alfred Kreymbourg. Their short fiction and sketches provided varied images of feminine resilience in a profession most novelists, except Phillips, had assured readers killed off those women who practiced it.

In 1912, Whitlock, a journalist, lawyer, and midwestern reform politician, published "The Girl That's Down," a tale which centers on Mace, an "old offender" who is constantly picked up for soliciting.[69] Whitlock deplores the social indifference that decrees her arrest while letting her customers off. To prove that the hardened prostitute would respond to a more compassionate system, he focuses on Mace's gratitude when a liberal judge lets her and another woman picked up for soliciting go free. Outside in the street, Mace suggests to her now cohort that they try a different life: "Not that way this morning, kid. We'll start the other way. It won't hurt to try" (230).

Although Mace is described as a cynical Night Court prostitute, Whitlock rather implausibly sentimentalized her response to the judge's leniency. No one had ever before "descended to her from the world above with a kind look, a helpful word, or even a cup of water" (219). What is more noteworthy about the tale is Whitlock's vision of a played-out Mace starting the world anew. Her world-weariness anticipates that of O'Neill's Anna Christie, though Mace is older and has lost the power to attract. In any event, her prospects are bleak indeed compared to the celebrity triumphs of Susan Lenox.

Quite different from Whitlock's tired streetwalker are the brash attention-seekers of John Reed's sketches in *The Masses*. Reed was an editor of the journal, founded in 1911 in the first flowering of Greenwich Village cultural defiance. For six years *The Masses,* dedicated to an "attack [on] old systems, old morals, old prejudices,"[70] opened its lively pages to socialists and anarchists, feminists and apologists of free love. Reed himself published everything from sympathetic portraits of the Mexican revolutionary Pancho Villa and of striking Paterson silk workers to stories of the war in Europe and character studies of free-spirited Tenderloin women. In the years prior to the Russian Revolution and the publication of *Ten Days That Shook the World* (1919) and his involvement in founding the Communist Party in America, Reed was less the doctrinaire political thinker that the free-wheeling social revolutionary. In the wry assessment of his one-time friend, the political commentator Walter Lippmann, the "central passion of his life...[was] an inordinate desire to be arrested."[71] As the self-appointed defender of Village Bohemianism, Reed was particularly disdainful of Progressive efforts to reform the working girl who sought love in the dance halls or the prostitute who sought customers in the street. Leave the promiscuous woman, Reed cautioned, to be herself, untrammeled by opprobrium or arrest.

Brand Whitlock's Police Court scenario ends with a prostitute inspired to self-reform by a compassionate judge. In Reed's 1913 *Masses* sketch, "A Taste of Justice," the prostitutes who are routinely given ten days for soliciting leave the courtroom as unregenerate as they entered.[72] Not particularly attractive or admirable, these "squat, hard-faced, 'cheap' girls [are] like dusty little birds wrapped too tightly in their feathers" (81). Kauffman would have rendered them pathetic. Phillips would have dwelled on the superior ones who beat the system. The Reed, they are women who "cursed at...or guyed [him]...according to whether or not they had any dinner" (8). With their "insolent laughter" and "intricate knowledge" of the Tenderloin, they know their world, he remarks admiringly, "perfectly."[73]

There was obviously a great period reluctance to discuss the prostitute as a prostitute, even among those like Kauffman and Phillips who claimed to produce documentary novels about her. It took a radical opponent of bourgeois morality like Reed to suggest that, save for the hazards of her profession, she was satisfied with life. As a group his prostitutes are energetic and accomplished sexual hucksters. As individuals, they are colorful personalities. Martha, for example, the voluble dance hall denizen of his 1913 vignette "Where the Heart Is," is a "reckless-mouthed" woman "insolently swinging her hips" who represents the "life-force indomitable."[74] Reed had tried to place "Where the Heart Is" in a number of magazines less radical than *The Masses,* but not surprisingly even the editors of the muckraking *Everybody's* magazine refused to print such unabashed praise of the *demi-monde.*[75] For Martha is no sorrowful white slave but a cheerful siren in tight clothing and a yellow-plumed hat, proud of her popularity with the college boys. She happily recounts to all who will listen that she has done the tour of Europe, from the red-light Place Pigalle to lucrative yacht trips with French aristocrats. Such experiences have mode her the *bon vivant* rather than the old hand, as if she cruised the world in search of life experiences rather than customers. Reed recognizes that her anecdotes mythify her encounters, but insists that the vitality with which she tells them renders her an artist in living.

Martha's Parisian counterpart Marcelle in "A Daughter of the Revolution" (1915) demonstrates her free-spiritedness in a similar fashion, meeting the demands of a precarious existence with a blend of charisma and chicanery.[76] Based on Reed's café encounter with a Parisian prostitute, the sketch is divided between an awareness that the profane Marcelle has been "soiled with too much handling" (5) and an admiration for her forceful personality and love of life. Reed points out that as the daughter and grand-daughter of revolutionaries Marcelle is a rebel in her own way, although her left-wing family had seen immorality, not economic liberation, in her decision to become a prostitute. The politically committed, however, are no more virtuous than the streetwalker. Her own father, not recognizing her, solicits her one day in the street. Life's injustice has only made Marcelle more vocal in her defense of what she does to live. She defends her occupation with ferocity: " 'Regret my life?' she flashed. . . '*Dame*, no, I'm free!' " (8).

Edna, the youthful title character of a lengthier 1916 sketch by Reed's Village acquaintance Alfred Kreymbourg, is another advocate of this method of achieving feedom. Like Reed, Kreymbourg did not so much create a fictional character as embellish on an actual encounter. *Edna, the Girl of the Street*, its title playing on Crane's more famous work, turns Kreymbourg's conversations with a Boston prostitute into the tale of a New York evening in which the narrator, Amos Lane, picks up two roving streetwalkers.[77] He treats them to a meal in a hotel restaurant and repairs to a room with one of them—but only to pay for the story of her life.

Kreymbourg, who had foreseen the story would run afoul of Sumner's anti-vice forces, vainly attempted to ward off censorship by confining Edna's sexual aggression to her few whispered hints. He also tacked on a moralistic message about Lane's desire to rescue her from herself. Since the sketch included a hotel room scene in which Edna expressed contentment with her life, the Vice Society immediately confiscated the 350 copies of the published story and hauled the editor and publisher off to court for selling obscene material. Frank Crane, who had defended the serialized *Susan Lenox* in the pages of *Hearst's* magazine, came to the defense of the work. So did George Bernard Shaw, who as the author of *Mrs. Warren's Profession* was no stranger to censorship. The defenders prevailed and the obscenity case was dismissed, although *Edna* fell swiftly from notoriety to obscurity.[78] If Kreymbourg's sketch is mentioned now at all, it is as a victory over American censorship rather than as the depiction of an anti-type of the white slave.

As *Edna* opens, the autobiographical narrator, whom Kreymbourg defends by calling him a "sociologist," wanders the Tenderloin and, when he encounters Edna and a female friend, plays the hesitant customer. Edna's stream of talk does little to mask her profit motive, but her slangy raillery shapes the false gaiety of the evening. As energetic as she is businesslike, Edna is a version of Crane's predatory Nell without the hostility. Lane tries to explain away Edna's professionalism by pointing out, as did other American writers of the day, that she seems so innocent: "How could such a fresh fun-loving face...belong to the profession? [Surely,] Edna, at the most, was just an everyday girl" (12).

As if she were setting a naive vice commission straight, Edna presents her life story as a transit from department store exploitation to small acting parts to what she considers the lucrative New York streets. In contrast to Susan Lenox, who pragmatically envisions prostitution as a short-term survival measure, Edna joins Reed's prostitutes as an apologist for her profession. Prostitution brings liberty, not the least of which is sexual, for "It'd be hell to sleep with the same fellow every night" (26). Having let a woman utter one of the most controversial lines in the fiction of the time, Kreymbourg immediately evades the idea of sexual independence suggested by this line and takes refuge in a redemption scheme. Lane "must save her now; after would be too late" (26). When she foils his narrator's missionary attempt by asking for money, Lane pays her for her time, and leaves her remunerated and impenitent.

Although David Graham Phillips was the only well-known novelist of his time to receive both critical and popular acclaim for his not-so-scarlet woman, he was not the only one to explore the idea. Whitlock's saddened rest-seekers, Reed's café philosophers, and Kreymbourg's sidewalk optimists were glimpsed in works which gave voice to the streetwalker as a survivor who knew when to ply the trade and when to leave it. *The Masses,* which Reed contributed to and helped edit, also published other portraits of the survivalist streetwalker, from recyclings of the nineteenth-century "wicked city" convention of the embittered cynic to visions of Harold Frederic's saintly prostitute. In 1914, William Rose Benet's poem, "Poor Girl," offered defiantly bitter women who ridiculed the society which scapegoated them.[79] In contrast, Horatio Winslow's "A Daughter of Delight" (1911) pictures a slangy posturer like Reed's Martha and Marcelle whose bravado heightens the poignance of her life.[80] She covers over the truth of her life with tall tales, striking the narrator as "at once amusing pitiful" (9). Frank Shay's 1913 playlet "The Machine" depicts a more hunted creature, trapped by the corrupt mechanism of a legal system which disregards both her pleas to be sent to a reformatory and the pimp hovering to secure her release.[81] The image of the prostitute as sacrifical lamb is further developed in James Henle's 1915 sketch, "Nobody's Sister."[82] In Henle's exculpatory vision, the prostitute has the "courage of the meek and the charity born of suffering" (10). She provides an almost religious comfort to those "she must receive" (10), and is unjustly scorned for earning a living the only way she knows how.

As this short survey of Whitlock, Reed, and their contemporaries reveals, Phillips was not alone in romanticizing the prostitute. They too shifted their gaze from her sexual activity and extolled her will to live, whether it surfaced as the confident self-assertion of a Martha or an Edna or the quiet endurance of the woman who is nobody's sister. Only Phillips, though, transformed her survival story into a romance of manly incorruptibility. Susan Lenox is distinct from the shopworn hustlers, free-spirited posturers, judicial victims, or kindly altruists envisioned by other writers. These women had courageously accepted or overcome the scarring experiences of the trade. Susan Lenox can leave behind the profession to which all the rest are tied. Phillips's myth is that she has won an endurance contest, not involved herself in a debasing life. Thus the prostitutes of Reed and Kreymbourg live; however implausibly, Phillips's heroine triumphs.

* * * * *

With Susan Lenox, the prostitute in American literature had traveled far from the seduction victim who can neither rescue herself from social ostracism nor from corrosive guilt. Reginald Wright Kauffman had already reshaped the nineteenth century's moralistic seduction melodrama to a certain extent. Unlike Maggie and her sisters, his Mary Denbigh tries to fight back, seeking facts about the trade rather than the oblivion of the remorseful outcast. She even avenges herself on her abductor by using the venereal weapons at her command. Still, if exhaustion rather than masochism brings her to the door of death, her doom is no less familiar.

Phillips was the only mainstream American novelist to reject this Progressive version of the harlot's progress tale. Susan's rise to wealth is even in a way reminiscent of Horatio Alger: pluck and luck enable her too to ascend. Compared to the permanently marginal prostitutes depicted in the vignettes of those like Reed, Phillips's streetwalker-turned-celebrity is no Socialist indictment of the American dream. Yet Phillips had attempted something radical nonetheless: he had tried to imagine a prostitute who reshaped the circumstances of her oppression by deriving psychic profit from the rough lessons of the sex trade. His description of the street as her school has a strikingly modern quality. Ironically, however, he exempts his heroine from the sexual duplicity of which he accuses the respectable woman. The heroic prostitute becomes his ideal type, combined street fighter, boyish optimist, and lady. An ill-assorted mixture of masculine and feminine, neither as a man nor as a woman is her innocence informed by her experience.

Of all the writers under scrutiny in this study, David Graham Phillips's offered the most complicated response to the conflict about female sexuality. Divided between his late-Victorian insistence that women be virtuous and his conviction that all women were carnally flawed, between his need for a female hero and his belief in woman's unheroic nature, Phillips's misogyny encompassed society wives and journalists, heiresses and businesswomen. Only in the unlikely figure of the prostitute could Phillips find the heroine he sought. Her adversarial relations with the men who tried to control her made her for Phillips the atypical woman, the manly woman, the woman as hero. Phillips's peers and predecessors had defended the prostitute by erasing the sexuality they felt still needed punishment. Phillips, in contrast, carried her defense much further, proclaiming her purity and rewarding her with success. But to do so, he was compelled to alter woman's flawed nature itself. The ambivalence that the prostitute as a sexual being had occasioned in writers from Miller through Kauffman was no less present in Phillips's work. As man rather than woman, virgin rather that harlot, she remained as improbably asexual as ever.

Chapter Seven
Fallen Women in the Minds of Men

Once I was pure as the snow, but I fell— —
Fell, like a snowflake, from Heaven to Hell— —
Fell, to be trampled as filth on the street— —
Fell, to be scoffed at, spit on, and beat;
Praying, cursing, wishing to die,
Selling my soul to whoever would buy.
Dealing in shame for a morsel of bread;
Hating the living and fearing the dead.
     from Cortland Myers, *Midnight in a Great City*

I planned to "assignate" until spring, for I had found out that the expenses of private women were not half so large as those of women in public houses.
     from *Madeleine, An Autobiography*

In 1919, two years after John Sumner's Vice Society assault on Phillips's *Susan Lenox,* a work appeared which drew his fire once more. It was the autobiography of "Madeleine," an authentic survivor of the rigors of the sex trade. Employing much the same language of attack he had directed at Phillips's novel, Sumner called *Madeleine* "one of the worst and most dangerous books of the day."[1] Within weeks of the autobiography's publication, Sumner took Harper and Brothers to court. By early 1920, the publishers had withdrawn from circulation this anonymous chronicle of fifteen years of brothel life in the cities of the Midwest and on the Canadian frontier.

A few years before, Sumner had exerted a great influence on another prominent publisher, Appleton and Company, in the battle to suppress *Susan Lenox.* (Two decades earlier in 1896, Appleton had tried to ward off Sumner's predecessor Comstock by bowdlerizing *Maggie.*) But the censors' influence was waning. *Madeleine* was, in fact, cleared of obscenity charges, a development which historians have linked to a loosening of American attitudes toward sexuality in literature.[2] Despite the legal victory, an over-cautious Harper's decided against reissuing the book. As a result, this saga of a veteran prostitute-madam was consigned to an obscurity from which it only emerged a few years ago.

167

Considering the idealized or otherwise unrealistic images produced by the prostitute's male imaginers in the thirty years prior to *Madeleine*, its suppression was unfortunate. Here was no tearful penitent, no suicidal sinner destroyed by "the life," no vice commission witness recounting the terrors of white slavery. A woman who, at least by her account, "refused to be crushed" (327), Madeleine represents a far more credible version of the prostitute-as-survivor than the mythic heroine Susan Lenox. She has Susan's fighting spirit and scorn of condemnation, but never ascends the heights of urban celebrity. She seems, simply, to have quietly quit the trade. In further contrast to the Amazonian Susan, Madeleine left prostitution having known venereal disease, which prostitutes called a "dose," and still struggling with severe addictions to gambling and drink. Nor did Madeleine discount the psychic assault on the self which her experiences had exacted from her. After a decade on the street and in houses from Chicago to Butte to the Northwest Territory, she had amassed enough to run a Canadian brothel and even retire on the profits. But by then she was "at war with society...with every man's hand against [her]" (304). Although affluent enough, she had lost all ties to her family and her more devoted former clients. She was, in addition, a seemingly hopeless alcoholic who recalled telling herself that she would only stop drinking when she was dead. Imitating the model her father, whose drinking increased as he aged, had provided her, she seemed more self-destructive as a capitalist madam than she had ever been as a raw brothel girl.

Historian Marcia Carlisle has remarked, though, that Madeleine's self-interest, not her desire for self-annihilation, is at the center of her narrative.[3] If she was not quite Phillips's invulnerable protagonist, neither was she Fawcett's ruined Cora Strang. At 34, after a decade and a half in commercialized sex, Madeleine engineered her exit. She pragmatically embraced religion, at least long enough to wean herself from drink, and entered the respectable world she had avoided for so long.

Despite her claim than she preferred her new life of "decency and usefulness" (325), Madeleine was silent about what that life included. Moreover her narrative, like that of her contemporary Nell Kimball and memoirist-madams of the ensuing decades like Pauline Tabor, did not condemn but celebrate her past.[4] She proudly provided an insider's taxonomy of the profession: the varieties of brothels, colleagues, madams, customers, local officials, prostitutes' proscriptions and superstitions. Occasionally she donned the Progressive mantle to deplore the bordello as a "House of Bondage" (194). But she was merely pointing out the repulsiveness of a given patron or requested sex act or the monotony of the brothel routine. In contrast to the Mary Denbighs of Progressive fiction who cried out against the system which kept prostitutes hostage and stole their earnings, Madeleine focused on the fair profit women could earn in a "decent" house. She further contended that "old-timers," so far from being used up or in the river, could earn money because they had more expertise. From the perspective of a middle-rung prostitute who spent some time as a streetwalker, Madeleine disdained the stereotypes of sin and retribution which fueled the period literature. Even when admitting that contact with a "great unwashed brute" (218) was the lot of Norma, a street prostitute she knew, she added that the woman— no teen ingenue, assuredly—survived by stealing from the drunkards with whom she slept.

Madeleine's was a calm acceptance of the system which, after all, as a madam she learned to exploit. On the other hand, given her candor about her dangerous habits and experiences, she was angry at the prejudices concerning prostitutes: the charges of alcoholism, disease, degeneracy, and mental illness, the conviction that reform was unlikely. She had no illusions, however, about motive. She chided those like the authors studied here who believed in Virtue Betrayed. Here she remarked with characteristic force:

> I met the public prostitute, the clandestine prostitute, and the occasional prostitute...I met the girl from the sheltered home and the girl who had been allowed to run wild; the girl who had sold her honor for bread, and the girl who had sold it for luxury and fine clothes. I met the girl who should have been a nun, and those others who were predestined by ancient conditions for the life of a harlot.
>
> But the one girl I never met in all these years and in all the cities and countries that I visited was the pure girl who had been trapped and violated and sold into slavery... (238)

This sweeping denial of involuntary prostitution, so at odds with the melodramatic conventions of writers from Miller to Phillips, bolstered her claim that she knew "all there [was] to be known about prostitution" (321). Although her eyewitness history debunked the *idée fixe* of the Progressive era, and by implication the harlot's progress tale of the preceding century, by 1919, once the white slave hysteria was dissipated, no one really disputed her arguments. With the respected Judge Ben Lindsey providing an introduction, no one claimed her narrative was fraudulent or even ghost-written.[5] In fact, the *New York Times* reviewer condemned her book largely because it was so matter-of-fact, and did not illuminate the social problem of prostitution. "She was simply choosing," the writer added in disgust, "the easiest way to get money."[6] Even the more tolerant *New Republic* astutely pointed out that she consistently romanticized her effect on customers and involvement in the vice world.[7]

Madeleine's self-creation illustrates the paradox at the heart of the whole subgenre of the prostitute's confessional. The more she revealed, the more she confused her readers, for the revelations were full of contradictions, delusions, and fantasies. She said she entered the trade to support the child she would soon have yet insisted she could have stayed indefinitely with generous friends. She claimed she remained a prostitute to send money to her family, yet admitted: "It was not possible for me to send them much money, for I had no way of accounting for the possession of it" (154). She affected to despise the men for whom she counterfeited passion, but glorified in being "the most sought-after girl in town, [who] rejoiced in [her] popularity" (179). There was more romanticizing as well. Every brothel she worked in was beautiful and no madam ever cheated her. Once she became a madam herself, she contended she inspired fanatical devotion in her subordinates and scrupulous honesty in the girls. A former client, she bragged, supposedly pursued only her for a decade, wanting her to leave the trade and remain with him, but she preferred her "independence."

"Lying was a part of the profession" (45), Madeleine conceded, and the inconsistencies of her narrative reflect that. In spite or because of her evasions and rationalizations, she managed to convey in her writing her hard-headed acceptance of the life she had chosen. In this she differed, of course, from many of her less adaptive peers. The miserable Margaret von Staden supplied a plaintive account of the vise-like grip in which San Francisco pimps kept her for years. The embittered Lydia Pettengill Taylor lashed out at men for leading her astray and respectable women for sneering at her. And the compassionate Maimie Pinzer wrote letters to her benefactress revealing a true resolve to save young women from the ravages of venereal disease and the pain of family condemnation.[8] Madeleine was certainly none of these women. Nor was she an introspective narrator, able to see her urge to sexual rebellion as a response to a father who forbade it. She wrote, "It was his most reverent assertion that no woman of his own or my mother's name had ever borne the breath of reproach"(25). But she was unwilling to analyze his influence on her or the extent to which, from a Freudian perspective, her early lovers and clients were "debased father figures needed to deny the existence of the one and only parental object of her infantile love."[9] The period was beginning to tabulate case histories of prostitutes and to look to the family—if not yet to such concepts as the Oedipal complex—as the crucible of delinquent behavior. Madeleine, in effect, was avoiding psychological implications.[10]

Nevertheless, her narrative voice gave expression to a woman who had navigated a dangerous youth and had spent her womanhood negotiating the sale of her body to clients and employers with interests fundamentally opposed to her own. Of the writers discussed in this study, all but Phillips shy away from depicting such a type and he balks at making Susan sound the professional. An even more striking contrast to *Madeleine* can be found in a vignette that the well-known observer of the underclass, Jacob Riis, included among his collected stories of slum life, published in 1898. The story appeared in print at the time Madeleine had been ten years a prostitute and was successfully managing her first house.[11] The sketch employs the stereotype of the bestial prostitute familiar to readers of Miller, Fawcett, and the mid-century thriller. More importantly, it reveals that, like the novelists of the day, even compassionate reformers could not escape their fear of the prostitute nor break away from the conventions which embodied it. To Riis's vignette we now briefly turn.

* * * * *

Among his many contributions to urban reform, Riis was an advisor to the Tenement House Committee of 1894, dedicated to upgrading the unwholesome conditions of the New York slum. Richard Watson Gilder, the man who turned down the uncensored *Maggie* for publication, was also a committee member. Riis found it as difficult as Gilder to extend compassionate interest in the poor to the Bowery streetwalker. An often sentimental observer of tenement life, Riis only refers in passing to her in *How the Other Half Lives*. There he alludes to New York's "army of profligate women" as if begrudging them further attention.[12] The book's only other reference is equally fleeting. Ready to penetrate the dark recesses of places like Mulberry Bend and Bottle Alley, Riis, nevertheless, shudders at the female frequenters of a stale-beer dive: "To the women—unutterable horror of the suggestion—the place was free" (62).

Nine years after *How the Other Half Lives*, Riis published *Out of Mulberry Street*, tales of tenement life. He overcame his distaste for the subject enough to include "Nigger Martha's Wake," the tale of prostitute's suicide. But when Riis tried to imagine the woman he had, almost a decade before, either condemned in passing or captured almost accidentally in photos of the derelict inmates of Police Court lodging houses, this time he translated his "unutterable horror" into horrified utterance. Unlike the self-serving but quite human commentator of *Madeleine*, Riis's prostitute is a creature as loathsome as any found in the mid-century urban thriller or the adaptations by Miller and Fawcett.

Elsewhere in *Out of Mulberry Street* Riis praises the innocence of slum children and the sometime kindliness of the police with a sentimental insistence. Stories like "Merry Christmas in the Tenements" transform needy children into paragons inspiring the older toughs to make Christmas sacrifice for them. In a variant, the teenaged central character of "The Kid," perceived as an old offender by the law, pauses in his flight from the police to rescue a child from an oncoming streetcar— at the cost of his freedom. If in that tale Riis finds the law unjust to the Bowery outcast, "He Kept His Tryst" praises policeman Schultz, a humanitarian of the beat. Sincerely affected by the drifters he is compelled to reprimand, Schultz embodies Riis's own sympathy for the kind of "human wreck, in rum and rags" (86) who so often crossed his reportorial path. Other sketches, it is true, picture unfit parents, thieves, and neighborhood lunatics with less charity, but none of these slum misfits evoke the revulsion of "Nigger Martha."

As the sketch opens, the title character has just swallowed carbolic acid, a fittingly dreadful end to her hellish existence. Dwelling on her grotesquely blotched face rather than what she looked like before her rash act, Riis provides no humanizing detail. All that he can note is that a "remorse not to be borne" (107) propelled the drunken woman to suicide. Riis, however, offers no reflections on innocence betrayed. Instead he vents his scorn on the survivors, particularly two of Martha's Bowery cohorts, Cock-eyed Grace and Sheeny Rose. Pictured the day after Martha's wake egged on to confrontation by their colleagues, the women are so filled with hate that they try to draw blood from each other with hatpins. They even suspend their predatory interest in a "night's catch" (107) to give vent to the bestiality that propelled them to the streetwalker's life in the first place. The women try to blind each other with their hatpins, and engage in any other cruelty their "pent-up malice" (112) can release. Grace is attacking Rose, hated by the dead woman, for trying to attend the funeral. But Riis is less interested in motivation than in characterizing these women as "tigers," "fiends," and, when the police break up the fight and arrest them, "disheveled hags" (112). The slurs prefacing Martha's and Rose's names suggest that in Riis's rather racist and nativist view, they are the sullied representatives of troublesome minorities. Their behavior, however, brands them devils, not black or Irish women. Noting that their behavior is "appropriate" (113) given their profession, Riis does not even offer the seduction rationale of Miller or Fawcett to account for their frenzied conduct.

Riis once remarked to Richard Watson Gilder, who was far more interested in publishing his work on the slum than Crane's controversial *Maggie,* that he observed but did not invent.[13] The statement seems rather disingenuous. Suicides and vicious street fights among prostitutes were clearly facts of life on the Lower East Side, and Riis had the photographer's eye for such details. Yet in depicting these veterans of the trade as fiends, he played on a subliterary tradition which had little use for sociological observation. In Riis's artistic transformation, survival yields to suicide, friendship to bloody vendetta, human qualities to animal ones. The befriender of "the other half" proved no friend to one of its most obvious exemplars.

* * * * *

Imagining the prostitute was hard work for American writers. Contemplating the fiction of the day, that ambivalent Boston Brahmin, Henry Adams, complained that writers "used sex for sentiment, never for force."[14] Indeed, Jacob Riis exorcised his anxieties about the force of the Bowery harlot by bestializing her, then by shifting the focus to her non-sexual activity. Less inclined to study her than his male colleagues discussed here, Riis was much like them in his evasive response. However much Miller, Fawcett, Crane, Frederic, Kauffman, and Phillips claimed to comprehend the aggressively sexual figure of the prostitute, their claim camouflaged a deeper truth. They could not convincingly portray the woman who so threatened their late-Victorian ideal of feminine purity. They only resolved their conflict between exoneration of the innocent victim and condemnation of the carnal professional through a shared group of literary strategies. Instead of presenting the type of American woman whose sex activity was explicit, all of them sanitized her. They created no Madeleines. Late-nineteenth-century writers sensationalized or sentimentalized and killed off the prostitute while Progressives exaggerated her exploitation or romanticized her triumph over it. The lost souls, martyrs, didactic white slaves, and armor-plated heroines these writers depicted suggest more than a failure of imagination or the influence of censorship or the genteel tradition. Rather, such characterizations revealed a fearful denial of feminine sexuality, hired or otherwise. It was a legacy that would prove enduring.

Notes

Chapter 1

[1]With the coming of the war, government began to close down red-light districts to protect the troops from venereal disease. Prostitution, though not abolished, was driven underground. Social hygienists, psychologists, and criminologists became the new students of the social evil. The crusading fervor of the pre-war years took a new direction: now the drive was to incarcerate the prostitute rather than effect her moral reform.

[2]Charles Brockden Brown, *Arthur Mervyn or Memoirs of The Year 1793* [1798-1800], ed. Warner Berthoff (New York: Holt, Rinehart and Winston, 1962), Part II, Chapter 11; William Hill Brown, *The Power of Sympathy* (1789; rpt. Boston: New Frontiers Press, 1961), p. 46.

[3]Nathaniel Hawthorne, "My Kinsman, Major Molyneux" [1832], *The Celestial Railroad and Other Stories* (New York: Signet-New American Library, 1963), p. 36; Harriet Beecher Stowe, *We and Our Neighbors* (New York: J.B. Ford, 1875); Louisa May Alcott, *Work* (Boston: Roberts Brothers, 1873).

[4]Janis Stout, *Sodoms in Eden. The City in American Fiction before 1860* (Westport, Ct.: Greenwood Press, 1976), p. 40. See my second chapter for a discussion of the Gothic thriller.

[5]Prostitutes were sometimes minor characters in working girls' romances of the 80's and 90's, largely written by women. See Joanne J. Meyerowitz, *Women Adrift: Independent Wage Earners in Chicago, 1880-1930* (Chicago: University of Chicago Press, 1988), pp. 56, 60.

[6]On antebellum activity, see Carroll Smith-Rosenberg, "Beauty, the Beast and the Militant Woman," *A Heritage of Her Own,* ed. Nancy F. Cott and Elizabeth Pleck (New York: Simon and Schuster, 1979), pp. 197-221. Mid- and late-Victorian American women's anti-prostitution efforts are chronicled in the *National Purity Congress: Papers, Addresses, Portraits,* ed. Aaron M. Powell (Baltimore: National Purity Alliance, 1896). Progressive era activity is described in Ruth Rosen, *The Lost Sisterhood. Prostitution in America, 1900-1918* (Baltimore: Johns Hopkins University Press, 1982), Chapter 4. On Butler, see E. Moberly Bell, *Josephine Butler. Flame of Fire* (London: Constable, 1962) and Judith Walkowitz, *Prostitution and Victorian Society: Women, Class and the State* (Cambridge: Cambridge University Press, 1980), pp. 90-112.

[7]Quoted in "Dramatizing Vice," *Literary Digest,* October 4, 1913, 578.

[8]Except for a Riis sketch to be discussed in Chapter 7 in which the black title character is killed off before the tale begins, the woman these writers envisioned was white. While there were countless exploited black and Chinese prostitutes, fiction and, with few exceptions, mainstream reform literature, seemed uninterested in them.

[9]As this is a literary study of the professional prostitute, Dreiser's *Sister Carrie* (1900) will not be included. The title character lives for a time as the mistress of a traveling salesman but is certainly not a courtesan, much less a street or brothel prostitute.

[10]Felice Flanery Lewis, *Literature, Obscenity, and Law* (Carbondale and Edwardsville: Southern Illinois University Press, 1976), p. 13.

[11]See also Carl Bode, "Columbia's Carnal Bed," *American Quarterly*, 15 (Spring, 1963), 53-64.

[12]Steven Marcus, *The Other Victorians. A Study of Sexuality and Pornography in Mid-Nineteenth-Century England* (1964; rpt. New York: Meridian Books, 1974), p. 272.

[13]See Hershel Parker and Brian Higgins, "Maggie's 'Last Night': Authorial Design and Editorial Patching," *Studies in the Novel*, 10 (Spring, 1978), 64-75.

[14]M.M. Marberry, *Splendid Poseur. Joaquin Miller, An American Poet* (New York: Thomas Y. Crowell), p. 168, evasively terms *The Destruction of Gotham* "a calumnious narrative of the iniquity of New York." To George A. Dunlap, *The City in the American Novel, 1789-1900* (1934; rpt. New York: Russell and Russell, 1965), p. 62, it is a "fantastic story" of "disease and death."

[15]See, for example, Walter F. Taylor, *The Economic Novel in America* (Chapel Hill: University of North Carolina Press, 1972), pp. 82-83. There is no mention of the prostitute in the book index. Walter B. Rideout, *The Radical Novel in the United States, 1900-1954* (Cambridge: Harvard University Press, 1956), pp. 67-69, also gives the subject short shrift. Stanley Harrison, *Edgar Fawcett* (New York: Twayne Publishers, 1972), does too.

[16]Fawcett's publishers seem to have begun the trend, routinely omitting mention of the title when advertising his later works. Stanley Kunitz, ed., *American Authors, 1600-1900* (New York: H.W. Wilson, 1938), continues it.

[17]On the novel as "unconventional," see Robert Spiller et al, eds. *Literary History of the United States* (New York: Macmillan, 1974), 4th ed. rev., p. 1120. Other oblique references appear in, for example, Thomas F. O'Donnell and Hoyt C. Franchere, *Harold Frederic* (New York: Twayne Publishers, 1961), p. 90. Feminist critics, in search of lost women writers, seem to bypass works by male writers on prostitution as well. A rare exception is Carol Hurd Green, "Stephen Crane and the Fallen Women," *American Novelists Revisited. Essays in Feminist Criticism*, ed. Fritz Fleischmann (Boston: G.K. Hall and Company, 1982), pp. 225-242. Green makes no allusion, however, to novelists other than Crane.

[18]Rideout, p. 68; F.C.S., Introduction, *The House of Bondage* (1910; rpt. Upper Saddle River, N.J.: Gregg Press, 1968), n.p.

[19] *Literary History*, pp. 1118, 1022.

[20]Louis Filler, "An American Odyssey: The Story of Susan Lenox," *Accent*, 1 (August, 1940), 28.

[21]Everett Carter, Introduction, Harold Frederic, *The Damnation of Theron Ware* [1896] (Cambridge: The Belknap Press of Harvard University Press, 1960), xxi.

[22]Joyce Warren, *The American Narcissus. Individualism and Women in Nineteenth-Century American Fiction* (New Brunswick, N.J.: Rutgers University Press), p. 3.

[23]For discussions of these forces and their effect on the American depiction of women, see Judith Fryer, *The Faces of Eve. Women in the Nineteenth-Century American Novel* (New York: Oxford University Press, 1976), Chapter 1, and Carolyn Heilbrun, "The Masculine Wilderness of the American Novel," *Saturday Review*, January 29, 1972, 41-44.

[24]Leslie Fiedler, *Love and Death in the American Novel*, rev. ed. (New York: Dell Publishing Company, 1960), p. 220.

[25]The comments on Melville are in Warren, p. 115; on Hawthorne, in Philip Rahv, "The Dark Lady of Salem," *Literature and the Sixth Sense*, intro. by Rahv (Boston: Houghton, Mifflin, 1969), p. 63.

[26]Fryer, p. 47.

[27]Oliver Wendell Holmes, *Elsie Venner* (1859; rpt. Boston: Houghton, Mifflin, 1891).

[28]Quoted in Lars Ahnebrink, *The Beginnings of Naturalism in American Fiction* (New York: Russell and Russell, 1961), p. 19.

[29]Mark Twain and Charles Dudley Warner, *The Gilded Age* [1872] (New York: Signet-New American Library, p. 288). Howells's *Mrs. Farrell* was published in 1875.

[30]The respective authors are Margaret Hungerford, Curtis Bond, and Richard Henry Savage. DuMaurier's *Trilby* appeared in 1894.

[31]William Dean Howells, "Criticism and Fiction" [1891], *"Criticism and Fiction" and Other Essays*, ed. Clara Marburg Kirk and Rudolf Kirk (New York: New York University Press, 1959), pp. 72, 73.

[32]Quoted in John Tebbel, *A History of Book Publishing in the United States*, vol. 2 (New York: R.R. Bowker, 1975), p. 627.

[33]Howells, "Decency...," p. 547.

[34]Malcolm Cowley, "Foreward: The Revolt Against Gentility," *After the Genteel Tradition*, ed. Cowley (1936; rpt. Carbondale: Southern Illinois University Press, 1964), pp. 9-10.

[35]H.H. Boyesen, *Social Strugglers* (New York: Charles Scribner's Sons, 1893), p. 266.

[36]Charles Dudley Warner, *The Golden House* (New York: Harper and Brothers, 1894), p. 60. Future references to this edition will appear in the text.

[37]James W. Sullivan, "Minnie Kelsey's Wedding," *Tenement Tales of New York* (New York: Henry Holt and Company, 1895). Future references to this edition will appear in the text.

[38]Lewis, p. 13.

[39]David J. Pivar, *Purity Crusade: Sexual Morality and Social Control* (Westport, Ct.: Greenwood Press, 1973), p. 33; Paul S. Boyer, *Purity in Print. The Vice-Society Movement and Book Censorship in America* (New York: Scribners, 1968).

[40] *Publishers' Weekly*, 13 (May 18, 1889), 665.

[41]Quoted in Tebbel, p. 627. I am indebted to Tebbel, pp. 609-634, and Boyer pp. 2-21, for information on censored titles.

[42]Quoted in Boyer, p. 17.

[43]Lewis, pp. 3-5, 24.

[44]Quoted in Alphonse R. Favreau, "The Reception of Daudet's 'Sapho' in the United States," *Papers of the Michigan Academy of Science, Arts and Letters*, 30 (1944), 133.

[45]I am indebted to Tebbel, p. 624 and Favreau, 581-588, for the facts of the *Sapho* controversy.

[46] *New York World*, October 31, 1905, 9.

[47]Quoted in Heywood Broun and Margaret Leech, *Anthony Comstock. Roundsman of the Lord* (New York: Charles and Albert Boni, 1927), p. 223.

[48]Tebbel, pp. 609-613. For the biographical material on Comstock, I am also indebted to Broun and Leech.

[49]Broun and Leech, p. 153.

[50]Quoted in Lewis, p. 12.

[51]Quoted in Broun and Leech, p. 134.

[52]Quoted in Lewis, p. 13; see Anthony Comstock, "Vampire Literature," *North American Review*, 153 (August, 1913), 160-171.

[53]"Anthony Comstock," *Dictionary of American Biography*, ed. Allen Johnson and Dumas Malone. Vol. 4 (New York: Charles Scribner's Sons, 1930), p. 331.

[54]Quoted in Isaac F. Marcosson, *David Graham Phillips and His Times* (New York: Dodd, Mead, 1932), p. 257.

55Mrs. John Sandford, *Woman, in Her Social and Domestic Character* (London: Longman, Rees, 1833), p. 8.

56For a thorough discussion of ideas still widely believed at the turn of the century, see Barbara Welter, "The Cult of True Womanhood: 1820-1860," *American Quarterly*, 18 (Summer, 1966), 151-174; See also Sheila Rothman, *Woman's Proper Place: A History of Changing Ideas and Practices, 1870 to the Present* (New York: Basic Books, 1978), pp. 21-26.

57 *Revolution*, 1 (June 25, 1868), 389.

58Warren, p. 152.

59William Dean Howells, "Editor's Easy Chair," *Harper's*, 111 (October, 1905), 794.

60George Kibbe Turner, "The City of Chicago. A Study of the Great Immoralities," *McClure's*, 28 (April 1907), 582.

61J. Richardson Parke, *Human Sexuality. A Medico-Literary Treatise* (Philadelphia: Professional Publishing Company, 1906), p. 10.

62William Sanger, *The History of Prostitution* (1858; rpt. New York: Medical Publishing Company, 1897), p. 488. For a similar argument in the Progressive era, see Allen Brandt, *No Magic Bullet. A Social History of Venereal Disease in the United States Since 1880* (New York: Oxford University Press, 1987), p. 268.

63Elizabeth Blackwell, "On Sexual Passion in Men and Women" [1894], in *Root of Bitterness*, ed. Nancy F. Cott (New York: E.P. Dutton, 1972), p. 300.

64Carl N. Degler, *At Odds: Women and the Family in America from the Revolution to the Present* (New York: Oxford University Press, 1980), Chapter 2.

65Peter Gay, *The Bourgeois Experience*, Vol. 1. (New York: Oxford University Press, 1984), p. 5.

66Neil Mc Kendrick, *"The Bourgeois Experience," New York Times Book Review*, January 8, 1984, 35.

67Quoted in Marcus, p. 29.

68Sanger, p. 488.

69Barbara Ehrenreich and Deirdre English, *Witches, Midwives and Nurses. A History of Women Healers* (Old Westbury, N.Y.: Feminist Press, 1973), p. 12.

70John A. Phillips, *Eve. The History of an Idea* (New York: Harper and Row, 1984), p. 45. See also H.R. Hays, *The Dangerous Sex: The Myth of Feminine Evil* (New York: Putnam, 1964), and Maximilian Rudwin, *The Devil in Legend* (New York: AMS Press, 1964).

71The Dekker play is the *The Honest Whore* [1608].

72Nancy F. Cott, "Passionlessness. An Interpretation of Victorian Sexual Ideology, 1750-1850," in *A Heritage of Her Own. Toward a New Social History of American Women*, ed. Nancy F. Cott and Elizabeth Pleck (New York: Simon and Schuster, 1979), pp. 162-181.

73Hays, p. 42.

74See, for example, Sanger, p. 565; Mary Terhune, *Eve's Daughters, or Common Sense for Maids* (New York: J.R. Anderson and H.S. Allen, 1882), p. 6; and Abraham Hummel and William F. Howe, *In Danger! Or, Life In New York* (New York: J. Ogilvie, 1888), p. 128.

75Quoted in Keith Thomas, "The Double Standard," *Journal of the History of Ideas*, 20 (1959), 197.

76Hummel and Howe, p. 125.

77Matthew Hale Smith, *Sunshine and Shadow in New York* (Hartford: J.B. Burr and Company, 1872), p. 366.

78 *Vices of a Big City. Existing Menaces to Church and Home* (New York: J.B. Clark, 1890), p. 30; James D. McCabe, *Lights and Shadows of New York Life* (Philadelphia: National Publishing Company, 1872), p. 596.

[79]For the pre-eminent study, see the Vice Commission of Chicago, *The Social Evil in Chicago* (1911; rpt. New York: Arno Press and The New York Times, 1970).

[80]For this and similar language, see Committee of Eighteen, *The Social Evil in Syracuse*, 1913; rpt. in *Prostitution in America: Three Investigations, 1902-1914.* (New York: Arno Press and The New York Times, 1976), pp. 69-79; George Kneeland [Vice Commission of 1913], *Commercialized Prostitution in New York City* (1913; rpt. Montclair, N.J.: Patterson Smith, 1969), p. 103; Chicago Vice Commission, pp. 46, 75, 95.

[81]Sanger, p. 492.

[82]Edward Crapsey, *The Nether Side of New York* (New York: Sheldon Publishing Company, 1872), p. 143.

[83]Buel, p. 78.

[84]Bracebridge Hemyng, *Those That Will Not Work*, Vol. 4, Henry Mayhew, *London Labour and the London Poor* (London: Griffin, Bohn and Company, 1862), p. 212.

[85]Elizabeth Evans, *The Abuse of Maternity* (Philadelphia: J.B. Lippincott, 1875), p. 118.

[86]B.O. Flower, "Prostitution within the Marriage Bond," *Arena*, 13 (1895), 61.

[87]Hemyng, p. 212.

[88]Annie Allen, "How to Save Girls Who Have Fallen," *Survey*, 23 (1910), p. 690.

[89]Maude E. Miner, *The Slavery of Prostitution* (New York: Macmillan, 1916), p. 36.

Chapter 2

[1]Notes of Garland's lectures on American literature and art, in Lars Ahnebrink, *The Beginnings of Naturalism in American Fiction* (New York: Russell and Russell, 1961), pp. 440-441.

[2]O.W. Frost, *Joaquin Miller* (New York: Twayne Publishers, 1967), pp. 92, 99; Benjamin Lawson, *Joaquin Miller* (Boise: Boise State University, 1979) pp. 7-8; Stanley Harrison, *Edgar Fawcett* (New York: Twayne Publishers, 1972), p. 17; "Edgar Fawcett," Stanley Kunitz, ed., *American Authors, 1600-1900* (New York: H.W. Wilson Company, 1938), p. 264.

[3]Joaquin Miller, *The Destruction of Gotham* (New York: Funk and Wagnalls, 1886); Edgar Fawcett, *The Evil That Men Do* (New York: Funk and Wagnalls, 1889). Future references to these editions will appear in the text.

[4]Introduction, *The Poetical Works of Joaquin Miller*, ed. Stuart P. Sherman (New York and London: G.P. Putnam's Sons, 1923), p. 35; Harrison, pp. 4, 6.

[5]Frost, p. 115.

[6]On Miller's myth of himself, see Lawson, pp. 3-7 and Frost, Chapter 1.

[7]"Songs of the Sierras," *The Complete Poetical Works of Joaquin Miller* [1871] (1897; rpt. New York: Arno Press and The New York Times, 1972). Future references to this edition by page rather than line will appear in the text. On the work's London popularity, see Van Wyck Brooks, *The Times of Melville and Whitman* (New York: E.P. Dutton, 1947), pp. 303-305.

[8]Joaquin Miller, *First Fam'lies of the Sierras* (Chicago: Jansen, McClurg and Company, 1876). Future references to this edition will appear in the text. Miller adapted the book lucratively for the stage in 1877 under the title *Danites of the Sierras*.

[9]There is no book-length biography of Fawcett. See Kunitz, pp. 263-264.

[10]Letter of Edgar Fawcett to [?] Hayne, November 3, 1877, in Stanley Harrison, "Through a Nineteenth-Century Looking Glass: The Letters of Edgar Fawcett," *Tulane Studies in English*, 15 (1967), 136.

[11]Edgar Fawcett, "Plutocracy and Snobbery in New York," *Arena*, 25 (July, 1891), 143.

[12]Edgar Fawcett, *Tinkling Cymbals* (Boston: James R. Osgood and Company, 1884), p. 13.

[13]Edgar Fawcett, *An Ambitious Woman* (Boston: Houghton, Mifflin, 1884), p. 3.

[14]Abraham Hummel and William F. Howe, *In Danger! Or Life in New York* (New York: J. Ogilvie, 1888), v.

[15]Arthur Pember, *Mysteries and Miseries of the Great Metropolis* (New York: D. Appleton, 1874), p. 15.

[16]Eugene Arden, "The Evil City in American Fiction," *New York History*, 35 (1954), 259.

[17]Arthur Schlesinger, "The City in American History," *Mississippi Valley Historical Review*, 27 (1940), 45.

[18]James D. McCabe, *Lights and Shadows of New York Life* (Philadelphia: National Publishing Company, 1872), p. 401.

[19]David S. Reynolds, *Beneath the American Renaissance: The Subversive Imagination in the Age of Emerson and Melville* (New York: Alfred A. Knopf, 1988), p. 82. A good discussion of authors like Judson, Ingraham, and Bradbury is in Janis Stout, *Sodoms in Eden. The City in American Fiction before 1860.* (Westport, Ct.: Greenwood Press, 1967), Chapter 4.

[20]George Ellington, *The Women of New York* (New York: New York Book Company, 1878), p. 6.

[21]See also Russel Nye, *The Unembarrassed Muse* (New York: Dial Press, 1970), p. 209.

[22]George Lippard, *The Quaker City, or The Monks of Monk Hall* [1845], ed. Leslie Fiedler (New York: Odyssey Press, 1970), p. 2.

[23]George Foster, *New York by Gaslight* (New York: DeWitt and Davenport, 1850) and *Celio, or New York Above-Ground and Under-Ground* (New York: Robert M. DeWitt, 1850); Joseph Holt Ingraham, *Frank Rivers; or, The Dangers of the Town* (New York: DeWitt and Davenport, 1853). Future references to these editions will appear in the text.

[24]Susanna Rowson, *Charlotte Temple* [1791], ed. Cathy N. Davidson (New York: Oxford University Press, 1986), p. 105.

[25]Leslie Fiedler, Introduction, George Lippard, *The Quaker City*, xiii.

[26]Reverend Peter Stryker, *The Lower Depths of the Great American Metropolis* (New York: n.p., 1866), p. 6.

[27]Osgood Bradbury, *Female Depravity; or, the House of Death* (New York: Robert M. DeWitt, 1857), p. 8. Future references to this edition will appear in the text.

[28]*The Life and Sufferings of Cecilia Mayo* (Boston: M. Aurelius, 1843), p. 16.

[29]James Buel, *Mysteries and Miseries of America's Great Cities* (San Francisco: A.L. Bancroft, 1883), p. 50.

[30]Pember, p. 3.

[31]Buel, p. 52.

[32]Quoted in Stout, p. 40.

[33]Z.C. [E.Z.] Judson, *The Mysteries and Miseries of New York: A Story of Real Life* (New York: Bedford and Company, 1848), pp. 12, 13.

[34]*The Destruction of Gotham*, back page.

[35]Nina Auerbach, *Woman and the Demon. The Life of a Victorian Myth* (Cambridge: Harvard University Press, 1982), p. 186.

[36]Quoted in Patricia Cooper, "Women Workers, Work Culture, and Collective Action in the American Cigar Industry, 1900-1919," *Life and Labor. Dimensions*

of American Working-Class Social History, ed. Charles Stephenson and Robert Asher (Albany: State University of New York, 1986), p. 196.

[37]On western toleration of the prostitute, see Reverend William Taylor, *California Life* (New York: Phillips and Hunt, 1882), p. 177 and Richard Lingeman, *Small Town America: A Narrative History from 1620 to the Present* (New York: G.P. Putnam, 1980), p. 267.

[38]Frost, p. 103.

[39]M.M. Marberry, *Splendid Poseur. Joaquin Miller, An American Poet* (New York: Thomas Y. Crowell, 1953), p. 168.

[40]Edgar Fawcett, "The Woes of the New York Working-Girl," *Arena,* 25 (December, 1891), 26-35. Future page references will appear in the text.

[41]Edgar Fawcett, *New York* (London and New York: F. Tennyson Nelly, 1898). Future references to this edition will appear in the text.

[42]Edmond de Goncourt, *La Fille Elisa* (1877; rpt. Paris: Calmann-Levy, n.d.), p. 19. The translation is mine.

[43]Edgar Fawcett, *The Confessions of Claud* (Boston: Ticknor and Company, 1887). Future references to this edition will appear in the text.

[44]Charles Dickens, *Oliver Twist* [1838] (New York: Penguin Books, 1966). Future references to this edition will appear in the text.

[45]Quoted in Harrison, *Edgar Fawcett,* p. 9.

[46]*Nation,* 43 (July 29, 1886), 102.

[47]*Literary World,* 21 (March 1, 1890), 71.

[48]Frost, p. 12.

[49]An allusion to Miller's desire for a utopian alternative to what Starr calls the "nightmare-world" of *Destruction of Gotham* appears in Kevin Starr, *Americans and the California Dream, 1850-1915* (New York: Oxford University Press, 1973), p. 288.

Chapter 3

[1]Stephen Crane, *Maggie: A Girl of the Streets* [text and criticism], ed. Thomas A. Gullason (1893; rpt. W.W. Norton and Company, 1974). This Norton Critical Edition is the only authoritative text of the original uncensored edition. Future references to it will appear in the text. On Crane's knowledge of the Tenderloin, see Olov W. Fryckstedt, "Stephen Crane in the Tenderloin," *Studia Neophilologica,* 34 (1962), 138; Robert W. Stallman, *Stephen Crane: A Biography* (New York: George Braziller, 1968), p. 26; John Berryman, *Stephen Crane* (New York: William Sloane Associates, 1950), p. 139.

[2]Letter of Frank W. Noxon to Max J. Herzberg, December 7, 1926, in *Stephen Crane: Letters,* ed. R.W. Stallman and Lillian Gilkes (New York: New York University Press, 1960), p. 335.

[3]Stallman, *Biography,* pp. 189, 228.

[4]Quoted in Thomas Beer, *Stephen Crane: A Study in American Letters* (New York: Alfred A. Knopf, 1923) p. 309 and, citing Beer, in Stallman, *Biography,* p. 189. Stanley Wertheim and Paul Sorrentino, the new editors of Crane's letters, doubt the authenticity of Crane's letter describing the Watts episode. Yet Stallman clearly does not, and the new editors' argument that Beer could have fabricated the incident seems weak given that Beer typically defended Crane against charges of patronizing prostitutes, or even befriending them. See the Introduction, *The Correspondence of Stephen Crane,* Vol. 1, ed. Wertheim and Sorrentino (New York: Columbia University Press, 1988), pp. 6-10.

[5]Letter of Frank Noxon to Max J. Herzberg, December 7, 1926, in *Stephen Crane: Letters,* p. 335.

[6]Stephen Crane, "Notes About Prostitutes" [1896], *The New York City Sketches of Stephen Crane,* ed. R.W. Stallman and E.R. Hagemann (New York: New York University Press, 1966), p. 260.

[7]For Crane's account of the affair, prefaced by a *Journal* description of it, see Stephen Crane, "Adventures of a Novelist," *New York Journal,* September 20, 1896, 17-18. See also Fryckstedt, and Stallman and Hagemann, "Preface," *New York City Sketches,* x-xii.

[8]Stallman, *Biography,* pp. 229-232, gives a full account of Dora's second arrest and the enmity of the New York police for Crane.

[9]Quoted in Stallman, *Biography,* p. 224.

[10]Stephen Crane, "Adventures of a Novelist," 17.

[11]Robert H. Davis, Introduction, *The Work of Stephen Crane,* Vol. 2, ed. Wilson Follett (New York: Russell and Russell, 1925), xvii-xviii.

[12]Letter of E.W. McCready to J.R. Stolper, January 22, 1934, Appendix, *Stephen Crane: Letters,* p. 339.

[13]On Crane's protective attitude toward Cora, see Stallman, *Biography,* pp. 240, 304. The Davis remark is quoted in Scott C. Osborn, "Stephen Crane and Cora Taylor: Some Corrections," *American Literature,* 26 (1954), 416. Osborn also quotes Davis's characterization of Cora as the "mistress of a brothel," 417.

[14]On Cora as "Mrs. Crane," see Lillian Gilkes, "Stephen Crane and the Harold Frederics," *The Serif,* 6 (December, 1969), 23. The relative was Helen Crane, "My Uncle, Stephen Crane," *American Mercury,* 31 (January, 1934), 28.

[15]Lillian Gilkes, *Cora Crane* (Bloomington: Indiana University Press, 1960), Chapter 8, passim.

[16]On the Reverend Crane, See Stallman, pp. 5-8. On Mrs. Crane's religiosity and aid to an unwed mother, see pp. 5 and 9.

[17]On Crane's prudery, see Stallman, *Biography,* pp. 47-48; see also editorial commentary, *Stephen Crane: Letters,* p. 9.

[18]Quoted in Stallman, *Biography,* p. 225.

[19]Quoted in Stallman, *Biography,* p. 74.

[20]Gilkes, *Cora Crane,* p. 34.

[21]Malcolm Cowley, "A Natural History of American Naturalism," *Documents of Modern Literary Realism,* ed. George J. Becker (Princeton: Princeton University Press, 1963), p. 443.

[22]Quoted in Stallman, *Biography,* p. 70. I am indebted to his Chapter 5 discussion of the facts concerning the publication of the 1893 *Maggie.*

[23]See Crane's letter to Ripley Hitchcock, February 4-6?, 1896, *Stephen Crane: Letters,* p. 112: He "dispensed with a goodly number of damns," but there is no evidence that he excised the solicitation scene himself. See also Hershel Parker and Brian Higgins, "Maggie's 'Last Night': Authorial Design and Editorial Patching," Stephen Crane, *Maggie: A Girl of the Streets* [text and criticism], ed. Gullason, pp. 234-245.

[24]David M. Fine, "Abraham Cahan, Stephen Crane and the Romantic Tenement Tale of the Nineties," *American Studies,* 14 (Spring, 1973), 102.

[25]Edward W. Townsend, *"Chimmie Fadden," Major Max and Other Stories* (1895; rpt. New York: Garrett Press, 1969), p. 3.

[26]Edward W. Townsend, *A Daughter of the Tenements* (New York: Lovell, Coryell, 1895). Future references to this edition will appear in the text.

[27]*Bookman,* 3 (November, 1895), 217.

[28]Charles Dudley Warner, *The Golden House* (New York: Harper and Brothers, 1894), p. 57.

[29]H.H. Boyesen, *Social Strugglers* (New York: Charles Scribner's Sons, 1893), p. 263.

[30]Stallman, *Biography*, p. 76.

[31]Larzer Ziff, *The American 1890s* (New York: Viking Press, 1966), p. 190.

[32]*New York Press*, October 17, 1896, 20.

[33]*Denver Republican*, July 26, 1896, 15.

[34]*Boston Journal*, June 2, 1896, 12.

[35]Quoted in Stallman, *Biography*, p. 72.

[36]Quoted in R.W. Stallman, ed., *Stephen Crane: A Critical Bibliography*, 1st ed. (Ames, Iowa: Iowa State University Press, 1972), p. 106.

[37]Quoted in Stallman, *Bibliography*, p. 106.

[38]Quoted in Stallman, *Bibliography*, p. 118.

[39]Matthew Hale Smith, *Sunshine and Shadow in New York* (Hartford: J.B. Burr, 1868), p. 377.

[40]James Buel, *Mysteries and Miseries of America's Great Cities* (San Francisco: A.L. Bancroft, 1883), p. 62.

[41]William Sanger, *The History of Prostitution* (1858; rpt. New York: Medical Publishing Company, 1897), 515.

[42]*Boston Times*, July 12, 1896.

[43]*Literary Digest*, 13 (August 8, 1896), 460.

[44]Donald B. Gibson, *The Fiction of Stephen Crane* (Carbondale and Edwardsville: Southern Illinois University Press, 1968), Chapter 2, passim; Thomas A. Gullason, "Tragedy and Melodrama in Stephen Crane's *Maggie*," *Maggie: A Girl of the Streets*, ed. Gullason, p. 248, calls Maggie "one of the most absent heroines in American literature."

[45]Sanger, p. 494.

[46]Emile Zola, *Nana* [1881]. (Paris: Fasquelle, 1974), p. 32. The translation is mine.

[47]See Chapter 2 for a discussion of the Judson and Mayo works; Edward Crapsey, *The Nether Side of New York* (New York: Sheldon Publishing Company, 1872), p. 14.

[48]Gibson, p. 29, makes a similar point.

[49]"A Desertion" [1900], *The New York City Sketches of Stephen Crane*, pp. 189-191. Future references to this edition will appear in the text.

[50]"A Desertion" [189?], *The New York Sketches*, pp. 260-261. Future references to this edition will appear in the text.

[51]"In the Tenderloin: A Duel Between An Alarm Clock and a Fatal Purpose" [1896], *The New York City Sketches of Stephen Crane*, pp. 159-162. Future references to this edition will appear in the text.

[52]Bernard Weinstein, "The Journalism of Stephen Crane." Unpub. Ph.D. diss., New York University, 1968, p. 183.

[53]"Yen-Nock Bill and His Sweetheart" [1896], *The New York City Sketches*, pp. 170-172. Future references to this edition will appear in the text.

[54]"The 'Tenderloin' As It Really Is" [1896], *The New York City Sketches*, pp. 162-167. Future references to this edition will appear in the text.

[55]"A Detail" [1896], *The New York City Sketches*, pp. 277-279. Future references to this edition will appear in the text.

[56]Davis, Introduction, xix.

[57]Davis, Introduction, xix.

[58]Lawrence E. Hussman, Jr., "The Fate of the Fallen Woman in *Maggie* and *Sister Carrie*," *The Image of the Prostitute in Modern Literature*, ed. Pierre L. Horn and Mary Beth Pringle (New York: Ungar, 1984), p. 96.

[59]Donald Pizer, "Stephen Crane's *Maggie* and American Naturalism," *Criticism*, 7 (Spring, 1965), 173.

[60]*Maggie: A Girl of the Streets*, Vol. 1, *The Works of Stephen Crane*, ed. Fredson Bowers (Charlottesville: The University Press of Virginia, 1969). Future references will appear in the text as the Virginia edition.

[61]On the Reverend Crane, see editorial commentary, *Stephen Crane: Letters*, p. 5; Reverend Thomas DeWitt Talmage, *The Masque Torn Off* (Chicago: J. Fairbanks and Company, 1879). Future references to this edition will appear in the text. Talmage refers to his "divine commission" in another anti-prostitution tract, *The Night Sides of City Life* (Chicago: J. Fairbanks, 1878), p. 8. See also Marcus Cunliffe, "The American Background of *Maggie*," *American Quarterly*, 6 (Spring, 1955), 37-38.

[62]Joseph S. Salemi, "Down a Steep Place into the Sea: Suicide in Stephen Crane's *Maggie*," *American Notes and Queries*, n.s.1 (April, 1988), 59.

[63]Carol Hurd Green, "Stephen Crane and the Fallen Women," *American Novelists Revisited: Essays in Feminist Criticism*, ed. Fritz Fleischmann (Boston: G.K. Hall and Company, 1982), p. 235.

[64]Wirt Sikes, *One Poor Girl. The Story of Thousands* (Philadelphia: J.B. Lippincott, 1869), p. 54. Future references to this edition will appear in the text.

[65]Eric Solomon, *Stephen Crane: From Parody to Realism* (Cambridge: Harvard University Press, 1967), pp. 23-25.

[66]*George's Mother*, Vol. 1, *The Works of Stephen Crane*, ed. Bowers. Future references to this edition will appear in the text.

[67]Letter of Frank W. Noxon to Max Herzberg, December 7, 1926, in *Stephen Crane: Letters*, p. 335.

Chapter 4

[1]Frederic's *Damnation* was listed in fifth place, Crane's *Red Badge* in eighth place in a survey of the ten best-selling novels of 1896. See Alice P. Hackett, *Fifty Years of Best Sellers, 1895-1945* (Boston: R.R. Bowker, 1945), p. 12.

[2]Harold Frederic, "Stephen Crane's Triumph," *New York Times*, September 26, 1896, 22; Stephen Crane, "Harold Frederic," *The Chap-Book*, 3 (1898), 358.

[3]There is no published biography of Frederic. The best source remains Paul Haines, "Harold Frederic." Unpub. Ph.D. diss., New York University, 1945. Biographical chapters appear in Thomas O'Donnell and Hoyt C. Franchere, *Harold Frederic* (New York: Twayne Publishers, 1961). See also Briggs, passim.

[4]A full account is given in Lillian B. Gilkes, "Stephen Crane and the Harold Frederics," *The Serif*, 5 (December, 1969), 21-48.

[5]Harold Frederic, *Gloria Mundi* (Chicago: Herbert S. Stone, 1899), p. 323. Future references to this edition will appear in the text.

[6]Alfred Kazin, *On Native Grounds. An Interpretation of Modern American Prose Literature* (New York: Doubleday and Anchor, 1956), p. 13, voices a common sentiment in calling Frederic "a pioneer realist." See also Austin Briggs, Jr., *The Novels of Harold Frederic* (Ithaca: Cornell University Press, 1969), passim. On Frederic as naturalist *manqué*, see Charles C. Walcutt, *American Literary Naturalism, A Divided Stream* (Minneapolis: University of Minnesota Press, 1956), p. 47.

[7]O'Donnell and Franchere, p. 19.

[8]William Acton, *Prostitution Considered in Its Moral, Social, and Sanitary Aspects* [1857] (1870 ed.; rpt. London: Frank Cass, 1972); Michael Pearson, *The Five Pound Virgins* (New York: The Saturday Review Press, 1972), Chapter 2.

[9]This Victorian era description of a "brazen-faced woman" is quoted in Francoise Basch, *Relative Creatures. Victorian Women in Society and the Novel* (New York: Schocken Books, 1974), p. 197.

[10]Taine is quoted in Pearson, p. 278, the *Saturday Review* in Pearson, p. 24.

[11]Lady Mary Jeune, "Saving the Innocents," *Fortnightly Review*, 44 (November, 1885), 669-682. See also F.K. Prochaska, *Women and Philanthropy in Nineteenth-Century England* (Oxford: The Clarendon Press, 1980).

[12]Edward J. Bristow, *Vice and Vigilance. Purity Movements in Britain Since 1700* (Totowa, N.J.: Rowman and Littlefield, 1977), Chapters 6 and 7; Judith Walkowitz, *Prostitution and Victorian Society: Women, Class and the State* (Cambridge: Cambridge University Press, 1980), p. 42; Ann R. Higginbotham, "Respectable Sinners: Salvation Army Rescue Work with Unmarried Mothers, 1884-1914," in *Religion in the Lives of English Women, 1760-1930*, ed. Gail Malmgreen (Bloomington: Indiana University Press, 1986), p. 229.

[13]Acton, p. 14; Raymond L. Schults, *Crusader in Babylon: W.T. Stead and the Pall Mall Gazette* (Lincoln: University of Nebraska Press, 1972), Chapter 5.

[14]"Down Among the Dead Men," *New York Times*, July 24, 1884, 1; "The New American President," *Pall Mall Budget*, 22 (November 14, 1884), 12-14. The *Budget* was the *Gazette's* weekly digest. Haines, p. 135n, establishes Frederic's authorship of the *Gazette* articles by citing a letter from Stead's private secretary commissioning Frederic to do them.

[15]O'Donnell and Franchere, p. 102.

[16]"Some Recollections of Harold Frederic," *Saturday Review* [London], 86 (October 29, 1898), p. 571.

[17]Biographical commentary, *Correspondence*, pp. 512-513. The articles were: "From a Saunterer in the Labyrinth," *Pall Mall Gazette*, 23 (July 18, 1885), 2, republished in the *Pall Mall Budget*, 22 (July 24, 1885), 22, and "Musings on the Question of the Hour," *Pall Mall Budget*, 23 (August 13, 1885), 11. References will be to the *Budget* articles and will appear in the text.

[18]Full accounts of the "Maiden Tribute" affair appear in Schults, Chapter 5, and Pearson, Chapters 7-9. I am indebted to them both.

[19]Harold Frederic, "Mr. Stead and His Work," *New York Times*, September 7, 1885, 5. Future references to this article will appear in the text.

[20]Harold Frederic, "Europe's War Drama," *New York Times*, February 21, 1897, 15.

[21]Frederic Whyte, *Life of W.T. Stead* (New York: Houghton, Mifflin, 1925), I, p. 179.

[22]Editor's introduction to Harold Frederic, "Musings on the Question of the Hour," 22.

[23]See Acton, pp. 30-31, for a similar vision of the prostitute.

[24]Harold Frederic, "Mr. Stead and His Work," 5.

[25]See Norris Magnuson, *Salvation in the Slums. Evangelical Social Work, 1865-1920* (Metuchen, N.J.: Scarecrow Press and the American Theological Library Association, 1977), Chapter 6; Higginbotham, passim.

[26]Pearson, p. 162; Joseph O. Baylen, "A Victorian's 'Crusade' in Chicago, 1893-1894," *Journal of American History*, 51 (December, 1964), 419. On Social Purity proceedings, see, for example, *National Purity Congress: Papers, Addresses, Portraits*, ed. Aaron M. Powell (Baltimore: American Purity Alliance, 1896).

[27]"Some Recollections of Harold Frederic," 571.

[28]"Harold Frederic, The Author of *Theron Ware*," *Current Opinion*, 20 (1896), 14.

[29]Editorial commentary, *Correspondence*, p. 9.

[30]"Some Recollections of Harold Frederic," 571.

[31]C. Lewis Hind, *More Authors and I* (New York: Dodd, Mead, 1922), p. 114.

[32]Everett Carter, "Introduction," Harold Frederic, *The Damnation of Theron Ware* [1896] (Cambridge, Mass.: The Belknap Press of Harvard University Press, 1960), xiii. References to this edition will appear in the text, as will references to the following

editions of Frederic's novels: *The Lawton Girl* (1890; rpt. Ridgewood, N.J.: Gregg Press, 1968), *Seth's Brother's Wife* (1886; rpt. Ridgewood, N.J.: Gregg Press, 1968), "Marsena" in *Harold Frederic's Stories of York State*, ed. Edmund Wilson (Syracuse: Syracuse University Press, 1966).

[33]Larzer Ziff, *The American 1890s: Life and Times of a Lost Generation* (New York: Viking, 1966), p. 209.

[34]Quoted in Haines, p. 147. Haines, whose dissertation excerpts Frederic's working notes, remains the only scholar to have seen them in entirety in the collection of Frederic's daughter Mrs. Eliot Keen. For information on the stages of composition of *The Lawton Girl* I am thus greatly indebted to him.

[35]Quoted in Haines, p. 132. Carey McWilliams, "Harold Frederic: 'A Country Boy of Genius,' " *University of California Chronicle*, 35 (January, 1933), 28, terms *Seth's Brother's Wife* "essentially Frederic's own story."

[36]Haines, p. 41.

[37]Outline in Haines, p. 277.

[38]Haines, p. 41. Briggs, p. 150n, speaks in passing of "Frederic's first-hand acquaintance with the bordellos of London."

[39]Outline in Haines, p. 278.

[40]For information on Frederic's working title and shift in emphasis regarding Jessica, I am again indebted to Haines, although he offers no comment on the change Frederic wrought in his title character.

[41]Quoted in Thomas O'Donnell, Stanton Garner and Robert H. Woodward, eds., *A Bibliography of Writings By and About Harold Frederic* (Boston: G.K. Hall, 1975), p. 145.

[42]William Wallace, "New Novels," *Academy*, 37 (May 17, 1890), 333.

[43]Quoted in O'Donnell et al, *Bibliography*, p. 144.

[44]Quoted in O'Donnell et al, *Bibliography*, p. 148.

[45]Quoted in O'Donnell et al, *Bibliography*, p. 146.

[46]"Summer Reading," *Critic* n.s. 13 (June 7, 1890), v.

[47]*Public Opinion*, 9 (May 31, 1890), 186.

[48]The phrase "the difficulties in the case" appears in a review quoted in O'Donnell et al, *Bibliography*, p. 144; the "social question" in "Recent Fiction," *Nation*, 51 (September 4, 1890), 195; the reference to "such people" in O'Donnell et al, *Bibliography*, p. 143.

[49]Reference to the "course" material is quoted in O'Donnell et al, *Bibliography*, p. 148; to the "seamy" in O'Donnell et al, *Bibliography*, p. 145; to the "unpleasant" in the *Manchester Guardian*, 8 April 1890, and to the "dingy" in "Recent Fiction," *Nation*, 195.

[50]Quoted in O'Donnell et al, *Bibliography*, p. 155.

[51]*Philadelphia Public Ledger*, May 13, 1890, 10.

[52]*Philadelphia Times*, June 23, 1890, 3.

[53]William Dean Howells, "Editor's Study," *Harper's Monthly* 31 (1890), 801.

[54]Quoted in O'Donnell et al, *Bibliography*, p. 153.

[55]O'Donnell and Franchere, p. 90.

[56]Briggs, p. 85.

[57]*Autobiography of Walter Besant* (New York: Dodd, Mead, 1902), p. 257.

[58]Martha Vicinus, *Independent Women. Work and Community for Single Women, 1850-1920* (Chicago: University of Chicago Press, 1985), p. 233.

[59]O'Donnell and Franchere, p. 19.

[60]Quoted in Haines, p. 10.

[61]On statistics regarding women's entry into social work, see Vicinus, p. 212; on Frederic's friendship with philanthropist Lady Jeune, see the biographical commentary, *Correspondence*, p. 48.

[62]Lady Jeune, 681.

[63]Harold Frederic, "Musings," 11.

[64]Quoted in Kathleen Heasman, *Evangelicals in Action. An Appraisal of Their Social Work in the Victorian Era* (London: Geoffrey Bles, 1962), p. 158. See also Bristow, pp. 5, 63.

[65]Quoted in E. Moberly Bell, *Josephine Butler, Flame of Fire* (London: Constable, 1962), p. 175. On Butler's earlier reclamations, see Josephine Butler, *An Autobiographical Memoir*, ed. George W. And Lucy A. Johnson (Bristol: J.W. Arrowsmith, 1913), pp. 63-64 and Pearson, p. 130.

[66]Josephine Butler, *Rebecca Jarrett* (London: Morgan and Scott, 1886), p. 9. Future references to this edition will appear in the text.

[67]Stead's remarks are quoted in Pearson, p. 127; a full account of the trial and Jarrett's part in it appears in Schults, Chapter 6.

[68]For description of Jarrett's exhortations, see Heasman, pp. 159, 161 and Bristow, p. 63.

[69]Harold Frederic, "Preface to a Uniform Edition," *In the Sixties* (1897), rpt. in *Correspondence*, p. 4.

[70]For a complete discussion see Sally Mitchell, *The Fallen Angel: Chastity, Class, and Women's Reading, 1835-1880* (Bowling Green, Ohio: Bowling Green University Popular Press, 1981), Chapter 1.

[71]Eric Trudgill, *Madonnas and Magdalens: The Origins and Development of Victorian Sexual Attitudes* (New York: Holmes and Meier, 1976), p. 289.

[72]Matilda Houstoun, *Recommended to Mercy*, 3 vols. (London: Saunders and Otley, 1863), II. 29. See also Mrs. Gaskell, *Ruth* [1853] (London: Dent-Everyman, 1967); Frances Trollope, *Jessie Phillips* (London: Henry Colburn, 1848); Wilkie Collins, *The New Magdalen* (New York: Peter Fenelon Collier, 1873).

[73]O'Donnell and Franchere, p. 143.

[74]Elizabeth Gaskell, *Mary Barton* [1848] (New York: W.W. Norton and Company, 1958), p. 117.

[75]See Francoise Basch, *Relative Creatures: Victorian Women in Society and the Novel* (New York: Schocken Books, 1974), p. 225 on the Dickensian female sinner's desire for expiration and death.

[76]"Recent Fiction," *Independent*, 43 (July 10, 1890), 966.

[77]"Gissing" [1895], rpt. in *Gissing: The Critical Heritage*, ed. Pierre Coustillas and Colin Partridge (London: Routledge and Kegan Paul, 1972), p. 258.

[78]"Gissing," p. 258.

[79]Harold Frederic, "Preface to a Uniform Edition," pp. 4-5.

[80]Briggs, p. 94.

[81]She is "evil" to Everett Carter, Introduction, *The Damnation of Theron Ware*, x; a "New Woman" to Briggs, p. 91; a "secular monastic" to Dorothy Y. Deegan, *The Stereotype of the Single Woman in American Novels* (New York: King's Crown Press, 1951), p. 138.

[82]Harold Frederic, *The Marketplace* (1899; rpt. Ridgewood, N.J.: Gregg Press, 1968). Future references to the edition will appear in the text.

[83]Gail Cunningham, *The New Woman and the Victorian Novel* (London: Macmillan, 1978), p. 3.

[84]Frederic Papers, Library of Congress, notes for the 1898 novel, *Gloria Mundi*, titled "The New Woman." Under "Mind and Habits," he remarked in a similar vein that the "less [woman] thinks and knows the more beauty she retains."

[85]Grant Allen, *The Woman Who Did* (London: John Lane, 1895). Publication facts appear in Lloyd Fernando, *"New Women" in the Late Victorian Novel* (University Park: Pennsylvania State University Press, 1977), p. 131.

[86]Patricia Stubbs, *Women and Fiction. Feminism and the Novel, 1880-1920* (Sussex: Harvester Press, 1979), p. 118.

[87]See Gilkes, 29-30 and biographical commentary, *Correspondence*, pp. 271, 327, 505. In contrast, most critics censor their discussion of Frederic's relations with Kate Lyon. See O'Donnell and Franchere, pp. 67-68 and Ziff, p. 208.

[88]"Harold Frederic, The Author of *Theron Ware*," 14.

[89]Joli Jensen, "Women as Typewriters," *Turn-of-the-Century Women*, 3 (Summer, 1986), 44.

[90]O'Donnell and Franchere, p. 106, note that Frederic took the manuscript of "Marsena" to a woman typist.

[91]Biographical commentary, *Correspondence*, p. 505; Briggs, p. 27n.

[92]Gilkes, 30.

[93]During her lengthy liaison with Frederic she appears to have published only one story, "Lorraine's Last Voyage," *New York Ledger*, 38 (September 28, 1895), 9-11. See also did research for Stephen Crane but received no payment. See Stanton B. Garner, "Kate Lyon—Author," *The Frederic Herald*, 1 (September, 1967), 2 and Gilkes, 30.

[94]Quoted in Gilkes, 30.

[95]Norman and Jeanne MacKenzie, *H.G. Wells. A Biography* (New York: Simon and Schuster, 1973), p. 112.

[96]On Ruth Frederic's withdrawal from school, and Kate's social ostracism, see Haines, pp. 210, 212.

[97]H.G. Wells, *Experiments in Autobiography* (New York: Macmillan, 1934), pp. 365, 364.

[98]"Some Recollections of Harold Frederic," 571.

[99]Quoted in Gilkes, 32.

[100]Harold Frederic, *March Hares* (New York: D. Appleton and Company, 1896). Future references to this edition will appear in the text.

[101]Briggs, p. 150.

[102]Harold Frederic, *Mrs. Albert Grundy: Observations in Philistia* (1896; rpt. Greenwood, Ct.: Meridian Company, 1969), pp. 133-134.

[103]Gilkes, 38.

Chapter 5

[1]Reginald Wright Kauffman, *The House of Bondage* (1910; rpt. Upper Saddle River, N.J.: Gregg Press, 1968). Future references to this edition will appear in the text.

[2]Walter B. Rideout, *The Radical Novel in the United States, 1900-1954* (Cambridge: Harvard University Press, 1956), p. 68. A brief discussion of Kauffman and the muckraking tradition is in Louis Filler, *Crusaders for American Liberalism* (1939; rev. ed., Yellow Springs, Ohio: Antioch Press, 1959), Chapter 22.

[3]Reginald Wright Kauffman, Introduction, *The Girl That Goes Wrong* (New York: Macaulay, 1911), pp. 3-5. Future references to this edition will appear in the text. On Kauffman as a researcher, see the *National Cyclopedia of American Biography* (New York: James T. White, 1965), Vol. 48, pp. 531-532 and "Writers and Their Work," *Hampton's*, 23 (August, 1909), 285.

[4]Interview with Kauffman, *New York Times*, November 5, 1911, 13; Reginald Wright Kauffman, "Explanation," *The Spider's Web* (New York: Moffat, Yard, 1913), passim. Future references to this edition will appear in the text.

[5]"White Slave Traffic," *Presentment of the Additional Grand Jury for the January Term of the Court of General Session...*, in *The House of Bondage*, pp. 477-480.

[6]Anna Garlin Spencer, "The Scarlet Woman," *Forum*, 49 (1913), 289.

[7]W.T. Stead, *If Christ Came to Chicago* (London: Temple House, 1895). See also Joseph O. Baylen, "A Victorian's 'Crusade' in Chicago, 1893-1894," *Journal of American History*, 51 (1964), 418-434.

[8]See Mark Thomas Connelly, *The Response to Prostitution in the Progressive Era* (Chapel Hill: University of North Carolina Press, 1980), passim; Roy Lubove, "The Progressives and the Prostitute," *Historian*, 24 (May, 1962), 308-329; Robert Riegel, "Changing American Attitudes Toward Prostitution (1800-1920)," *Journal of the History of Ideas*, 29 (1968), 437-452.

[9]The Vice Commission of Chicago, *The Social Evil in Chicago* (1911; rpt. New York: Arno Press and The New York Times, 1970), pp. 388-392.

[10]George Kneeland [Of the Vice Commission of 1913], *Commercialized Prostitution in New York City* (1913; rpt, Montclair, N.J.: Patterson Smith, 1969), ix.

[11]The Committee of Eighteen, Morals Survey Committee, *The Social Evil in Syracuse*, 1913 ed.; rpt. in *Prostitution in America: Three Investigations, 1902-1914* (New York: Arno Press and The New York Times, 1976), p. 26. See also the Vice Commission of Chicago, pp. 99, 104.

[12]The Vice Commission of Chicago, p. 43.

[13]Quoted in Caro Lloyd, "The Illinois Vice Commission," *The New Review*, 1 (April 12, 1913), 453.

[14]Elizabeth Butler, *Women and the Trades, 1907-1908* (New York: Russell Sage Foundation, 1909), pp. 305-306.

[15]Rheta Childe Dorr, *What Eight Million Women Want* (Boston: Small, Maynard, 1910), p. 223.

[16]George Kibbe Turner, "The Daughters of the Poor: A Plain Story of the Development of New York City as a Leading Center of the White Slave Trade...," *McClure's*, 34 (November, 1909), 59. See also his "The City of Chicago. A Study of the Great Immoralities," *McClure's*, 28 (April, 1907), 575-592. All textual references are to the 1909 article.

[17]Turner, "The Daughters of the Poor," 59.

[18]Turner, "The Daughters of the Poor," 59. See also Theodore Bingham, *The Real Facts About the White Slave Traffic* (Boston: Gorham Press, 1911). For a good discussion of the many myths surrounding the white slave, see Edward J. Bristow, *Prostitution and Prejudice: The Jewish Fight Against White Slavery, 1870-1939* (New York: Schocken Books, 1983), Introduction.

[19]Ruth Rosen, *The Lost Sisterhood: Prostitution in America, 1900-1918* (Baltimore: Johns Hopkins University Press, 1982), pp. 155, 124; Lubove, 313.

[20]Connelly, p. 30; *New York Times*, January 13, 1910.

[21]Reginald Wright Kauffman, *Jarvis of Harvard* (Boston: L.C. Page, 1901), p. 10. Future references to this edition will appear in the text.

[22]Reginald Wright Kauffman, Introduction, *The Girl That Goes Wrong*, p. 3.

[23]If he had known of it, Kauffman would have seen the 1894 Norris work in manuscript form, as Norris deemed it too controversial to publish. It appeared posthumously in 1914. Frank Norris, *Vandover and the Brute* (New York: Grove Press, n.d.). Future references to this edition will appear in the text.

[24]Frank Luther Mott, *A History of American Magazines, 1885-1905* (Cambridge: The Belknap Press of Harvard University Press, 1957), p. 688.

[25]See, for example, Ernest Poole, "Getting That Home: Told by Jan, the Big Polish Worker," *Saturday Evening Post*, July 7, 1906, 7-9, 28. Frank Norris's *The Pit* was originally serialized in the *Post*.

[26]See *The Literary World* [Boston], 33 (February 1, 1902), 27 and Kauffman's summary of outraged Brahmin opinion in the preface to *Jarvis*, vii, ix.

[27]*The Delineator*, 73 (January, 1909), 495.

[28]Russell was best known for his 1905 *Everybody's Magazine* articles exposing the Beef Trust. He wrote about crime, the slums, and corrupt railroad franchises, issues addressed in Kauffman novels such as *The Sentence of Silence* (1912) and *The Spider's Web* (1913).

[29]Dorr's *What Eight Million Women Want* includes many of her earlier *Delineator* pieces. She also wrote for *Hampton's*.

[30]Maude E. Miner, "Two Weeks in the Night Court," *Survey*, 22 (1909), 229-234.

[31]With the outbreak of the First World War, Kauffman joined the army as an officer, saw combat in France, and, invalided out in 1917, became a war correspondent. His collected reportage, *Our Navy at Work* (1918), and fiction like *Victorious* (1919) were billed as "by the author of *The House of Bondage*." By the time of his death in 1959, after a long and productive career as a newsman, he had written over fifty books, thirty of them novels. The fame of *The House of Bondage* was by now forgotten, a brief obituary acknowledging the book by listing it, without further comment, with a few other titles.

[32]*New York Times*, September 17, 1910, 511.

[33]*The Spider's Web*, ix. See also Filler, p. 291.

[34]*The Spider's Web*, ix; F.C.S., Introduction, *The House of Bondage*, n.p.

[35]Emma Goldman, "The White Slave Traffic," *Mother Earth*, 4 (January 1910), 346. A slightly altered version, titled "The Traffic in Women" [1917], is in *The Traffic in Women and Other Essays* (1917; rpt. New York: Times Change Press, 1970), p. 20.

[36]"Sex O'Clock in America," *Current Opinion*, 55 (1913), 113. An oblique negative reference to Kauffman appears in Agnes Repplier, "The Repeal of Reticence," *Atlantic Monthly*, 113 (March, 1914), 301.

[37]See Chapter Six. On Comstock's suppression of Daniel Carson Goodman's *Hagar Revelly*, which dealt with adultery, see *Publishers' Weekly*, January 3, 1914, 14 and February 14, 1914, 515-517. Goodman's reaction to Comstock is in the *New York Times*, June 20, 1915, 14.

[38]Connelly, p. 197n.

[39]*New York Times*, September 17, 1910, 511.

[40]Hutchins Hapgood, *Bookman*, 32 (October, 1910), 178.

[41]John Masefield, Preface, Reginald Wright Kauffman, *The Daughters of Ishmael* [British title of *The House of Bondage*] (London: Stephen Swift, 1911), vii. For a novel on English white slavery, see American expatriate Elizabeth Robins's *My Little Sister* (New York: Dodd, Mead, 1913).

[42]Brand Whitlock, *The Fall Guy* (Indianapolis: Bobbs-Merrill, 1912), p. 273. See also "Is White Slavery Nothing More Than A Myth?" *Current Opinion*, 55 (1913), 348, and George Creel, "Where Is the Vice Flight?" *Harper's Weekly*, 47 (October 19, 1914), 340-342.

[43]The Roe book was also published under titles like *The Great War on White Slavery, or, Fighting for the Protection of Our Girls* (Chicago: W. Walter, 1911). Future references to the W. Walter edition will appear in the text. Walter Reckless, *Vice in Chicago* (Chicago: University of Chicago Press, 1933), p. 38, cites Roe's version, then the girl's own matter-of-fact statement.

[44]Dorr, p. 209.

[45]*New York Times*, November 5, 1911, 13.

[46]The Vice Commission of Chicago, p. 193.

[47]The girl "tired of drudgery" is cited on p 172, the girl disliking a servant's life on p. 172, the "devil" on p. 168, the "easy life" philosopher on p. 168.

[48]Rosen, p. 145.

[49]*Madeleine: An Autobiography* (1919; rpt. New York: Persea Books, 1986); *Nell Kimball: Her Life as an American Madam,* ed. Stephen Longstreet [written in 1932] (New York: Macmillan, 1970). Both works, whose authorship has been authenticated, cover Progressive era prostitution.

[50]Reginald Wright Kauffman, "Introduction," *The Girl That Goes Wrong,* passim.

[51]Walter Hurt, *The Scarlet Shadow. A Story of the Great Colorado Conspiracy* (Girard, Kansas: The Appeal to Reason Press, 1907). Future references to this edition will appear in the text.

[52]Estelle Baker, *The Rose Door* [1911] Chicago: Charles H. Kerr, 1913). Future references to this edition will appear in the text.

[53]Virginia Brooks, *Little Lost Sister* (Chicago: Gazzolo and Ricksen, 1914). Future references to this edition will appear in the text.

[54]Reginald Wright Kauffman, *The Girl That Goes Wrong,* back page.

[55]Reginald Wright Kauffman, *The Sentence of Silence* (New York: Macaulay 1914). Future references to this edition will appear in the text.

[56]Lubove, 316.

[57]Eunice Lipton, "The Laundress in Nineteenth-Century French Culture," *Art History,* 3 (September, 1980), 303.

Chapter 6

[1]The chief biographies remain Isaac F. Marcosson's adulatory *David Graham Phillips and His Times* (New York: Dodd, Mead, 1932) and Abe C. Ravitz, *David Graham Phillips.* See also Paul C. Rodgers, Jr., "David Graham Phillips. A Critical Study." Unpub. Ph.D. diss., Columbia University, 1955.

[2]George Mowry, Introduction, David Graham Phillips, *The Treason of the Senate* (Chicago: Quadrangle Books, 1964), p. 23. The book reprints the 1906 *Cosmopolitan* articles.

[3]David Graham Phillips, *Susan Lenox: Her Fall and Rise,* Intro. by Robert W. Chambers (New York: D. Appleton and Company, 1917). Future references, which will appear in the text, will be to this unexpurgated edition, unless otherwise noted. When a given sentence or passage was omitted from the censored edition, the chapter will so indicate.

[4]Quoted in Marcosson, p. 257. On the censorship of *Susan Lenox,* see Marcosson, Chapter 8.

[5]This 1917 *Minneapolis Journal* review of *Susan Lenox* is quoted in Marcosson, p. 263.

[6]Marcosson, p. 254.

[7]"Invicta," *New Republic,* March 10, 1917, 169.

[8]Eric F. Goldman, "David Graham Phillips: Victorian Critic of Victorianism," *The Lives of Eighteen from Princeton,* ed. Willard Thorp (Freeport: Books for Libraries Press, 1968), p. 337.

[9]Review of *The Husband's Story, New York Times,* October 1, 1910, 535. See also "David Graham Phillips, A Novelist with a Vision," *Current Literature,* 52 (March, 1911), 327-329.

[10]"Invicta," 176.

[11]F.C.S., Introduction, David Graham Phillips, *A Woman Ventures* (1902; rpt. Upper Saddle River, N.J.: Gregg Press, 1970), n. p. Future references to this edition will appear in the text. See Marcosson for an extended discussion.

[12]David Graham Phillips, "The Union of Sixth Avenue and Broadway," *Harper's Weekly,* 35 (April 25, 1891), 302. Future references will appear in the text.

[13]David Graham Phillips, *The Great God Success* (1901; rpt. Ridgewood, N.J.: Gregg Press, 1967). Future references to this edition will appear in the text.

14The piece is reprinted in Marcosson, pp. 76-77. Future references will appear in the text.

15Lois Banner, *American Beauty* (New York: Alfred A. Knopf, 1983), pp. 40, 42, 75, 133.

16David Graham Phillips, *The Price She Paid* (New York: D. Appleton and Company, 1912); *Old Wives for New* (New York: Grosset and Dunlap, 1908). Future references to these editions will appear in the text.

17James R. McGovern, "David Graham Phillips and the Virility Impulse of the Progressives," *New England Quarterly*, 39 (1966), 335.

18David Graham Phillips, "Albert J. Beveridge," *Success*, 8 (August, 1905), 526. Future references will appear in the text.

19McGovern, 346.

20Alfred Kazin, *On Native Grounds. An Interpretation of Modern American Prose Literature*, rev. ed. (Garden City, N.Y.: Doubleday and Anchor, 1956), p. 71.

21David Graham Phillips, *The Fashionable Adventures of Joshua Craig* (New York: D. Appleton and Company, 1909), p. 6. Future references to this edition will appear in the text.

22Banner, p. 171.

23Quoted in "David Graham Phillips, A Novelist with a Vision," 327.

24"Current Fiction," *Nation*, 87 (March, 1909), 226.

25David Graham Phillips, *The Grain of Dust* (New York: D. Appleton and Company, 1911). *The Husband's Story* (New York: D. Appleton and Company, 1910), in which a bored man of power laments his idle wife, is far more typical of Phillips's plots. Future references to these editions will appear in the text.

26See, for example, his articles "Restless Husbands," *Cosmopolitan*, 51 (August, 1911), 419-425 and "What Is A Successful Wife?" *Delineator*, April, 1911, 265, 327-328. Future references to the *Delineator* article will appear in the text.

27David Graham Phillips, *Light-Fingered Gentry* (New York: D. Appleton and Company, 1907), p. 51.

28David Graham Phillips, *The Price She Paid* (New York: D. Appleton and Company, 1912). Future references to this edition will appear in the text.

29Ravitz, p. 101. For a good discussion of Phillips's attitude toward the Woman Question, see Ravitz, Chapter 6.

30Ida M. Tarbell, *The Business of Being a Woman* (New York: Macmillan, 1912), p. 63.

31Charlotte Perkins Gilman, *The Man-Made World* (New York: Charlton Company, 1911), pp. 163-177; Anna Garlin Spencer, *Woman's Share in Social Culture* (New York and London: Mitchell Kennerley, 1913), i-viii.

32Rosalind Rosenberg, *Beyond Separate Spheres. The Intellectual Roots of Modern Feminism* (New Haven: Yale University Press, 1982), xiv. See also Carol Hymowitz and Michaele Weissman, *A History of Women in America* (New York: Bantam Books, 1978), p. 228, and Spencer, passim.

33David Graham Phillips, *The Reign of Gilt* (New York: James Pott and Company, 1905), pp. 270-271. Future references will appear in the text.

34Joanna Russ, "Comment on 'Prostitution in Medieval Canon Law,'" *Signs*, 5 (Summer, 1977), 922.

35Rodgers, iii; Rupert Hughes, "David Graham Phillips," *Book News Monthly*, 25 (April, 1907), 507-510.

36Kazin, *On Native Grounds*, rev. ed., p. 81; Frank Luther Mott, *A History of American Magazines* (Cambridge, Mass.: The Belknap Press, 1938). Six of Phillips's novels were serialized in the *Saturday Evening Post*.

37H.L. Mencken, "The Leading American Novelist," *Smart Set*, 33 (January, 1911), 163-164.

[38]See for example, reviews of his work in the *Dial*, 47 (November 16, 1909), 386 and the *New York Times*, August 28 1909, 511.

[39]On Phillips's "indecency" and "vulgarity," see *Independent*, 64 (April 9, 1908), 808, *Nation*, 88 (March 4, 1909), 266, and Charlotte Harwood, "Fiction in a Lighter Vein," *Putnam's*, August 1, 1908, 621. On his "coarseness," see *Nation*, 86 (March 19, 1908), 264.

[40]C.E. Russell, "The Message of David Graham Phillips," *Book News Monthly*, 25 (April, 1907), 53.

[41]"Graham Phillips's Hygienic Novel," *New York Times*, April 4, 1908, 187.

[42]Marcosson, p. 254.

[43]Mott, p. 501.

[44]Marcosson, p. 256. See also his Chapter 8.

[45]Marcosson, p. 256. For a full account of the "battle for *Susan Lenox*," see Marcosson, Chapter 8.

[46]See especially "The Story of Susan Lenox," *Hearst's International Magazine*, 28 (October, 1916), 226 and 18 (March, 1916), 171.

[47]Mott, p. 501.

[48]Quoted in Paul S. Boyer, *Purity in Print. The Vice-Society Movement and Book Censorship in America* (New York: Charles Scribner's and Sons, 1968), p. 288n.

[49]Marcosson, p. 261; Ravitz, p. 179n.

[50]David Graham Phillips, *Susan Lenox: Her Fall and Rise*, Afterward by Elizabeth Janeway (1917; rpt. Carbondale and Edwardsville: Southern Illinois University Press, 1977), xix. A reprint of the bowdlerized Appleton edition, the text omits 100 pages of the original.

[51]Walter Kendrick, *The Secret Museum. Pornography in Modern Culture* (Viking, 1987), p. 161.

[52]Marcosson, p. 261.

[53]*New York Times*, February 25, 1917, 62,63. See also *Boston Evening Transcript*, March 3, 1917, 6.

[54]James Gerould, Review of *Susan Lenox*, *Bellman*, 22 (April 7, 1917), 385.

[55]"Invicta," 63.

[56]Frank Crane, Review of *Susan Lenox*, *Hearst's International Magazine*, 28 (September, 1915), 165; "The Contested Merits of David Graham Phillips's Posthumous Novel," *Current Opinion*, 62 (April, 1917), 274.

[57]Quoted in Marcosson, pp. 262-263.

[58]Arthur Hobson Quinn, *American Fiction* (New York: D. Appleton and Company, 1936), p. 645; Kenneth S. Lynn, *The Dream of Success: A Study of the Modern American Imagination* (Boston: Little, Brown and Company, 1955), Chapter 3, has only a slightly higher opinion of Phillips's talents.

[59]Marcosson, 249.

[60]Louis Filler, "An American Odyssey: The Story of Susan Lenox," *Accent*, 1 (Autumn, 1940), 28.

[61]Janeway, xvii.

[62]Ruth Rosen and Sue Davidson, eds., *The Maimie Papers* (Old Westbury, N.Y.: Feminist Press, 1977); Margaret von Staden, "My Story (The History of a Prostitute's Life in San Francisco," Ms., Schlesinger Library. The modern historian is Ruth Rosen, *The Lost Sisterhood. Prostitution in America, 1900-1918* (Baltimore: Johns Hopkins University Press, 1982), Chapter 8.

[63]Janeway, xii, likens her to Moll; Kazin, *On Native Grounds* [original edition] (New York: Reynal and Hitchcock, 1942), p. 108, compares Susan to Fielding's hero.

[64]R. W. B. Lewis, *The American Adam. Innocence, Tragedy and Tradition in the Nineteenth Century* (Chicago: Phoenix Books and the University of Chicago Press, 1958), p. 5.

[65]Leslie Fiedler, *Love and Death in the American Novel*, rev. ed. (New York: Dell Publishing Company, 1960), p. 18.

[66]Lewis, p. 61.

[67]"Miggles," [1870]. *Bret Harte's Stories of the Old West* (Boston: Houghton, Mifflin, 1940).

[68]Marcosson, p. 253.

[69]Brand Whitlock, "The Girl That's Down," *The Fall Guy* (Indianapolis: The Bobbs-Merrill Company, 1912). Future references to this edition will appear in the text.

[70]Quoted in Daniel Aaron, *Writers on the Left* (New York: Avon Books, 1961), p. 39. A good biography of Reed is Robert Rosenstone, *Romantic Revolutionary* (New York: Alfred A. Knopf, 1975).

[71]Walter Lippmann, "Legendary John Reed," *New Republic*, December 29, 1914, 15. See also Robert Hallowell, "John Reed," *New Republic*, November 7, 1920, 298-299.

[72]John Reed, "A Taste of Justice," *Masses*, 4 (April, 1913). Future references will appear in the text.

[73]John Reed, "Broadway Night," *Masses*, 8 (May, 1916), 20.

[74]John Reed, "Where the Heart Is,", *Masses*, 4 (January, 1913), 8.

[75]Rosenstone, p. 89.

[76]John Reed, "A Daughter of the Revolution," *Masses*, 6 (February, 1915). Future references will appear in the text.

[77]Alfred Kreymbourg, *Troubadour* (New York: Boni and Liveright, 1925), pp. 104-105, discusses the prototype for his *Edna, the Girl of the Street* (New York, n.p., 1919). Future references to Kreymbourg's privately printed edition will appear in the text.

[78]I am indebted to Kreymbourg, *Troubadour*, pp. 106-109, for this account of the attempt to censor *Edna*.

[79]William Rose Benet, "Poor Girl," *Masses*, 5 (April, 1914), ll.

[80]Horatio Winslow, "A Daughter of Delight," *Masses*, 2 (November, 1911), 8-9 and December, 1911, 6-7.

[81]Frank Shay, "The Machine," *Masses*, 4 (August, 1913), 9.

[82]James Henle, "Nobody's Sister," *Masses*, 6 (January, 1915), 10. Future references will appear in the text.

Chapter 7

[1]*Madeleine, An Autobiography* (1919; rpt. New York: Persea Books, 1986), Intro. Marcia Carlisle. Future references to this edition will appear in the text. The irate Sumner is quoted in Paul S. Boyer, *Purity in Print. The Vice-Society Movement in America* (New York: Scribners, 1968), p. 50.

[2]Boyer, Chapter 2.

[3]Carlisle, Introduction to *Madeleine*, vi.

[4]*Nell Kimball, her Life as an American Madam*, ed. Stephen Longstreet [written 1932] (New York: Macmillan, 1970). Future references to this edition will appear in the text. There are many parallels between the lives of the two women, including early promiscuity as rebellion against parental discipline, voluntary entry into a midwestern brothel, and "upward mobility" as a madam. Unlike Madeleine's, Kimball's narrative is filled with profanity. On prostitution in the 1930's and 40's, see Pauline Tabor, *Pauline's* (Louisville, Ky.: Touchstone Publishing Company, 1971).

[5]Carlisle, vi.

[6]*New York Times*, November 16, 1919, 662.

[7]*New Republic*, December 24, 1919, 25.

[8]Margaret von Staden, "My Story (The History of a Prostitute's Life in San Francisco)," Ms., Schlesinger Library; Lydia Pettengill Taylor, *From Under the Lid* (Portland: Glass and Prud'homme, 1938); *The Maimie Papers,* ed. Ruth Rosen and Sue Davidson (Old Westbury, N.Y.: Feminist Press, 1977).

[9]Arnold S. Maerov, "Prostitution: A Survey and Review of Twenty Cases," *Psychiatric Quarterly,* 39 (1965), 680. See also Charles Winick and Paul Kinsie, *The Lively Commerce. Prostitution in the United States* (Chicago: Quadrangle Books, 1971), p. 85.

[10]See C. Aronovici, *Unmarried Girls with Sex Experience* (Philadelphia: Bureau for Social Research of the Seybert Institute, 1915) and Jean Weidensall, *The Mentality of the Criminal Woman* (Baltimore: Warwick and York, 1916).

[11]Jacob Riis, "Nigger Martha's Wake," *Out of Mulberry Street* (1898; rpt. Upper Saddle River, N.J.: Gregg Press, 1970). Future references to this edition will appear in the text.

[12]Jacob Riis, *How the Other Half Lives* (1890; rpt. New York: Dover, 1971), p. 189. With a prudery fanatical by modern standards, Riis praised a "gentle and refined woman who, left in direst poverty to earn her own living among strangers, threw herself from her attic window, preferring death to dishonor" (183). Future references to this edition will appear in the text.

[13]James B. Lane, *Jacob A. Riis and the American City* (Port Washington, N.Y.: Kennikat Press, 1974), p. 83.

[14]Quoted in Jeffrey F. Thomas, "Bret Harte and the Power of Sex," *Western American Literature,* 8 (1973), 91.

Bibliography

I. Fiction, Sketches, Poetry, and Drama on the Prostitute, Fallen Woman, and Seductress

Alcott, Louisa May. *Work*. Boston: Roberts Brothers, 1873.

Allen, Grant. *The Woman Who Did*. London: John Lane, 1895.

✗Baker, Estelle. *The Rose Door*, 1911. Chicago: Charles H. Kerr, 1913.

Benet, Stephen Vincent. "Poor Girl." *Masses*, 5 (April, 1914), 11.

Bond, A. Curtis. *Mrs. Sparks of Paris*. New York: Pollard and Moss, 1888.

Bradbury, Osgood. *Female Depravity; or, the House of Death*. New York: Robert DeWitt, 1857.

Brooks, Virginia. *Little Lost Sister*. Chicago: Gazzolo and Ricksen, 1914.

Brown, William Hill. *The Power of Sympathy*, 1789; rpt. Boston: New Frontiers Press, 1961.

Chopin, Kate. *The Awakening*, 1899. New York: Capricorn Books, 1964.

Collins, Wilkie. *The New Magdalen*. New York: Peter Fenelon Collier, 1873.

Crane, Stephen. *Active Service*, 1900. Vol. 3, *The Works of Stephen Crane*, ed. Fredson Bowers. Charlottesville: University Press of Virginia, 1976.

———— "A Desertion," 189? [unfinished sketch]. *The New York City Sketches of Stephen Crane*, ed. R.W. Stallman and E.R. Hagemann. New York: New York University Press, 1966.

———— "A Desertion," 1900. *The New York City Sketches*.

———— "A Detail," 1896. *The New York City Sketches*.

———— "In the Tenderloin," 1896. *The New York City Sketches*.

———— *Maggie: A Girl of the Streets* [text and criticism], 1893 ed., ed. Thomas A. Gullason. Norton Critical Edition. New York: W.W. Norton and Company, 1974.

———— *Maggie: A Girl of the Streets*, 1896 ed. Vol. 1, *The Works of Stephen Crane*, ed. Bowers, 1969.

———— "Notes About Prostitutes," 1896 [unfinished sketch]. *The New York City Sketches*.

———— "The Tenderloin As It Really Is," 1896. *The New York City Sketches*.

———— "Yen-Nock Bill and His Sweetheart," 1896. *The New York City Sketches*.

Daudet, Alphonse and Adolphe Belot. *Sappho*, trans. Elizabeth Beall Ginty. New York: F. Pullman, 1895.

———— *Sapho*. [Typescript of Clyde Fitch adaptation, 19?]. Berg Collection, New York Public Library.

Dickens, Charles. *David Copperfield*, 1850. New York: New American Library, 1962.

———— *Oliver Twist*, 1838. New York: Penguin Books, 1966.

Dreiser, Theodore. *Sister Carrie*, 1900. New York: Penguin Books, 1986.

DuMaurier, George. *Trilby*, 1894. New York: Dent Dutton, 1969.

Fawcett, Edgar. *The Evil That Men Do*. New York: Funk and Wagnalls, 1889.

Foster, George. *Celio, or New York Above-Ground and Under-Ground.* New York: Robert M. DeWitt, 1850.

———. *New York by Gaslight.* New York: Dewitt and Davenport, 1850.

Foster, Hannah W. *The Coquette,* 1797; rpt., ed. Cathy N. Davidson. New York: Oxford University Press, 1986.

Frederic, Harold. *The Damnation of Theron Ware,* 1896. Cambridge: The Belknap Press of Harvard University Press, 1960.

———. *Gloria Mundi.* Chicago: Herbert S. Stone, 1899.

———. *The Lawton Girl,* 1890; rpt. Ridgewood, N.J.: Gregg Press, 1968.

———. *March Hares.* New York: D. Appleton, 1896.

———. *The Marketplace,* 1899; rpt. Ridgewood, N.J.: Gregg Press, 1968.

———. "Marsena," 1894. *Harold Frederic's Stories of York State,* ed. Edmund Wilson. Syracuse: Syracuse University Press, 1966.

———. *Seth's Brother's Wife,* 1886; rpt. Ridgewood, N.J.: Gregg Press, 1968.

Gaskell, Elizabeth. *Mary Barton,* 1848. New York: W.W. Norton and Company, 1958.

———. *Ruth,* 1853. London: Dent-Everyman, 1967.

Gissing, George. *The Unclassed,* 1884. Sussex: The Harvester Press, 1976.

Goncourt, Edmond de. *La Fille Elisa,* 1877. Paris: Calmann-Levy, n.d.

Harte, Bret. "Miggles," 1870. *Bret Harte's Stories of the Old West.* Boston: Houghton, Mifflin, 1940.

———. "The Outcasts of Poker Flat," 1870. *Bret Harte's Stories of the Old West.*

Hawthorne, Nathaniel. "Rappaccini's Daughter," 1844. *The Celestial Railroad and Other Stories.* New York: New American Library, 1963.

———. *The Scarlet Letter,* 1850. New York: Holt, Rinehart and Company, 1960.

Henle, James. "Nobody's Sister." *Masses,* 6 (January, 1915), 10.

Holmes, Oliver Wendell. *Elsie Venner,* 1859. Boston: Houghton, Mifflin, 1891.

Houstoun, Matilda. *Recommended to Mercy.* 3. vols. London: Saunders and Otley, 1863.

Howells, William Dean. *Mrs. Farrell,* 1875. New York: Harper and Brothers, 1921.

Hungerford, Margaret. *A Modern Circe.* Philadelphia: Lippincott, 1887.

Hurt, Walter. *The Scarlet Shadow. A Story of the Great Colorado Conspiracy.* Girard, Kansas: The Appeal to Reason Press, 1907.

Ingraham, Joseph Holt. *Frank Rivers; or, The Dangers of the Town.* New York: DeWitt and Davenport, 1853.

Judson, Z.C. [E.Z.]. *The Mysteries and Miseries of New York: A Story of Real Life.* New York: Belford & Company, 1848.

Kauffman, Reginald Wright. *The Girl That Goes Wrong.* New York: Macaulay, 1911.

———. *The House of Bondage,* 1910; rpt. Upper Saddle River, N.J.: Gregg Press, 1968.

———. *Jarvis of Harvard.* Boston: L.C. Page, 1901.

———. *The Sentence of Silence.* New York: Macaulay, 1914.

———. *The Spider's Web.* New York: Moffat, Yard, 1913.

Kreymbourg, Alfred. *Edna, the Girl of the Street.* New York, n.p., 1917.

Life and Sufferings of Cecilia Mayo. Boston: M. Aurelius, 1843.

Lippard, George. *The Quaker City, or, The Monks of Monk Hall,* ed. Leslie Fiedler. 1845. New York: Odyssey Press, 1970.

Miller, Joaquin. *The Danites in the Sierras; a drama in four acts.* Chicago, Jansen, McClurg and Company, 1881.

———. *The Destruction of Gotham.* New York: Funk and Wagnalls, 1886.

———. *First Fam'lies of the Sierras.* Chicago: Jansen, McClurg and Company, 1876.

———. "Songs of the Sierras," 1871. *The Poetical Works of Joaquin Miller,* 1897; rpt. New York: Arno Press and the New York Times, 1972.

Norris, Frank. *Vandover and the Brute,* 1914. New York: Grove Press, n.d.

Odell, Samuel W. *Delilah.* New York: Hunt and Easton, 1891.

["Once I was pure as the snow"], in Cortland Myers, *Midnight in a Great City.* New York: Merrill Publishing Company, 1895, p. 141.

Parish, Grant. *Décolleté Washington.* Baltimore: John Cox's Sons, 1892.

Phillips, David Graham. "Foolish Girls Who Rouge," 1890; rpt in Isaac F. Marcosson, *David Graham Phillips and His Times.* New York: Dodd, Mead, 1932, pp. 76-77.

———. *The Great God Success,* 1901; rpt. Ridgewood, N.J.: Gregg Press, 1967.

———. *Susan Lenox: Her Fall and Rise* [unexpurgated edition]. 2 vols. Intro. by Robert W. Chambers. New York: D. Appleton and Company, 1917.

———. *Susan Lenox: Her Fall and Rise* [unexpurgated 1917 edition]. 2 vols. in 1; rpt. Carbondale and Edwardsville: Southern Illinois University Press, 1977.

———. "The Union of Sixth Avenue and Broadway," *Harper's Weekly,* 35 (April 25, 1891), 302.

Phillips, John A. *Eve. The History of an Idea.* New York: Harper and Row, 1984.

Reed, John. "Broadway Night." *Masses,* 8 (May, 1916), 19-20.

———. "A Daughter of the Revolution." *Masses,* 6 (February, 1916) 5-8.

———. "A Taste of Justice." *Masses,* 4 (April, 1913), 8-9.

———. "Seeing Is Believing." *Masses,* 5 (December, 1913), 14-16.

———. "Where the Heart Is." *Masses,* 4 (January, 1913), 8-9.

Riis, Jacob. "Nigger Martha's Wake." *Out of Mulberry Street,* 1898; rpt. Upper Saddle River, N.J.: Gregg Press, 1970.

Robins, Elizabeth. *My Little Sister,* New York: Dodd, Mead, 1913.

Rosen, Lew. *Grisette.* New York: John Delany, 1889.

Rowson, Susanna. *Charlotte Temple,* 1791; rpt. ed. Cathy N. Davidson. New York: Oxford University Press, 1986.

Savage, Richard Henry. *A Daughter of Judas.* Chicago and New York: F. Tennyson Nelly, 1894.

———. *Delilah of Harlem.* New York: The American News Company, 1893.

Shay, Frank. "The Machine." *Masses,* 4 (August, 1913), 9.

Sikes, Wirt. *One Poor Girl. The Story of Thousands.* Philadelphia: J.B. Lippincott, 1869.

Stead, W.T. *If Christ Came to Chicago.* London: Temple House, 1895.

Stowe, Harriet Beecher. *We and Our Neighbors.* New York: J.B. Ford, 1875.

Totten, Joseph Byron. *The House of Bondage,* 1913. Typescript, Theater Collection, Lincoln Center Library of the Performing Arts, New York Public Library.

Trollope, Frances. *Jessie Phillips.* London: Henry Colbourn, 1848.

Twain, Mark. *Roxy,* 1878; rpt. Ridgewood, N.J.: Gregg Press, 1968.

Twain, Mark and Charles Dudley Warner. *The Gilded Age,* 1872. New York: New American Library, 1969.

Verses for My Tombstone—If I Should Have One," in James Buel, *Mysteries and Miseries of America's Great Cities.* San Francisco: A.L. Bancroft, 1883, pp. 87-88.

Whitlock, Brand. "The Girl That's Down." *The Fall Guy.* Indianapolis: Bobbs-Merrill, 1912, 213-230.

Winslow, Horatio. "A Daughter of Delight." *Masses,* 2 (January, 1911), 8-9; 2 (December, 1911), 6-7.

Zola, Emile. *Nana,* 1881. Paris: Fasquelle, 1974.

II. Fiction on Urban Issues and Woman's Role

Brown, Charles Brockden. *Arthur Mervyn, or Memoirs of the Year 1793,* 1798-1800. New York: Holt, Rinehart and Winston, 1962.

Boyesen, H.H. *Social Strugglers.* New York: Charles Scribner's Sons, 1893.

Crane, Stephen. *George's Mother,* 1896. Vol. 1, *The Works of Stephen Crane,* ed. Fredson Bowers. Charlottesville: University Press of Virginia, 1969.

Fawcett, Edgar. *An Ambitious Woman.* Boston: Houghton, Mifflin, 1884.

————. *The Confessions of Claud.* Boston: Ticknor and Company, 1887.

————. *Miriam Balesteir.* Chicago: Belford, Clarke and Company, 1888.

————. *New York.* London and New York: F. Tennyson Nelly, 1898.

————. *Tinkling Cymbals.* Boston: James R. Osgood and Company, 1884.

"Getting That Home: Told by Jan, the Big Polish Worker," *Saturday Evening Post,* July 7, 1906.

Lyon, Kate. "Lorraine's Last Voyage." *New York Ledger,* 38 (September 28, 1895), 9-11.

Phillips, David Graham. *A Woman Ventures,* 1902; rpt. Upper Saddle River, N.J.: Gregg Press, 1970.

————. *The Fashionable Adventures of Joshua Craig.* New York: D. Appleton and Company, 1909.

————. *The Grain of Dust.* New York: D. Appleton and Company, 1911.

————. *The Great God Success,* 1901; rpt. Ridgewood, N.J.: Gregg Press, 1967.

————. *The Hungry Heart.* New York: D. Appleton and Company, 1909.

————. *The Husband's Story.* New York: D. Appleton and Company, 1910.

————. *Light-Fingered Gentry.* New York: D. Appleton and Company, 1907.

————. *Old Wives for New.* New York: Grosset and Dunlap, 1908.

————. *The Price She Paid.* New York: D. Appleton and Company, 1912.

Riis, Jacob. *Out of Mulberry Street,* 1898; rpt. Upper Saddle River, N.J.: Gregg Press, 1970.

Sheldon, Charles. *In His Steps.* New York: F.M. Lupton, 189?.

Sullivan, James W. *Tenement Tales of New York.* New York: Henry Holt and Company, 1895.

Townsend, Edward W. *"Chimmie Fadden," Major Max and Other Stories,* 1895; rpt. New York: Garrett Press, 1969.

————. *A Daughter of the Tenements.* New York: Harper and Brothers, 1899.

Warner, Charles Dudley. *The Golden House.* New York: Harper and Brothers, 1894.

III. Criticism, Biography, and Writings on Censorship and the Prostitute in Literature

Aaron, Daniel. *Writers on the Left.* New York: Avon Books, 1965.

"Anthony Comstock," *Dictionary of National Biography,* ed. Alan Johnson and Dumas Malone. Vol. 4. New York: Charles Scribner's Sons, 1930, pp. 330-331.

Arden, Eugene. "The Evil City in American Fiction." *New York History,* 35 (1954), 259-279.

Auerbach, Nina. *Woman and the Demon. The Life of a Victorian Myth.* Cambridge: Harvard University Press, 1982.

Basch, Francoise. *Relative Creatures. Victorian Women in Society and the Novel.* New York: Schocken Books, 1974.

Beer, Thomas. *Stephen Crane: A Study in American Letters.* New York: Alfred A. Knopf, 1923.

Berryman, John. *Stephen Crane.* New York: William Sloane Associates, 1950.

Bode, Carl. "Columbia's Carnal Bed." *American Quarterly,* 15 (Spring, 1963), 53-64.

Bowers, Fredson. Introduction. *The Collected Works of Stephen Crane,* vol. 1. Charlottesville: University Press of Virginia, 1977.

Boyer, Paul S. *Purity in Print. The Vice-Society Movement in the United States.* New York: Scribners, 1963.

Briggs, Austin, Jr. *The Novels of Harold Frederic.* Ithaca: Cornell University Press, 1969.

Brooks, Van Wyck. *The Times of Melville and Whitman.* New York: E.P. Dutton, 1974.

Broun, Heywood and Margaret Leech. *Anthony Comstock. Roundsman of the Lord.* New York: Albert and Charles Boni, 1927.

Carter, Everett. Introduction. Harold Frederic, *The Damnation of Theron Ware.* Cambridge: The Belknap Press of Harvard University Press, 1960.

Comstock, Anthony. "Vampire Literature." *North American Review,* 103 (August, 1891), 160-171.

"The Contested Merits of David Graham Phillips's Posthumous Novel." *Current Opinion,* 62 (April, 1917), 274-275.

Cooper, Frederick Taber. Review of *The Husband's Story. Bookman,* 35 (August, 1912), 632.

Cowley, Malcolm. "Foreward: The Revolt Against Gentility." *After the Genteel Tradition,* ed. Cowley, 1936; rpt. Carbondale: Southern Illinois University Press, 1963, 3-20.

———. "A Natural History of American Naturalism." *Documents of Modern Literary Realism,* ed. George J. Becker. Princeton: Princeton University Press, 1963, pp. 429-451.

Craig, Alec. *Suppressed Books.* Cleveland and New York: World Publishing Company, 1963.

Crane, Frank. "Susan Lenox." *Hearst's International Magazine,* 28 (September, 1915), 165.

Crane, Helen. "My Uncle, Stephen Crane." *American Mercury,* 31 (January, 1934), 24-29.

Crane, Stephen. "Adventures of a Novelist." *New York Journal,* September 20, 1896, 16-17.

———. *The Correspondence of Stephen Crane.* 2 vols. ed. Stanley Wertheim and Paul Sorrentino. New York: Columbia University Press, 1988.

———. "Harold Frederic." *The Chap Book,* 3 (1898), 358-359.

Cunliffe, Marcus. "Stephen Crane and the American Background of *Maggie.*" *American Quarterly,* 7 (Spring, 1955), 31-44.

Cunningham, Gail. *The New Woman and the Victorian Novel.* London: Macmillan, 1978.

"Current Fiction: *The Fashionable Adventures of Joshua Craig.*" *Nation,* 88 (March 4, 1909), 226.

"Current Fiction: *The Husband's Story.*" *Nation,* 88 (October 13, 1910), 339.

"David Graham Phillips, A Novelist With a Vision." *Current Literature,* 52 (March, 1911), 327-329.

Davis, Robert H. Introduction, *The Work of Stephen Crane*. Vol. 1. ed. Wilson Follett. New York: Russell and Russell, 1925.

Deegan, Dorothy Yost. *The Stereotype of the Single Woman in American Novels*. New York: King's Crown Press, 1951.

"Dramatizing Vice." *Literary Digest,* October 4, 1913, 578-580.

"Dramatizing Vice." *Publishers' Weekly,* May 18, 1889, 665.

Dunlap, George A. *The City in the American Novel, 1789-1900*, 1934; rpt. New York: Russell and Russell, 1965.

"Edgar Fawcett." *American Writers, 1600-1900*, ed. Stanley Kunitz. New York: H.W. Wilson Company, 1938, pp. 263-264.

F.C.S. Introduction. Reginald Wright Kauffman, *The House of Bondage,* 1910; rpt. Upper Saddle River, N.J.: Gregg Press, 1968.

Favreau, Alphonse R. "The Reception of Daudet's 'Sapho' in the United States." *Michigan Academy of Science Arts and Letters Papers,* 30 (1944), 581-588.

Fernando, Lloyd. *"New Women" and the Late Victorian Novel*. University Park: Pennsylvania State University, 1977.

Fiedler, Leslie. Introduction. George Lippard, *The Quaker City,* ed. Fiedler, 1845; rpt. New York: Odyssey Press, 1970.

——— *Love and Death in the American Novel*. rev.ed. New York: Dell, 1966.

Filler, Louis. "An American Odyssey. The Story of Susan Lenox." *Accent,* 1 (Autumn, 1940), 22-29.

Fine, David M. "Abraham Cahan, Stephen Crane, and the Romantic Tenement Tale of the Nineties." *American Studies,* 14 (Spring, 1973), 95-107.

Fortenberry, George, Stanton Garner and Robert H. Woodward, eds. *The Correspondence of Harold Frederic*. Fort Worth: Texas Christian University, 1977.

Frederic, Harold. "Gissing," 1895; rpt. *Gissing: The Critical Heritage,* ed. Pierre Coustillas and Colin Partridge. London: Routledge and Kegan Paul, 1972, 255-259.

——— *Mrs. Albert Grundy: Observations in Philistia,* 1896; rpt. Greenwood, Ct.: Meridian Company, 1969.

——— "The New Woman." [notes for *Gloria Mundi*] Frederic Papers, Library of Congress.

——— "Preface to a Uniform Edition," 1879; rpt. in *The Correspondence of Harold Frederic,* ed. George Fortenberry et al. Fort Worth: Texas Christian University, 1977.

——— "Stephen Crane's Triumph." *New York Times,* September 26, 1896, 22.

Frost, O.W. *Joaquin Miller*. New York: Twayne Publishers, 1967.

Fryckstedt, Olov W. "Stephen Crane in the Tenderloin." *Studia Neophilologica,* 24 (1962), 135-163.

Fryer, Judith. *The Faces of Eve. Women in the Nineteenth-Century American Novel*. London and New York: Oxford University Press, 1976.

Garland, Hamlin. [American literature and art: lecture notes], Lars Ahnebrink, *The Beginnings of Naturalism in American Fiction*. New York: Russell and Russell, 1961, pp. 440-441.

Garner, Stanton."Kate Lyon—Author." *The Frederic Herald,* 1 (September, 1967), 2.

Gerould, James. "Susan Lenox." *Bellman,* 22 (April 7, 1917), 385.

Gibson, Donald B. *The Fiction of Stephen Crane*. Carbondale and Edwardsville: Southern Illinois University Press, 1968.

Gilkes, Lillian. *Cora Crane.* Bloomington: Indiana University Press, 1960.

———. "Stephen Crane and the Harold Frederics." *The Serif,* 5 (December, 1969), 21-48.

Goldman, Eric R. "David Graham Phillips: Victorian Critic of Victorianism." *The Lives of Eighteen from Princeton,* ed. Willard Thorp. Freeport, N.Y.: Books for Libraries Press, 1968, pp. 318-332.

Goodman, Daniel Carson. [Reply to Anthony Comstock]. *New York Times,* June 20, 1915, 14.

"Graham Phillips's Hygienic Novel." *New York Times,* April 4, 1908, 187.

Green, Carol Hurd. "Stephen Crane and the Fallen Women." *American Novelists Revisited. Essays in Feminist Criticism,* ed. Fritz Fleischmann. Boston: G.K. Hall and Company, 1982, pp. 225-242.

Gullason, Thomas A. "Tragedy and Melodrama in Stephen Crane's *Maggie.*" *Maggie: A Girl of the Streets,* ed. Gullason, pp. 245-253.

Hackett, Alice P. *Fifty Years of Best Sellers, 1895-1945* (Boston: R.R. Bowker, 1945).

"*Hagar Revelley* Not Immoral." *Publishers' Weekly,* February 14, 1914, 515-517.

Haines, Paul. "Harold Frederic." Unpub. Ph.D. diss., New York University, 1945.

Hapgood, Hutchins. Review of *The House of Bondage, Bookman,* 32 (October, 1910), 178.

"Harold, Frederic, The Author of *Theron Ware.*" *Current Opinion,* 20 (1898), 14.

Harrison, Stanley. *Edgar Fawcett.* New York: Twayne Publishers, 1972.

———. "Through a Nineteenth-Century Looking Glass: The Letters of Edgar Fawcett." *Tulane Studies in English,* 15 (1967), 107-157.

Harwood, Charlotte. "Fiction in a Lighter Vein." *Putnam's,* August, 1908, 619-623.

Heilbrun, Carolyn. "The Masculine Wilderness of the American Novel." *Saturday Review,* 55 (January 29, 1972), 41-44.

Hind, C. Lewis. *More Authors and I.* New York: Dodd, Mead, 1922.

Howells, William Dean. "Criticism and Fiction" [1891]. *"Criticism and Fiction" and Other Writings,* ed. Clara Marburg Kirk and Rudolph Kirk. New York: New York University Press, 1959.

———. "Editor's Easy Chair." *Harper's Monthly,* 49 (October, 1905), 794-797.

———. "Editor's Study." *Harper's Monthly,* 31 (1890), 801.

Hughes, Rupert. "David Graham Phillips." *Book News Monthly,* 25 (April, 1907), 5-7-510.

"*The Husband's Story:* A Portrait of an American Wife." *New York Times,* October 1, 1910, 535.

Hussman, Lawrence E. "The Fate of the Fallen Woman in *Maggie* and *Sister Carrie.*" *The Prostitute in Modern Literature,* ed. Peirre L. Horn and Mary Beth Pringle. New York: Ungar, 1984, pp. 91-100.

"Invicta." *New Republic,* March 10, 1917, 167-170.

Janeway, Elizabeth. "Afterward," David Graham Phillips, *Susan Lenox: Her Fall and Rise* [expurgated 1917 edition]. 2 vols. in 1. rpt. Carbondale and Edwardsville: Southern Illinois University Press, 1977.

Katz, Joseph. "Eroticism in American Literary Realism." *Studies in American Fiction,* 5 (Spring, 1977), 35-50.

Kauffman, Reginald Wright. "Explanation." *The Spider's Web.* New York: Moffat, Yard, 1913.

———. Introduction. *The Girl That Goes Wrong.* New York: Macaulay, 1911.

Kazin, Alfred. *On Native Grounds. An Interpretation of Modern American Prose Literature.* New York: Doubleday and Anchor, 1956.

Kendrick, Walter. *The Secret Museum. Pornography in Modern Culture.* New York: Viking, 1987.

"Kennerley Clerk Fined." *Publishers' Weekly,* January 3, 1914, 14.

Kreymbourg, Alfred. *Troubadour.* New York: Boni and Liveright, 1925.

Lawson, Benjamin. *Joaquin Miller.* Boise, Idaho: Boise State University, 1979.

"The Lawton Girl." *Manchester Guardian,* April 8, 1890.

"The Lawton Girl." *Philadelphia Public Ledger,* May 13, 1890, 10.

"The Lawton Girl." *Philadelphia Times,* June 23, 1890, 3.

Lewis, Felice Flanery. *Literature, Obscenity, and Law.* Carbondale: Southern Illinois University Press, 1976.

Lewis, R.W.B. *The American Adam: Innocence, Tragedy, and Tradition in the Nineteenth Century.* Chicago: Phoenix Books and University of Chicago Press, 1955.

Lynn, Kenneth. *The Dream of Success: A Study of the Modern American Imagination.* Boston: Little, Brown and Company, 1955.

McCready, E.W. Letter to B.J.R. Stolper, January 22, 1934, *Stephen Crane: Letters,* ed. R.W. Stallman and Lillian Gilkes. New York: New York University Press, 1960, p. 339-340.

McGovern, James R. "David Graham Phillips and the Virility Impulse of the Progressives." *New England Quarterly,* 39 (1966), 334-355.

MacKenzie, Norman and Jeanne MacKenzie. *H. G. Wells. A Biography.* New York: Simon and Schuster, 1973.

Mc Williams, Carey. "Harold Frederic: 'A Country Boy of Genius.' " *University of California Chronicle,* 35 (January, 1933), 21-34.

Marberry, M.M. *Splendid Poseur. Joaquin Miller, an American Poet.* New York: Thomas Y. Crowell, 1953.

Marcosson, Isaac F. *David Graham Phillips and His Times.* New York: Dodd, Mead, 1932.

Marcus, Steven. *The Other Victorians. A Study of Sexuality and Pornography in Mid-Nineteenth-Century England.* 1964; rpt. New York: Meridian Books, 1974.

Mencken, H.L. "The Leading American Novelist." *Smart Set,* 33 (January, 1911), 163-164.

"Mr. Goodman on Morals." *New York Times,* June 20, 1915, 14.

Mitchell, Sally, *The Fallen Angel. Chastity, Class, and Women's Reading, 1835-1880.* Bowling Green, Ohio: Bowling Green University Popular Press, 1981.

Mott, Frank Luther. *Golden Multitudes, The Story of Best Sellers in the United States.* New York: Macmillan, 1947.

———— *A History of American Magazines, 1885-1905.* Cambridge: The Belknap Press, 1957.

Mowry, George. Introduction. David Graham Phillips, *The Treason of the Senate,* 1906. Chicago: Quadrangle Books, 1964.

Noxon, Frank. Letter to Max J. Herzberg, December 7, 1926, *Stephen Crane: Letters,* ed. R.W. Stallman and Lillian Gilkes. New York: New York University Press, 1960, pp. 334-339.

Nye, Russel. *The Unembarrassed Muse. The Popular Arts in America.* New York: Dial Press, 1970.

O'Donnell, Thomas and Hoyt Franchere. *A Bibliography of Writings By and About Harold Frederic.* Boston: G.K. Hall, 1975.

———— *Harold Frederic.* New York: Twayne Publishers, 1961.

Osborn, Scott C. "Stephen Crane and Cora Taylor: Some Corrections." *American Literature*, 26 (1956), 416-417.

Parker, Hershel, and Brian Higgins. "Maggie's 'Last Night': Authorial Design and Editorial Patching." Stephen Crane, *Maggie: A Girl of the Streets* [text and criticism], rpt. of 1893 ed., ed. Thomas A. Gullason. Norton Critical Edition. New York: W.W. Norton and Company, 1974, pp. 234-245.

Payne, William Morton. Review of *The Husband's Story. Dial*, 47 (November 6, 1909), 386-387.

Pizer, Donald. "Stephen Crane's *Maggie* and American Naturalism." *Criticism*, 7 (Spring, 1965), 170-190.

Rahv, Philip. "The Dark Lady of Salem." *Literature and the Sixth Sense*, ed. Rahv. Boston: Houghton, Mifflin, 1969, pp. 55-75.

"Recent Fiction." *Independent*, 43 (July 10, 1890), 966.

"Reginald Wright Kauffman." *National Cyclopedia of American Biography*. New York: James T. White, 1965, vol. 48, pp. 531-532.

Repplier, Agnes. "The Repeal of Reticence." *Atlantic Monthly*, 113 (March, 1914), 297-304.

Review of *The Destruction of Gotham. Nation*, 43 (July 29, 1886), 102.

Review of *The Evil That Men Do. Literary World*, 21 (March 1, 1890), 71.

Review of *The Fashionable Adventures of Joshua Craig. Dial*, 46 (April 16, 1909), 264.

Review of *The Hungry Heart. New York Times*, August 28, 1909, 511.

Review of *The Husband's Story. Nation*, 91 (October 31, 1910), 339.

Review of *Jarvis of Harvard. Literary* World [Boston], 33 (February 1, 1902), 27.

Review of *Maggie. Bookman*, November 3, 1895, 217.

Review of *Maggie. Boston Journal*, June 21, 1896, 12.

Review of *Maggie. Denver Republican*, July 26, 1896, 15.

Review of *Maggie. Literary Digest*, 13 (August 8, 1896), 460.

Review of *Maggie. New York Press*, October 17, 1896, 20.

Review of *Mrs. Warren's Profession. New York World*, October 28, 1905, 9.

Review of Phillips's fiction. *Independent*, 64 (April 9, 1909), 386.

Review of Phillips's fiction. *Nation*, 88 (March 4, 1909), 263 and 86 (March 19, 1908), 264.

Review of *Susan Lenox. Boston Transcript*, March 3, 1917, 6.

Review of *Susan Lenox. New York Times Book Review*, 22 (February 25, 1917), 62-63.

Review of *Susan Lenox. Current Opinion*, 62 (April, 1917), 274.

Reynolds, David S. *Beneath the American Renaissance: The Subversive Imagination in the Age of Emerson and Whitman*. New York: Alfred a. Knopf, 1988.

Rideout, Walter. *The Radical Novel in the United States, 1900-1954*. Cambridge: Harvard University Press, 1956.

Rodgers, Paul C. "David Graham Phillips. A Critical Study." Unpub. Ph. D. diss., Columbia University, 1955.

Russell, C.E. "The Message of David Graham Phillips." *Book News Monthly*, 35 (April, 1907), 511-513.

Salemi, Joseph S. "Down a Steep Place into the Sea: Suicide in Stephen Crane's *Maggie*." *American Notes and Queries* n.s. 1 (April, 1988), 58-61.

"Sex O'Clock in America." *Current Opinion*, 55 (1913), 113.

Sherman, Stuart P. Introduction. *The Poetical Works of Joaquin Miller*, ed. Sherman. New York and London: G.P. Putnam's Sons, 1923.

Solomon, Eric. *Stephen Crane: From Parody to Realism.* Cambridge: Harvard University Press, 1967.

"Some Recollections of Harold Frederic." *Saturday Review* [London], 86 (October 29, 1898), 571-572.

Spiller, Robert, et al. *Literary History of the United States,* 4th ed. rev. New York and London: Macmillan, 1974.

Stallman, R.W. *Stephen Crane: A Biography.* New York: George Braziller, 1968.

——. *Stephen Crane: A Critical Bibliography,* 1st ed. Ames, Iowa: Iowa State University Press, 1972.

——. and E.R. Hagemann. Preface. *The New York City Sketches of Stephen Crane,* ed. Stallman and Hagemann. New York: New York University Press, 1966.

Stout, Janis, *Sodoms in Eden. The City in American Fiction before 1860.* Westport, Ct.: Greenwood Press, 1976.

Stubbs, Patricia. *Women and Fiction. Feminism and the Novel, 1880-1920.* Sussex: Harvester Press, 1979.

"Summer Reading." *Critic* n.s. 13 (June 7, 1890), v.

Taylor, Walter F. *The Economic Novel in America.* Chapel Hill: University of North Carolina Press, 1942.

Tebbel, John. *A History of Book Publishing in the United States.* Vol. 2. New York: R.R. Bowker, 1975.

Thomas, Jeffrey F. "Bret Harte and the Power of Sex." *Western American Literature,* 8 (1973), 91-109.

Tobin, A.I. and Elmer Gertz. *Frank Harris. A Study.* New York: Haskell House, 1970.

Trachtenberg, Alan. "Experiments in Another Country: Stephen Crane's City Sketches." *Southern Review,* 10 (Spring, 1974), 265-285.

Trudgill, Eric. *Madonnas and Magdalens: The Origins and Development of Victorian Sexual Attitudes.* New York: Holmes and Meier, 1976.

Walcutt, Charles C. *American Literary Naturalism, A Divided Stream.* Minneapolis: University of Minnesota Press, 1956.

Wallace, William. "New Novels." *Academy,* 37 (May 17, 1890), 333.

Walling, Anna S. "David Graham Phillips, The Last Years of His Life." *Saturday Evening Post,* 184 (October 21, 1911), 19-20.

Warren, Joyce. *The American Narcissus. Individualism and Women in Nineteenth Century American Fiction.* New Brunswick, N.J.: Rutgers University Press, 1984.

Weinstein, Stanley. "The Journalism of Stephen Crane." Unpub. Ph.D. diss., New York University, 1968.

Wells, H.G. *Experiments in Autobiography.* New York: Macmillan, 1895.

Wertheim, Stanley and Paul Sorrentino. Introduction. *The Correspondence of Stephen Crane,* ed. Wertheim and Sorrentino. 2 vols. New York: Columbia University Press, 1988.

Wilson, Edmund. "Editor's Foreward." *Harold Frederic's Stories of York State.* Syracuse: Syracuse University Press, 1966.

"Writers and Their Work." *Hampton's,* 23 (August, 1909), 285.

Wyman, Margaret. "The Rise of the Fallen Woman." *American Quarterly,* 3 (Summer, 1951), 167-173.

Ziff, Larzer. *The American 1890s: The Life and Times of a Lost Generation.* New York: Viking, 1966.

IV. Historical and Background Materials on Female Sexuality, the City, and the Status of Women

Acton, William. *Prostitution Considered in Its Moral, Social, and Sanitary Aspects*, 1857. rpt. of 1870 ed. London: Frank Cass, 1972.

Allen, Annie. "How to Save Girls Who Have Fallen." *Survey*, 21 (1910), 684-696.

Aronovici, C. *Unmarried Girls with Sex Experience*. Philadelphia: Bureau for Social Research of the Seybert Institute, 1915.

Banner, Lois. *American Beauty*. New York: Alfred A. Knopf, 1983.

Baylen, Joseph O. "A Victorian's 'Crusade' in Chicago, 1893-1984." *Journal of American History*, 51 (December, 1964), 418-434.

Bell, E. Moberly. *Josephine Butler. Flame of Fire*. London: Constable, 1962.

Besant, Walter. *Autobiography of Walter Besant*. New York: Dodd, Mead, 1902.

Bingham, Theodore. *The Real Facts About the White Slave Traffic*. Boston: Gorham Press, 1911.

Blackwell, Elizabeth. "On Sexual Passion in Men and Women," 1894, in *Root of Bitterness*. ed. Nancy F. Cott. New York: E.P. Dutton, 1972, pp. 293-303.

Boyer, Paul S. *Urban Masses and Moral Order in America, 1820-1920*. Cambridge: Harvard University Press, 1978.

Brandt, Alan. *No Magic Bullet. A History of Venereal Disease in the United States Since 1880*. New York: Oxford University Press, 1987.

Bremner, Robert. *From the Depths: The Discovery of Poverty in the United States*. New York: New York University Press, 1956.

Bristow, Edward J. *Prostitution and Prejudice. The Jewish Fight Against White Slavery*. New York: Schocken Books, 1983.

———. *Vice and Vigilance. Purity Movements in Britain Since 1700*. Totowa, N.J.: Rowman and Littlefield, 1977.

Buel, James. *Mysteries and Miseries of America's Great Cities*. San Francisco: A.L. Bancroft, 1883.

Butler, Elizabeth. *Women and the Trades, 1907-1908*. New York: Russell Sage Foundation, 1909.

Butler, Josephine. *An Autobiographical Memoir*, ed. George W. and Lucy A. Johnson. Bristol: J.W. Arrowsmith, 1913.

———. *Rebecca Jarrett*. London: Morgan and Scott, 1886.

Campbell, Helen. *Darkness and Daylight; Lights and Shadows of New York Life*. Hartford: Hartford Publishing Company, 1897.

Carlisle, Marcia. Introduction to *Madeleine, An Autobiography*. rpt. 1919 ed. New York: Persea Books, 1986.

Committee of Eighteen, Morals Survey Committee. *The Social Evil in Syracuse*, 1913; rpt. *Prostitution in America: Three Investigations, 1902-1914*. New York: Arno Press and the New York Times, 1976.

Connelly, Mark Thomas. *The Response to Prostitution in the Progressive Era*. Chapel Hill: University of North Carolina Press, 1980.

Cooper, Patricia. "Women Workers, Work Culture, and Collective Action in the American Cigar Industry, 1900-1919." *Life and Labor. Dimensions of American Working Class History*, ed. Charles Stephenson and Robert Asher. Albany: State University of New York, 1986, pp. 190-204.

Cott, Nancy. "Passionlessness. An Interpretation of Victorian Sexual Ideology, 1750-1850." *A Heritage of Her Own. Toward a New Social History of American Women*, ed. Cott and Elizabeth Pleck. New York: Simon and Schuster, 1979, pp. 162-181.

Crapsey, Edward. *The Nether Side of New York.* New York: Sheldon Publishing Company, 1872.

Creel, George. "Where Is the Vice Flight?" *Harper's Weekly,* 47 (October 19, 1914), 340-342.

Degler, Carl N. *At Odds: Women and the Family in America from the Revolution to the Present.* New York: Oxford University Press, 1980.

Dorr, Rheta Childe. *What Eight Million Women Want.* Boston: Small, Maynard, 1910.

Ehrenreich, Barbara and Deirdre English. *Witches, Midwives and Nurses. A History of Women Healers.* Old Westbury, N.Y.: Feminist Press, 1973.

Ellington, George. *The Women of New York.* New York: New York Book Company, 1878.

Evans, Elizabeth. *The Abuse of Maternity.* Philadelphia: J.B. Lippincott, 1875.

Fawcett, Edgar. "Plutocracy and Snobbery in New York." *Arena,* 25 (1891), 142-151.

―――― "The Woes of the New York Working-Girl." *Arena,* 25 (1891), 26-35.

Filler, Louis. *Crusaders for American Liberalism,* 1939; rev. ed., Yellow Springs, Ohio: Antioch Press, 1959.

Fishbein, Leslie. "Harlot or Heroine? Changing Views of Prostitution, 1870-1920." *Historian,* 43 (1980), 23-35.

Flower, B.O. "Prostitution within the Marriage Bond." *Arena,* 3 (1895), 59-73.

Frederic, Harold. "Down Among the Dead Men." *New York Times,* July 24, 1884, 1.

―――― "From a Saunterer in the Labyrinth." *Pall Mall Budget,* 22 (July 24, 1885), 22.

―――― "The New American President." *Pall Mall Budget,* 22 (November 14, 1884), 12-14.

―――― "Mr. Stead and His Work." *New York Times,* September 7, 1885, 5.

―――― "Musings on the Question of the Hour." *Pall Mall Budget,* 23 (August 13, 1885), 11-12.

Gay, Peter. *The Bourgeois Experience,* Vol. 1. New York: Oxford University Press, 1984.

Gilman, Charlotte Perkins. *The Man-Made World.* New York: Charlton Company, 1911.

Goldman, Emma. "The White Slave Traffic." *Mother Earth,* 4 (January, 1910), 344-351.

Hallowell, Robert. "Legendary John Reed." *New Republic,* November 7, 1920, 298-299.

Hays, H.R. *The Dangerous Sex: The Myth of Feminine Evil.* New York: Putnam, 1964.

Heasman, Kathleen. *Evangelicals in Action. An Appraisal of Their Social Work in the Victorian Era.* London: Geoffrey Bles, 1962.

Hemyng, Bracebridge. *Those That Will Not Work.* Vol. 4 of Henry Mayhew, *London Labour and the London Poor.* London: Griffin, Bohn and Company, 1862.

Higginbotham, Ann R. "Respectable Sinners: Salvation Army Rescue Work with Unmarried Mothers: 1884-1914." *Religion in the Lives of English Women, 1760-1930,* ed. Gail Malmgreen. Bloomington: Indiana University Press, 1986, pp. 216-233.

Hummel, Abraham and William F. Howe. *In Danger! Or, Life in New York.* New York: J.S. Ogilvie, 1888.

Hymowitz, Carol and Michaele Weissman. *A History of Women in America*. New York: Bantam Books, 1980.

"Is White Slavery Nothing More Than A Myth?" *Current Opinion*, 55 (1913), 848.

Jeune, Lady Mary. "Saving the Innocents." *Fortnightly Review*, 44 (November, 1885), 669-682.

Kneeland, George. *Commercialized Prostitution in New York City*, 1913; rpt. Montclair, N.J.: Patterson Smith, 1969.

Lane, James B. *Jacob A. Riis and the American City*. Port Washington, N.Y.: Kennikat Press, 1974.

Lewis, Dio. *Our Girls*. New York: Harper and Brothers, 1871.

Lingeman, Richard. *Small Town America: A Narrative History from 1620 to the Present*. New York: G.P. Putnam, 1980.

Lippmann, Walter. "Legendary John Reed." *The New Republic*, December 20, 1914, 15-16.

Lipton, Eunice. "The Laundress in Nineteenth-Century French Culture." *Art History*, 3 (September, 1980), 295-313.

Lloyd, Caro. "The Illinois Vice Commission." *The New Review*, 1 (April 12, 1913), 453-458.

Lubove, Roy. "The Progressives and the Prostitute." *Historian*, 24 (May, 1962), 308-329.

"Madeleine." Nation, December 24, 1919, 662.

"Madeleine." New York Times, November 16, 1919, 662.

Madeleine, An Autobiography, 1919. Intro. by Marcia Carlisle. rpt. New York: Persea Books, 1986.

Maerov, Arnold S. "Prostitution: A Survey and Review of Twenty Cases." *Psychiatric Quarterly*, 39 (1965), 675-701.

Magnuson, Warren. *Salvation in the Slums. Evangelical Social Work, 1865-1920*. Metuchen, N.J.: Scarecrow Press and the American Library Association, 1977.

McCabe, James D. *Lights and Shadows of New York Life*. Philadelphia: National Publishing Company, 1872.

Mc Kendrick, Neil. *"The Bourgeois Experience." New York Times Book Review*, January 8, 1984.

Meyerowitz, Joanne J. *Women Adrift: Independent Wage Earners in Chicago, 1880-1930*. Chicago: University of Chicago Press, 1988.

Miner, Maude. *The Slavery of Prostitution*. New York: Macmillan, 1916.

———. "Two Weeks in Night Court." *Survey*, 22 (1909), 229-234.

Myers, Cortland. *Midnight in a Great City*. New York: Merrill Publishing Company, 1895.

Nell Kimball, Her Life as an American Madam, ed. Stephen Longstreet. New York: Macmillan, 1970.

Parke, J. Richardson. *Human Sexuality. A Medico-Literary Treatise*. Philadelphia: Professional Publishing Company, 1908.

Pearson, Michael. *The Five Pound Virgins*. New York: Saturday Review Press, 1972.

Pember, Arthur. *Mysteries and Miseries of the Great Metropolis*. New York: D. Appleton and Company, 1874,

Phillips, David Graham. "Albert J. Beveridge." *Success*, 8 (August, 1905), 526-528.

———. *The Reign of Gilt*. New York: James Pott and Company, 1905.

———. "Restless Husbands." *Cosmopolitan*, 51 (August, 1911), 419-425.

———. "What Is A Successful Wife?" *Delineator*, 77 (April, 1911), 265-66.

Pivar, David J. *Purity Crusade: Sexual Morality and Social Control, 1868-1900.* Westport, Ct.: Greenwood Press, 1973.

Powell, Aaron M., ed. *National Purity Congress. Papers and Addresses.* Baltimore: National Purity Alliance, 1896.

Prochaska, F.K. *Women and Philanthropy in Nineteenth-Century England.* Oxford: The Clarendon Press, 1980.

Reckless, Walter. *Vice in Chicago.* Chicago: University of Chicago Press, 1933.

Riegel, Robert. "Changing American Attitudes Toward Prostitution (1800-1920)." *Journal of the History of Ideas,* 29 (1968), 437-452.

Riis, Jacob. *How the Other Half Lives,* 1890; rpt. New York: Dover, 1971.

Roe, Clifford G. *The Great War on White Slavery, or Fighting for the Protection of Our Girls.* Chicago: W. Walter, 1911.

Rosen, Ruth. *The Lost Sisterhood. Prostitution in America, 1900-1918.* Baltimore: John Hopkins University Press, 1982.

———— and Sue Davidson, eds. *The Maimie Papers.* Old Westbury, N.Y.: Feminist Press, 1977.

Rosenberg, Rosalind. *Beyond Separate Spheres. The Intellectual Roots of Modern Feminism.* New Haven: Yale University Press, 1982.

Rosenstone, Robert. *Romantic Revolutionary. A Biography of John Reed.* New York: Alfred A. Knopf, 1975.

Rothman, Sheila. *Woman's Proper Place: A History of Changing Ideas and Practices, 1870 to the Present.* New York: Basic Books, 1978.

Rudwin, Maximilian. *The Devil in Legend.* New York: AMS Press, 1970.

Russ, Joanna. "Comment on 'Prostitution in Medieval Canon Law.'" *Signs,* 5 (Summer, 1977), 922-923.

Ryan, Mary P. *Womanhood in America from Colonial Times to the Present.* New York: New Viewpoints, 1975.

Sandford, Mrs. John. *Woman, in Her Social and Domestic Character.* London: Longman, Rees, 1833.

Sanger, William. *The History of Prostitution,* 1858; rpt. New York: Medical Publishing Company, 1897.

Schults, Raymond L. *Crusader in Babylon: W.T. Stead and the Pall Mall Gazette.* Lincoln: University of Nebraska Press, 1972.

Smith, Matthew Hale. *Sunshine and Shadow in New York.* Hartford: J.B. Burr, 1868.

Smith-Rosenberg, Carroll. "Beauty, the Beast, and the Militant Woman." *A Heritage of Her Own,* ed. Nancy F. Cott and Elizabeth Pleck. New York: Simon and Schuster, 1979, pp. 197-221.

Spencer, Anna Garlin. "The Scarlet Woman." *Forum,* 49 (1913), 276-289.

———— *Woman's Share in Social Culture.* New York and London: Mitchell Kennerley, 1913.

Starr, Kevin. *Americans and the California Dream, 1850-1915.* New York: Oxford University Press, 1973.

Stryker, Peter. *The Lower Depths of the Great American Metropolis.* New York: n.p., 1866.

Tabor, Pauline. *Pauline's.* Louisville, Ky.: Touchstone Publishing Company, 1971.

Talmage, Thomas DeWitt. *The Masque Torn Off.* Chicago: J. Fairbanks and Company, 1879.

———— *The Night Side of City Life.* Chicago: J. Fairbanks and Company, 1878.

Tarbell, Ida. *The Business of Being a Woman.* New York: Macmillan, 1917.

Taylor, Lydia Pettengill. *From Under the Lid.* Portland: Glass and Prud'homme, 1938.

Taylor, William. *California Life.* New York: Phillips and Hunt, 1882.

Terhune, Mary. *Eve's Daughters, or, Common Sense for Maids.* New York: J.R. Anderson and H.S. Allan, 1882.

Thomas, Keith. "The Double Standard." *Journal of the History of Ideas,* 20 (1959), 195-216.

Turner, George Kibbe. "The City of Chicago: A Study of the Great Immortalities." *McClure's,* 28 (April, 1907), 575-592.

———. "The Daughters of the Poor: A Plain Story of the Development of New York City as a Leading Center of the White Slave Trade...." *McClure's,* 34 (November, 1909), 45-61.

Vice Commission of Chicago, *The Social Evil in Chicago,* 1911; rpt. New York: Arno Press and the New York Times, 1970.

Vices of a Big City. Existing Menaces to Church and Home. New York: J.E. Clark, 1890.

Vicinus, Martha. *Independent Women. Work and Community for Single Women, 1850-1920.* Chicago: University of Chicago Press, 1985.

Von Staden, Margaret. "My Story (The History of a Prostitute's Life in San Francisco)." Ms., Schlesinger Library, Radcliffe College.

Warner, Marina. *Alone of All Her Sex. The Myth and Cult of the Virgin Mary.* New York: Alfred A. Knopf, 1976.

Warren, John. *Thirty Years' Battle with Crime,* 1875; rpt. New York: Arno Press, 1970.

Weidensall, Jean. *The Mentality of the Criminal Woman.* Baltimore: Warwick and York, 1916.

Welter, Barbara. "The Cult of True Womanhood, 1820-1860." *American Quarterly,* 18 (Summer, 1966), 151-174.

"The White Slave Traffic." *Outlook,* 95 (1910), 545-546.

"The White Slave Traffic." *Presentment of the Additional Grand Jury,* Appendix to Reginald Wright Kauffman, *The House of Bondage,* pp. 477-480.

Whyte, Frederic. *Life of W.T. Stead.* 2 vols. New York and Boston: Houghton, Mifflin, 1925.

Winick, Charles and Paul Kinsie. *The Lively Commerce. Prostitution in the United States.* Chicago: Quadrangle Books, 1971.

Index